HARDPRESS.NET
HOME OF HARD-TO-FIND BOOKS

The Artist & Tradesman's Guide
by John Shepard

Address:
HardPress
8345 NW 66TH ST #2561
MIAMI FL 33166-2626
USA
Email: info@hardpress.net

SIGILLVM · ACADEMIÆ · HARVARDIANÆ · CHRISTO · ET · ECCLESIÆ · IN · NOV · ANG

THE
ARTIST & TRADESMAN'S GUIDE.

EMBRACING

SOME LEADING FACTS & PRINCIPLES OF SCIENCE,

AND A VARIETY OF MATTER ADAPTED TO THE WANTS

OF THE

ARTIST, MECHANIC, MANUFACTURER,

AND

MERCANTILE COMMUNITY

TO WHICH IS ANNEXED

AN ABSTRACT OF TONNAGE, DUTIES,

CUSTOM-HOUSE TARES, AND ALLOWANCES.

Commerce and Manufactures—the main sheet anchor of a nation.

By *John Shepard?*

UTICA:
PRINTED BY WILLIAM WILLIAMS.
No. 60, Genesee Street.

1827.

Northern District of New York, to wit:

BE IT REMEMBERED, That on the eighth day of November, in the fifty-first year of the independence of the United States of America, A. D. 1827, *John Shepard*, of the said district, hath deposited in this office the title of a book, the right whereof he claims as proprietor, in the words following, to wit.

"The Artist and Tradesman's Guide; embracing some leading facts and principles of science, and a variety of matter adapted to the wants of the artist, mechanic, manufacturer, and mercantile community. To which is annexed an abstract of tonnage, duties, custom-house tares and allowances. Commerce and manufactures—the main sheet anchor of a nation."

In conformity to the act of the Congress of the United States, entitled "An act for the encouragement of learning, by securing the copies of maps, charts, and books, to the authors and proprietors of such copies, during the times therein mentioned;" and also to the act entitled "An act supplementary to an act entitled 'An act for the encouragement of learning, by securing the copies of maps, charts, and books, to the authors and proprietors of such copies during the times therein mentioned,' and extending the benefits thereof to the arts of designing, engraving, and etching, historical and other prints."

R. R. LANSING,
Clerk of the District Court of the United States,
for the Northern District of New York.

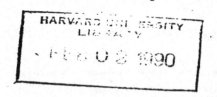

ADVERTISEMENT.

An apology is due to our subscribers for the delay which has occurred in the publication of this work. The time required to prepare and arrange the materials, has been much greater than was anticipated; nor after the labour and care bestowed, can we presume to declare every article perfect. Our object has been to render the work practically useful, rather than to make a display of science and fine writing—to the latter of which we make no pretence. If the merchant and the mechanic are benefitted by our exertions, and we have the vanity to believe that they will be, we have not "laboured for nought," but shall reap a rich reward in the reflection that we have in any degree been useful to those classes of community, who are the bone and sinews of our republic. To them we commit, without further remark, this little manual.

THE AUTHOR.

Nov. 1827.

CONTENTS.

CONTENTS.

WEIGHTS AND MEASURES.

1 Gallon measure (cong.) contains	8 pints,
8 pints	16 ounces,
1 ounce,	8 drachms,
1 drachm,	60 minims.

WEIGHT OF DRY SUBSTANCES.

1 pound contains	12 ounces,
1 ounce,	8 drachms,
1 drachm,	60 grains,
1 Scruple,	20 grains.

It is customary to distinguish quantities of fluid from dry substances, by prefixing the letter f. (fluid) when an ounce or drachm is mentioned in medical works; but in the prescriptions or formulæ, in this work, it was considered unnecessary, as the slightest acquaintance with the substances to be used will point out what is implied.

ARTIST AND TRADESMAN'S GUIDE.

CHAPTER I.

INTRODUCTION.

To the manufacturer, chemistry has lately become fruitful of instruction and assistance. In the arts of brewing, tanning, dying, and bleaching, its doctrines are important guides. In making soap, glass, pottery, and all metallic wares, its principles are daily applied, and are capable of a still more useful application, as they become better understood. Indeed every mechanic art, in the different processes of which heat, moisture, solution, mixture or fermentation is necessary, must ever keep pace in improvement with this branch of philosophy. Finally, there is scarcely an art of human life, which the science of chemistry is not fitted to subserve; scarcely a department of human inquiry, either for health, pleasure, ornament, or profit, which it may not be made in its present improved state, eminently to promote. To illustrate the science fully, in all its parts, would require more pages than this work is designed to contain; therefore, we shall be confined to some of the leading principles, and most useful practical operations, which it embraces.

CHAPTER II.

THE GENERAL PRINCIPLES OF CHEMISTRY.

The science of chemistry naturally divides itself into three parts; a description of the component parts of bodies, or of *elementary* or simple substances as they are called,—a description of the compound bodies formed by the union of simple substances, and an account of the nature of the power which produces these combinations. This power is known in chemistry by the name of affinity, or chemical attraction. By simple substances is not meant what the ancient philosophers called elements of bodies, as fire, air, earth, and water, nor particles of matter incapable of farther diminution or division. They signify merely bodies that have never been decomposed, or formed by art. The simple substances of which a body is composed are called the *constituent* parts of that body; and in decomposing it, we separate its constituent parts. If on the contrary we *divide* a body by cutting it to pieces, or even by grinding it to the finest powder, each of these small particles will consist of a portion of the general constituent parts of the whole body; these are called the *integrant* parts. *Compound* bodies are formed by the combination of two or more simple substances with each other. Attraction is that unknown force which causes bodies to approach each other. Its most obvious instances are the gravitation of bodies to the earth; that of the planets towards each other, and the attractions of electricity and magnetism. But that attraction which comes under the more immediate cognizance of chemists, subsists between the particles of bodies; and when it operates between particles of the same species, it is called the attraction of *cohesion*, or the attraction of aggregation; but

B

when between the particles of different substances, it is called the attraction of composition, chemical attraction, or chemical affinity. The attraction of cohesion, then is the power which unites the *integrant* particles of a body: the attraction of composition, that which combines the constituent particles. When particles are united by the attraction of cohesion, the result of such a union is a body of the same kind as the particles of which it is formed; but the attraction of composition, by combining particles of a dissimilar nature, produces compound bodies quite different from any of their constituents. If, for instance, you pour upon a piece of copper, placed in a glass vessel, some of the liquid called nitrous acid, (aqua fortis) for which it has a strong attraction, every particle of the copper will combine with a particle of the acid, and together they will form a new body, totally different from either the copper or nitrous acid. If you wish to decompose the compound which you have thus formed, present it to a piece of iron, for which the acid has a stronger affinity than for copper; and the acid will quit the copper to combine with the iron, and the copper will be then what the chemists call *precipitated*, that is to say, it will be thrown down in its separate state, and reappear in its simple form. In order to produce this effect, dip the blade of a knife into the fluid, and when you take it out, you will observe, that, instead of being wetted with a bluish liquid like that contained in the glass, it will be covered with a thin coat of copper.

It will be most conducive to science to consider all those substances as simple, which no mode of decomposing has yet been discovered. Simple substances naturally divide themselves into two classes. Those which belong to the first class are of too subtile a nature to be confined to any vessels which we possess. They do not seriously affect the most delicate balance, and have received therefore the name of *imponderable* bodies. The second class of bodies may be confined in proper vessels, may be exhibited in a separate state, and their weights or other properties may be determined. They have received the name of *ponderable* bodies. The imponderable bodies at present supposed to exist are four, light, heat or caloric, electricity, and magnetism. The first three are intimately connected with chemistry, but magnetism has with it no known connexion.

CHAPTER III.

CALORIC. Chemists have agreed to call the matter of heat *Caloric*, in order to distinguish it from the sensation which this matter produces. Caloric has a tendency to diffuse itself equally among all substances that come in contact with it. If the hand be put upon a hot body, part of the caloric leaves the hot body, and enters the hand; this produces the sensation of *heat*. On the contrary, if the hand be put upon a cold body, part of the caloric contained in the hand leaves the hand to unite with the cold body; this produces the sensation of *cold*. Cold therefore is nothing but a negative quality, simply implying the absence of the usual quantity of caloric. Caloric is uniform in its nature; but there exists in all bodies, two portions very distinct from each other. The one is called *sensible* heat, or free caloric; the other *latent* heat, or combined caloric. Sensible caloric is the nature of heat disengaged from other bodies, or, if united, not *chemically* united with them. *Latent* caloric is that portion of the matter of heat, which makes no *sensible* addition to the temperature of the bodies in which it exists. Wrought iron, though quite cold, contains a large portion of *latent* caloric; and if it be briskly hammered for some time on an anvil, it will become red hot, by the action of this species of caloric, which by the percussion of hammering is now evolved and forced out as *sensible* heat. Caloric pervades all bodies; and this is not the case with any other substance with which we are acquainted. It combines with different substances, however, in very different proportions; and for this reason one body is said to have a greater *capacity* for caloric than another. When gaseous substances become liquid, or liquid substances solid, by this change of state, they lose in a great measure their capacity for caloric. During the slacking of quick lime, the caloric which is involved escapes from the water, in consequence of its changing from a liquid to a solid form, by its union with the lime. When solid bodies become liquid or gaseous, their capacity for caloric is proportionably increased. If you place a glass of water in a mixture of equal quantities of snow and salt, during their conversion to a liquid, the water will be frozen in consequence of parting with its caloric to supply the increased capacity of the mixture. The portion of caloric necessary to raise a body to any given temperature, is called SPECIFIC caloric. The instrument in common use for measuring the temperature of bodies, is called a thermometer. Fahrenheit's is generally used in the United States. When a thermometer is brought in contact with any substance, the mercury expands or contracts till it acquires the same temperature; and the height at which the mercury stands in the tube, indicates the exact temperature of the substance to which it has been applied. It will not show the absolute caloric in substances; for it cannot measure that portion which is latent, or chemically combined with any body. Caloric is the cause of fluidity in all substances capable of becoming fluids, from the heaviest metal to the lightest gas. It insinuates itself among their particles and invariably separates them in some measure from each other. Thus ice is converted into water, and by a further portion of caloric into steam. We have reason to believe that every solid substance on the face of the earth might be converted to fluid of a very high temperature in peculiar circumstances. Some bodies give out their superabundant caloric much sooner than others. Iron is a quicker conductor of caloric than glass, and glass than wood. If you take a piece of iron in one hand and a piece of wood in the other, the iron feels cold, the wood warmer, though the thermometer shows that their temperature is the same. Substances usually become more dense by the loss of caloric; but the freezing of water is a sticking *exception* to this general law of nature, and is a memorable instance of the wisdom and provident care of the Almighty, when he established the laws of the universe.

Abstract caloric from steam until but 212 degrees remain, according to Fahrenheit's scale, and it will become water. Take away 180 degrees more, leaving but 32, and it will become ice. All gases and liquids would become solids, if caloric were abstracted to a certain degree, till at length all things would become permanently solid as the oldest primitive rocks.

Water does not require 212 degrees of heat for converting it into vapour; it has been made to boil at 67 degrees, which is 31 below blood heat. Therefore it requires 145 degrees of heat to resist the pressure of the atmosphere. From the following experiment we are taught, that combined caloric does not excite the sensation of heat nor affect the thermometer: Put a piece of tinder in the end of the piston of the fire syringe, made of cotton cloth dipped in a very strong solution of salt petre, and well dried—force down the piston suddenly and the tinder will take fire. Caloric was combined with the air in the syringe before it was compressed, which did not excite the sensation of heat nor imflame the tinder. There is so much caloric in the combination of air, water and other substances about us, that if it were capable of producing the ordinary effects of heat, the whole human family would be burned in a day. From the principle that caloric expands solids as well as gases, the variation in length of pendulums of clocks and balance wheels of watches, according to the varying temperature of the weather, causing them to run faster in cold and slower in hot weather, can be accounted for. .

That caloric expands liquids is clearly demonstrated by the fact, that spirits guage more in warm, and less in cold weather. The experiment may easily be tried by placing a barrel of rum in the sun, nearly full; if the thermometer ranges high, the liquor will soon run over. Then place it in a cold cellar, let it remain awhile, and the reverse will be evident.

An iron stove quickly gives off caloric heat into a room, and as soon cools. A brick Russian stove, must be heated a great while before it begins to give off caloric, and will not cool in a long time. Clothes made of wool and silk are slow conductors of caloric; those made of flax conduct rapidly—stone is a better conductor of caloric than brick. A stone house has its rooms sooner heated in summer and cooled in winter, than a brick house. A white earthen tea pot will keep tea hot longer than a black one—a bright tin coffee pot will keep coffee hot longer than a jappaned one. We are kept cooler in summer with light coloured clothes and warmer in winter, than with those which are dark coloured; for our bodies being warmer than the air in cold weather, caloric passes out through our clothes, but the hot rays of the sun in summer pass through our clothes inwardly.

CHAPTER IV.

WATER. Water is composed of 88 parts by weight of oxygen, and 12 of hydrogen in every 100 parts of the fluid. It is found in four states, namely: Solid, or ice; liquid, or water; vapour, or steam; and in a state of composition with other bodies. Its most simple state is that of ice, and the difference between liquid water or vapour and ice, is merely that the water contains a larger portion of caloric than ice, and that vapour is combined with still a greater quantity than water. However long we boil a fluid in an open vessel we cannot make it in the smallest degree hotter than its boiling point, for the; vapour absorbs the caloric, and carries it off as it is produced. It is owing to this that all evaporation produces cold. An animal might be frozen to death in the midst of summer by repeatedly sprinkling ether upon him, for its evaporation would shortly carry off the whole of his vital heat. Water thrown on burning bodies acts in the same way—it becomes in an instant converted into vapour and by thus depriving them of a large portion of their caloric, the fire, as we term it, is extinguished. Vapour occupies a space eight hundred times greater than it does when in the form of water—and the expansive force of steam is found by experiment to be much greater than that of gun powder. There is no reason to disbelieve that in time, steam may be applied to many useful purposes of which we have no idea.

Water is said to be in a state of *composition* with other bodies, because in many cases it becomes one of their *component* parts. It is combined in a state of solidity in marble, in chrystals, in spars, in gems, and in many alkaline, earthy, and metallic salts, both natural and artificial, to all of which substances it imparts hardness, and to most of them transparency. Near the poles water is always solid; there it is similar to the hardest rocks, and may be formed by the chisel of the statuary, like stone. It becomes still more solid in the composition called mortar, and in cements, having parted with more of its caloric in that combination than in the act of freezing. If you take some ground plaster of Paris, fresh calcined, and mix it with a little water, the affinity of the plaster for the water is so great, that in a few minutes the whole will be converted to a solid.

CHAPTER V.

EARTHS AND ALKALIES. Earths are such incombustible substances as are not ductile, are mostly insoluble in water or oil, and preserve their constitution in a strong heat. Notwithstanding the varied appearance of the earth under our feet, and the mountainous parts of the world, whose diversified strata present to our view substances of every texture and shade, the whole is composed of only nine primitive earths; and as three of these occur but seldom, the variety produced by the other six becomes the more remarkable. One of the most valuable earths with which we are acquainted is silex, or pure flint. It is the most durable article in the state of gravel for the formation of roads. It is a necessary ingredient in earthen ware, porcelain and cements; it is the basis of glass, and of all nitrous substances. It is white, inodorous, and insipid, in its pure state, and the various colours which it assumes in different substances, proceed from the different ingredients with which it is mixed. Alumine obtained its name from its being the base of the salt called alum. It is distributed over the earth in the form of clay, and on account of its aptitude for moulding into different forms and its property of hardening in the fire, is employed for various useful purposes. In making earthen ware, a due proportion both of silex and alumine are necessary; for if alumine alone were used, the ware could not be sufficiently burnt without shrinking too much, and even cracking; and a great excess of silex would lessen the tenacity and render the ware brittle. Lime is never found pure in nature; it is obtained by decomposing calcareous matters by the action of fire, which deprives them of their acid. In its pure state it is used in many of the arts. It is employed by the farmers as a manure; and by bleachers, tanners, ironmasters and others in their several manufactures, and in medicine. The use of lime in agriculture may be attributed to its property of hastening the dissolution of all vegetable and animal matters, and of imparting to the soil a power of retaining a quantity of moisture necessary for the nourishment and vigorous growth of the plants. Magnesia, besides being the basis of several salts is of great use in medicine; and is employed by the manufacturers of enamels and porcelain. The alkalies are distinguished by an acrid and peculiar taste, they change the blue juices of vegetables to a green, and the yellow to a brown and have the property of rendering oil miscible with water. They form various salts by combination with acids, act as powerful caustics, when applied to the flesh of animals, and are soluble in water. Potash and soda have been called fixed alkalies, because they will endure a great heat without being volatilized; and yet in a very high temperature they are dissipated in vapour. They are compounds of metallic substances, called potassium, sodium and oxygen. They have various uses in surgery and medicine, and are employed in large quantities by the glassmaker, the dyer, the soapmaker, the colourmaker, and by many other manufacturers. Ammonia is so extremely *volatile* as to exhale at all known temperatures. When combined with carbonic acid, it takes a concrete form, and a beautiful white colour, and is known in commerce by the name of volatile salts. With muriatic acid it forms what is termed sal ammonia, which is employed in many of our manufactures, particularly by dyers to give a brightness to certain colours. In tinning metals it is of use to cleanse the surfaces, and prevent them from oxydizing by the heat which is given to them in the operation. Ammonia is furnished from all animal substances by decomposition. The horns of cattle, especially those of deer, yield it in abundance, and it is from this circumstance that a solution of ammonia in water has been termed hartshorn.

Besides the nine earths above enumerated, we have now *thorina*, which is a raw earthy substance lately discovered. A new alkali, called *lithia*, has recently been discovered, which, like potash and soda, is found to be a metallic oxyde; its base is called *lithium*. Three new vegetable alkalies have also been discovered, called morphia, picrotoxine, and vanqueline. Clay, as it exists in soils is commonly called *argillaceous* earth, and lime in soils is called *calcareous* earth.

ACIDS AND SALTS. The name acid, in the language of chemists, has been given to all substances, whether liquids or solids, which produce that sensation on the tongue which we call sour. Most of the acids owe their origin to the combination of certain substances with oxygen; and they have the property of changing the blue, green, and purple vegetables to red, and of combining with alkalies, earths, and metallic oxydes, so as to compose the compounds termed *salts*. The acids were formerly divided into three classes, mineral, vegetable, and animal; but the more useful and scientific way of dividing them, is into two classes only. The undecomposible acids, and those which are formed with two principles, are comprised in the first class; while those acids which are formed with more than two principles compose the second class. Sulphuric acid, in commerce called oil of vitriol, is procured by burning sulphur in contact with some substance containing oxygen, and becomes acidified. That peculiar acid which is called muriatic is usually obtained from muriate of soda, which is the chemical name of common salt. Carbonic acid is a combination of carbon and oxygen, formerly called fixed air, on account of its being intimately combined in chalk, brimstone, and other substances. (See also the article carbonic acid gas.) The number of acids that are well known amount to more than 40, and their uses are so many and important, that it is impossible to name them. They are indispensable to various arts and manufactures; they are employed for culinary purposes, and for medicine; they act an important part in the great laboratory of nature and form a great proportion of the mountainous districts of the globe in their various combinations. The precise number of the salts is not known, but they probably amount to more than two thousand. The different salts are known from each other by the peculiar figure of their crystals, by their taste, and other distinctive or specific characters. Their crystalization is owing to the abstraction of the heat or water by which they were displaced. Crystalized salts are liable to changes in their appearance by exposure to the atmosphere. Some have so great an affinity for water, that they absorb it with avidity from the atmosphere, and thus becoming moist or liquid they are said to deliquence. Others having less affinity for water than atmospheric air has, lose their water or crystalization by exposure, and readily fall into powder. Such salts are said to effloresce. Salts have not only the property of dissolving in water, but by exposure to great heat they will melt; and they require different degrees of heat to put them into a state of fusion, as well as different quantities of water for their solution. Many of the salts are to be found native, and the carbonates, sulphates, and the muriates, are the most frequent. Chalk, limestone, and marble, are all included in the term carbonate of lime. Few salts are more copiously disseminated than the sulphate of lime, particularly in the city of Paris, and hence its name, plaster of Paris. Of the native muriates, muriate of lime occurs with rock salt, and muriate of magnesia occurs in abundance in sea water; and muriate of soda not only exists in immense quantities in the ocean, but vast mountains in different parts of the world, are entirely formed of this salt. Nitrate of potash, known by the more familiar name of nitre, or salt petre, is collected in various parts of the globe. Phosphate of lime which is the basis of animal bones, exists native in Hungary, and, composes several entire mountains in Spain. Mountains of salt were probably formed in very remote ages, and by processes of which we can form no idea. It may be supposed, however, that the changes have been slow and gradual; for several of the native salts exhibit marks of regularity and beauty in their crystalization, which cannot be imitated by art.

CHAPTER VI.

SIMPLE COMBUSTIBLES. Most of the simple substances are combustible, or bear some relation to combustion. Light and caloric are evolved during combustion. Oxygen is the principal agent; and hydrogen, sulphur, phosphorus, carbon, and the metals are the subjects, or instruments of this process. Hydrogen gas may be combined with water, sulphur, phosphorus or carbon. When combined with phosphorus it forms phosphuretted hydrogen gas, which takes fire when it comes in contact with atmospheric air. The elastic substance called carburetted hydrogen gas, is carbon dissolved in hydrogen, it has also been called heavy inflammable air. It is this gaseous compound which has occasioned so many dreadful accidents to miners, who call it fire damp. It is procured from pit coal by dry distillation, and from its inflammability and brilliant flame, it has been used for lighting streets, shops, manufactories and light houses on the sea coast. The rate at which it is obtained is comparatively trifling compared with oil and tallow.

Phosphorus is a solid inflammable substance, which burns at a very low temperature when in contact with oxygen gas or atmospheric air. Many amusing experiments can be performed with it; but it must be handled with extreme caution. If you fix a piece of solid phosphorus in a quill, and write with it upon paper, the writing in a dark room will appear beautifully luminous. If the face or hands be rubbed with phosphuretted ether, they will appear in a dark place as though on fire, without danger or sensation of heat. Pure carbon is known only in the diamond; but carbon in a state of charcoal may be procured by heating to redness a piece of wood closely covered with sand in a crucible, so as to preserve it while in the fire, and afterwards, while cooling, from the action of the atmosphere. It is capable of forming various combinations, but charcoal is that with which we are most famil-

iar.   Carbon is not only a component part, but it forms nearly the
whole of the solid basis of all vegetables, from the most delicate flower in the garden, to the huge oak of the forest.   It not only constitutes the basis of the woody fibre, but is a component part of sugar,
and of all kinds of wax, oils, gums, and resins, and of these again how
great is the variety! It is imagined that most of the metals may be
combined with carbon; but at present we know of only its combination with iron.   In one proportion it forms cast-iron, in another steel,
and in a third plumbago, generally, though improperly, called black
lead.   There is no lead in its composition.   Cast iron contains about
one forty-fifth of its weight of carbon.   Steel is combined with about
one part of carbon in two hundred of iron, and plumbago, or carburet
of iron, has been found to consist of nearly nine parts of carbon to
one of iron.   Wrought iron differs from cast iron, in being deprived
of its carbon and oxygen, by continued heat and repeated hammering,
which renders the metal malleable.   Steel is made of wrought iron, by
various processes, whereby the metal resumes a small portion of the
carbon, and acquires a capacity of receiving different degrees of hardness.   The metals are generally procured from beneath the surface
of the earth, in a state of combination either with other metals, or with
sulphur, oxygen or acids; though a few of them have been found in
a state of purity.   Metals are the great agents by which we can examine the recesses of nature; and their uses are so multiplied, that
they have become of the greatest importance in every occupation of
life.   They are the instruments of all our improvements, of civilization
itself, and are even subservient to the progress of the human mind
towards perfection.   They differ so much from each other, that nature
seems to have had in view all the necessities of man, in order that she
might suit every possible purpose his ingenuity can invent or his wants
require.   We not only receive this great variety from the hand of nature, but these metals are rendered infinitely valuable by various other properties which they possess;—by their combustibility, their solu-
bility in fluids, their combinations with various substances, and by their
union with each other, whereby compounds and alloys are formed, extremely useful in a variety of arts, manufactures, and other requisites
of life.   By combining them with oxygen we can invest them with *new*
properties, and are enabled to employ them to promote the progress of
the fine arts, by imitating the master pieces of creation in the production of artificial salts, gems, and chrystals, of every colour and of every shade. ~

The following is an enumeration of the classification of the simple bodies in general.
1, Comprehending the imponderable agents, *Heat or Caloric, Light, and Electricity.*
11. Comprehending agents capable of uniting with inflammable bodies, and in most instances of effecting their combustion,—*Oxygen, Choliae,* and *Iodine.*   Many learned chemists
have doubted whether chorine and iodine were supporters of combustion, any further than
they contain oxygen.   They are classed among the simple bodies, because they have not as
yet, been resolved into other ingredients.   The name chorine is simply expressive of its
greenish colour, and iodine of its violet colour.   111. Comprehending bodies capable of uniting with oxygen, and forming with its various compounds,—2. *Hydrogen,* forming water.
2. Bodies forming acids.   *Nitrogen,* forming nitric acid, *Sulphur,* forming sulphuric acid,
Phosphorus, forming phosphoric acid, *Carbon,* forming carbonic acid, *Boron,* forming bo-
ric acid, *Fluorine,* forming fluoric acid.   3. Metallic bodies which have been divided into
the seven following classes.   1st. The metals which combine with oxygen and form alkalies.
These are *potassium, sodium* and *lithium.*   The volatile alkali ammonia has been found by
Sir Humphrey Davy to be a triple compound of nitrogen, hydrogen and oxygen.   20. Those
metals which by combining with oxygen form the alkaline earths; viz. *calcium, magnesium.*

borium and *strontium.* Calcium is the base of lime, magnesium of magnesia, and so on. The metallic substances are of the colour of silver. 30. Those metals which by combining with oxygen constitute the remainder of the earths. These are *silicum, alumium, zirconium, glucinum, yttrium* and *thorinum.* These are presumed metals; for the earths, of which they are supposed to constitute the bases, have been as yet but partially decomposed; respecting some of them but little is known. 4th. The metals which absorb oxygen and decompose water at a high temperature. These are *iron, tin, zinc, cadmium* and *manganese.* 5th. Those metals which absorb oxygen at different temperatures, but do not decompose water at any temperature. This class is composed of twelve distinct metals, viz. *osmium, cerium, tellurium, titanium, uranium, nickel, cobalt, copper, lead, antimony, bizmuth* and *mercury.* 6th. Those metals which do not decompose water, but absorb oxygen and thereby convert it into acids. These are *arsenic, molybdenum, tungsten, chromium, columbium* and *selenium.* 7th. Those metals which do not decompose water, nor absorb oxygen from the atmosphere at any temperature. These are *platina, gold, silver, palladium, rhodium* and *iridium.*

OXYDES AND COMBUSTION. Any metal or combustible body, which is combined with less oxygen than is sufficient to render it *acid*, is usually called an *oxyde*. Whenever a substance is converted into an oxyde, we say it is oxydized. The mineral, the animal, and vegetable kingdoms, all furnish matters which are convertible into oxydes by an union with oxygen. Metallic oxydes are formed in several ways, the chief of which are by the access of atmospheric air, by the decomposition of water, and by the decomposition of acids. Iron may be mentioned as a familiar example of metals becoming oxydized by atmospheric air. It is well known that when this metal is exposed to air and moisture it acquires rust, or in other words its surface is converted to an oxyde, in which state, the metal will be found to have acquired an increase of weight. Common red lead, which is a true oxyde of lead, is made by melting that metal in ovens so constructed as to have a free access to atmospheric air. Gold, silver and platina, cannot be oxydized, unless in a very high temperature; and with respect to other metals, they not only differ in their capacity for oxygen, but also their attraction for it, so that one will often rob the other, thus reducing the first oxyde to its primitive metallic form. If you dissolve some quicksilver in nitric acid, and after dropping a little of the solution upon a bright piece of copper, gently rub it with a piece of cloth, the mercury will precipitate itself upon the copper, which will be completely silvered. With regard to the oxyde of nitrogen, the first degree of oxydizement produces *nitrous* oxyde; a further portion of oxygen, nitric oxyde, and they are both in a state of gas. Nitrous oxyde gas bears the nearest resemblance of any other to that of the atmospheric air. It will support combustion even better than common air; it is respirable for a short time, and it is absorbed by water. Persons who have inhaled this gas have felt sensations similar to that produced by intoxication. In some people it produces involuntary muscular motion, and a propensity to leaping and running, in others involuntary fits of laughter; and in all high spirits, and the most exqisitely pleasurable sensations, without any subsequent feelings of debility. (It is readily procured by exposing chrystals of nitrate of ammonia, in a retort to the heat of a lamp, by which means the ammoniacal salt is decomposed, and this gas is evolved.) Combustion may be defined to be a process by which certain substances decompose oxygen gas, absorb its base and suffer its caloric to escape in the state of sensible heat. The agency of oxygen in combustion is attributable to its affinity for combustible bodies. The combustible having a greater affini-

C

ty to oxygen than the oxygen has to caloric, the oxygen gas is decomposed, and its oxygen combines with the ignited body, which is
caloric, becoming free, is diffused among the surrounding bodies.
Whenever we burn a combustible body, a continued stream of atmospheric air flows towards the fire place, to occupy the vacancy left by
the air that has undergone decomposition, and which, in its turn, becomes decomposed also. Hence a supply of caloric is furnished without intermission, till the whole of the combustible is saturated with
oxygen. As the combustible burns, *light* is disengaged, and the more
subtile parts, now converted by caloric into gas, are dissipated in that
state. When the combustion is over, nothing remains but the earthy
parts of the combustible, and that portion which is converted by the
process, into an oxyde or an acid. The smoke which arises from a common fire is chiefly water in the state of vapour, with a mixture of carburetted hydrogen and bituminous substances; part of the water comes
from the moisture of the fuel; and the other part is formed during combustion, by the union of the hydrogen of the combustible with the oxygen of the atmosphere. The agency of oxygen in combustion may
be demonstrated by placing a lighted candle under a glass vessel inverted upon a plate of water. It will be seen that the candle will go
out as soon as it has consumed all the oxygen contained in the included air, and that the water will rise up in the vessel to fill the vacancy.
In the decomposition of atmospheric air by combustion, it is natural to
ask, what becomes of the nitrogen gas? As the oxygen becomes fixed in the combustible body, its caloric is disengaged, a part of which
combines with the nitrogen, and carries it off in the form of rarified
nitrogen gas. When bodies are burnt, none of their principles are
destroyed. We have reason to think that every particle of matter is
indestructible, and that the process of combustion merely decomposes
the body, and sets its several component parts at liberty, to separate
from each other, to form other new and varied combinations. It was
said of old, that the Creator *weighed* the dust and *measured* the water,
when he made the world. The first quantity is here still; and though
man can gather and scatter, move, mix and unmix, yet he can destroy
nothing; the dissolution of one thing is a preparation for the being,
and the bloom, and the beauty of another. Something gathers up *all*
the fragments and nothing is lost.

CHAPTER VII.

ELECTRICITY. The surface of the earth, and of all the bodies with
which we are acquainted, is supposed to contain or possess a power of
exciting or exhibiting a certain quantity of an exceedingly subtile agent,
called the electric fluid or power. The quantity usually belonging to
any surface, is called its natural share, and then it produces no sensible effects; but when any surface becomes possessed of more, or of
less than its natural quantity, it is electrified, and it then exhibits a variety of peculiar and surprising phenomena, ascribed to the power called electric. All those bodies which transmit or conduct electricity
from one surface to another, are called conductors, and those surfaces which will not transmit the electric power, are called electrics or
non-conductors. The general class of conductors comprehends me-

tals, ores, and fluids, in their natural state, except air and oils. Vitrified and resinous substances, amber, sulphur, wax, silk, cotton, and feathers are electrics or non conductors.—Many of these, such as glass, resin and air, become conductors by being heated. When a surface is supposed to have more than its natural quantity of this fluid, it is said to be *positively* electrified, and when less than its natural share, to be *negatively* electrified. When any electrified conductor is wholly surrounded by non-conductors, so that the electric fluid cannot pass from it along conductors to the earth, it is said to be *insulated*. The human body is a good conductor of electricity ; but if a person stand on a cake of resin, or on a stool supported by glass legs, the electric fluid cannot pass from him to the earth, and if he is touched by another person standing on the ground, a sparkling appearance and noise will be exhibited. Two surfaces, both positively or both negatively electrified, *repel* each other ; and two substances, of which one is positively and the other negatively electrified, *attract* each other. Opposite electricities always accompany each other, for if any surface become positive, the surface with which it is rubbed becomes negative ; and if any surface be rendered positive, the *nearest* conducting surface will become negative. When one side of a *conductor* receives the electric fluid its whole surface is instantly pervaded ; but when an *electric* or *non conductor* is presented to an electrified body, it becomes electrified on a small spot only. If to one side of a pane of glass you communicate positive electricity, the opposite side will become negatively electrified, and the plate is then said to be *charged*. These electricities cannot come together, unless a communication, by means of conductors, is made between the sides of the glass ; and if their union be made through the human body, it produces an affection of the nerves called an electric shock. As the excitation which is produced by rubbing with the hand on a tube or plate of glass, is not only very laborious, but inadequate to the production of any material quantity of electric fluid, machines have been constructed of various forms for this purpose.—Some of the experiments which may be made with an electrical machine are necessary for illustrating the laws of electricity, and others are merely entertaining. If the inside of a glass tumbler be electirified by presenting it to a pointed wire, extending from the prime conductor, and then placed over a few pitch balls laid upon a table, the balls will immediately begin to leap up along the sides of the glass, and then back on the table ;—they are attracted and repelled by the electrified inside surface of the glass, the electricity of which they gradually conduct to the table. If a person having long hair, not tied up, be placed upon an insulated stand, and, by means of a chain, be connected with the prime conductor, when the machine is put in motion, the hairs on his head, by repelling each other, will stand out in a most surprising manner. A piece of sponge, filled with water, and hung to the conductor, when electrified in a dark room, exhibits a most beautiful appearance. If a piece of sealing wax be fastened to a wire, and the wire be fixed into the end of the conductor, and the wax lighted, the moment the machine is worked, the wax will fly off in the finest threads imaginable. Take a two ounce phial, half full of olive oil, pass a slender wire through the cork, and let the end of it be so bent as to touch the glass just below the surface of the oil ; then place

your thumb opposite the point of the wire in the phial, and, if in that
position, you take a spark from the charged conductor, the spark, in
order to reach your thumb, will actually perforate the glass. In this
way holes may be made all round the phial.——Substances should be
warmed and experiments made when the wind is northerly, and the atmosphere dry, to produce the best effect.

By means of the Leyden Phial, a hundred persons may receive a
shock at the same instant, and electric fluid, on the same principle,
might be conveyed many miles in a moment of time. The electric
fluid may be made to appear in the form of a vivid flash, accompanied
with a loud report, with this phial. But the greatest discovery that
was ever made in electricity, was reserved for Dr. Franklin, of America. Franklin brought the supposition that a similarity existed between lightning and the electric fluid to the test, and proved the truth
of it by means of a boy's kite covered with a silk handkerchief instead
of paper, and some wire fastened in the upper part, which served to
collect and conduct the fluid. When he raised this machine into the
atmosphere, he drew electric fluid from the passing clouds, which de-
scended through the flaxen string of the kite, as a conductor, and was
afterwards drawn from an iron key, which he tied to the line at a small
distance from his hand; from this experiment originated the formation
of a conductor to secure buildings from the effects of lightning.

When aqueous vapour is condensed, the clouds formed are usually
more or less electrical, and the earth below them being brought into an
opposite state, a discharge takes place, when the clouds approach within a certain distance, constituting lightning, and the collapsing of the
air, which is rarified in the electric circuit, is the cause of the thunder,
which is more or less intense, and of longer or shorter duration, according to the quantity of the air acted upon, and the distance of the
place where the report is heard from the point of the discharge.

GALVANISM. Galvanism is another mode of exciting electricity.
In electricity the effects are chiefly produced by mechanical action, but
the effects of Galvanism are produced by the chemical action of bodies
upon each other. When it was observed, that common electricity, even
that of lightning, produced vivid convulsions in the limbs of recently
killed animals, it was ascertained that metallic substances, by mere
contact, under particular circumstances, excited similar commotions.
It was found essential that the forces of metals employed should be of
different kinds. Apply one piece of metal to the nerve of the part,
and the other to the muscle, and afterwards connect the metals, either
by bringing them together, or connecting them by an arch of metallic
substance; every time this connexion is formed, a convulsion takes
place. The greatest muscular contractions are found to be produced
by zinc, silver, and gold. A person may be made sensible of this kind
of electric action by the following experiments. . If he place a piece
of one metal, as a half crown above, and a piece of some other metal,
as zinc, below his tongue, by bringing the outer edge of these pieces in
contact, he will perceive a peculiar taste, and in the dark will see a
flash of light. If he put a slip of tin foil upon the bulb of one of his
eyes, and a piece of silver in his mouth, by causing these pieces to
communicate, in a dark place a faint flash will appear before his eyes.
Galvani supposed that the virtues of this new agent resided in the

nerves of the animal, but Volta showed that the phenomena did not depend on the organs of the animal, but upon the electrical agency of the metals, which is excited by the moisture of the animal, whose organs were only a delicate test of the presence of electric influence. The conductors of the galvanic fluid are divided into the perfect, which consist of metallic substances and charcoal, and imperfect, which are water and oxydated fluids, as the acids and all the subtances that contain these fluids. To render the Galvanic, or more properly, the Voltaic power sensible, the combination must consist of three conductors of the different classes. When two of the three conductors are of the first class, the combination is said to be of the first order ; when otherwise, it is said to be of the second order. If a piece of zinc be laid upon a piece of copper, and upon the copper a piece of flannel, moistened with a solution of salt water, a *circle* of the first class is formed ; and then, if three other pieces be laid on these in the same order, and repeated several times, the whole will form a pile or *battery* of the first order. The effects may be increased to any degree by a repetition of the same simple combination. The following is a cheap and easy method of constructing a Voltaic pile. Cast 20 or 30 pieces of zinc, of the size of a cent ; take as many cents and as many pieces of paper or woollen cloth cut in the same shape, and dip in a solution of salt and water. In building the pile, place a piece of zinc, wet paper, the superabundant water being pressed out, after which the copper ; then zinc, paper, and copper, and so on, until the whole is finished. The sides of the pile may be suppported with rods of glass, or varnished wood fixed in the board on which it is built. Having wet both hands touch the lower part of the pile with one hand, and the upper part with the other, constant little shocks of electricity will be felt until one hand be removed. If the hand be brought back, a similar repetition of shocks will be experienced. Hold a silver spoon in one hand, and touch with it the battery in the lower part, then touch the upper part with the tongue ; the bitter taste is extreme. If the end of the spoon be put under the eyebrow, close to the ball of the eye, a sensation will be felt like the burning of red hot iron, but which ceases the instant the spoon is removed. The plates will soon become oxydated, and require cleaning in order to make them act.

CHAPTER VIII.

LIGHT.

Light is derived from the sun in the solar system. This is called solar or celestial light. It is also derived from terrestrial objects; as from combustion, friction, chemical attraction, &c. which is called terrestrial light. It is generally accompanied with caloric. Every ray of common light contains in itself seven different kinds; these may be best separated by a triangular glass prism, but the same operation may be performed with a tumbler of water. The seven kinds of light differ in two remarkable characteristics; they are of different colours, and degrees of refrangibility; viz. red, orange, yellow, green, blue, indigo and violet. The red is least refrangible; the violet most; and the intermediates vary in their degree of refrangibility according to this order of succession. The different colouring of bodies depends on the different kinds of light which they reflect to the eye. White bodies reflect all kinds of light; black, reflect none: the different kinds, according to the arrangement of the constituent atoms of bodies reflecting them, not according to the nature of those bodies.

Example 1. Prepare the following solutions: 1. Sugar of lead dissolved, 1 to 50 of water per weight. 2. Pearlash, 1 to 4 of water. 3. Corrosive sublimate, 1 to 30 of water. 4. Copperas, 1 to 6 of water. 5. Sulphuric acid, 1 to 12 of water. 6. 1 to 100 of water. 7. Strong liquid of ammonia. 8. Tincture of red cabbage. 9. Tincture of galls. 10. Prusiate of potash. 11. Nitrate of mercury, made of 1 of mercury to 4 of nitric acid, to which add twice as much water. By mixing these liquids we make red—1 of 5 with 1 of 8. Orange, 4 of 3 with 1 of 2; limpid with 1 of 5. Yellow, 4 of 11 with 1 of 2. Green, 3 of 8 with 1 of 2; ruby red, with 1 of 5. Blue, 3 of 6 with 1 of 7; limpid with 1 of 5. Indigo, 1 of 4 with 1 of 10. Violet, add the red to the indigo. White, mix 3 of 1 with 1 of 2. Black, 3 of 9 with 1 of 4; limpid with 1 of 5.

These liquids either reflect different colours before they are mixed, from those which they reflect afterwards, or reflect no colour as some of them are limpid. It follows as a necessary conclusion, that colouring is not inherent in matter, but depends on the peculiar arrangement of the constituent atoms. As colours are changed by the various applications of the laws of chemical affinity, dyers, limners, &c. ought to be well acquainted with them.

Example 2. Rub two pieces of white quartz slightly together in the dark, and they will become luminous.

There are other bodies which absorb and give off light, as rotten wood, putrid fish, some artificial preparations, &c. Snow absorbs light by day, which it gives off at night—thus light is radiated from many substances, which seem not to belong to the class of luminous bodies. The particles of light are so extremely minute, that although they are projected in different directions, and cross each other, yet they are never known to interfere, or impede each others course. It is still a disputed point, however, whether light be a substance composed of particles like other bodies. In some respects it is obedient to the laws which govern bodies; in others it appears independent of them: thus, though its course is guided by the laws of motion, it does not seem to be influenced by the laws of gravity. It has never been discovered to have weight, though a variety of interesting experiments have been made in order to ascertain that point. Some have supposed that the rays of light, instead of being particles, consist of the undulations of an elastic medium, which fills all space, and which produces the sensation of light in the eye, just as the vibrations of the air produce the sensation of sound to the ear. Most of the phenomena may be accounted for by either hypothesis; but that of their being particles applies more happily to some of the facts respecting the modifications of light by refraction and reflection. Twilight is occasioned partly by refraction, but chiefly by reflection of the sun's rays by the atmosphere, and it lasts till the sun is eighteen degrees below the horizon. Were no atmosphere to reflect and refract the sun's rays, only that part of the heavens would be luminous in which the sun is placed; and if we could live without air, and should turn our backs to the sun, the whole heavens would appear as dark as in the night. In this case also, a sudden transition from the brightest sunshine to dark night, would immediately take place upon the setting of the sun.

CHAPTER IX.

OXYGEN GAS—*Vital Air.* Put a quantity of oxymuriate of potash into a small glass retort, to which is adapted a bent tube to collect the gas, and which passes beneath a bell glass filled with water; the retort is gradually heated; the air in the apparatus is expelled, the salt melts, is decomposed, and we obtain all the oxygen that enters into the composition of chloric acid and the potash—there remains in the retort a chlorulet of potassium. One hundred grains of the oxymuriate, yields thirty-nine grains of oxygen gas.

The Atmosphere, is composed of two distinct substances, termed oxygen and nitrogen gas. It is not a chemical *compound,* but a mere mixture of these gaseous substances in the proportion of 21 of the former and 79 of the latter. It contains, also, about one part in every thousand of carbonic acid gas, a considerable portion of water in a state of elastic vapour, and several adventitious substances. Oxygen is an element, or simple substance generally diffused through nature, though like caloric it does not exist by itself. It takes its name from two Greek words signifying that which produces or generates acids, because one of its general properties is to form acids by combining with different substances, which are called the bases of the several acids. Its different combinations are essential to animal life and combustion. Acted upon or combined with caloric it becomes oxygen gas, which is distinguished from all other gaseous matter by several important properties. Inflammable substances burn in it, under the same circumstances as in common air, but with vastly greater vividness. If a taper, the flame of which has been extinguished, the wick only remaining ignited, be plunged into a bottle filled with it, the flame will instantly be rekindled, and be very brilliant, and accompanied by a crackling noise. If a steel wire, or thin file, having a sharp point, armed with a bit of wood in a state of inflammation be introduced into a jar filled with the gas, the steel will take fire, and its combustion will continue, producing a most brilliant phenomenon. Oxygen gas is a little heavier than atmospheric air, and from its being absolutely necessary to the support of animal life, has been called vital air.

NITROGEN GAS. Phosphorus is inflamed in a given quantity of air—this gives up all its oxygen and the nitrogen is set free. For this purpose we set on fire a small bit of phosphorus, placed on a brick, which has been previous fixed on the shelf of a pneumatic trough, and which ought to be so elevated, that the phosphorus may be above the water in the trough, and, of course, in contact with the air. As soon as the phosphorus is inflamed, it should be covered with a large bell-glass full of atmospheric air, which dips into the water of the trough—the phosphorus, now in contact only with the air of the vessel, robs it of all its oxygen, forms phosphoric acid, which we see under the appearance of a very dense cloud, and a great amount of caloric and light is extricated; the air dilated by the heat which is produced, partly escapes in large bubbles : at the expiration of one or two minutes, the phosphorus goes out, and the process is terminated. The apparatus is left in the same situation, and the water is seen to rise in the bell-glass until this is cool ; the phosphoric acid is completely dissolved, and the interior of the apparatus, before nebulous and very opaque, regains its transparency. The nitrogen gas, which remains above the water, ought to be shaken sometimes with that fluid to remove any phosphoric acid it may retain, and particularly to decompose a portion of phosphuretted nitrogen gas which always is formed in the process, and which, thus agitated, abandons the phosphorus. Very pure nitrogen gas can be obtained by passing a stream of chlorine gas through liquid ammonia inclosed in a bottle.

Nitrogen is a substance diffused through nature, and particularly in animal bodies. It is not to be found in a solid or liquid state; but combined with caloric, it forms nitrogen, or as the French chemists call it on account of its being so destructive of life, *azotic gas*, in which no animal can breathe, or any combustible burn. It is uninflammable and somewhat lighter than atmospheric air, and though by itself it is so noxious to animals, it answers an important end, when mixed with oxygen gas in atmospheric air. Were it not for this large quantity of nitrogen in the atmosphere, the stimulating power of the oxygen would cause the blood to flow with too great rapidity through the vessels; the consequence of which would be, that the life of man would not be protracted to the length it now is. The vermilion colour of the blood is owing to the inhalation of oxygen gas. When the dark purple blood of the veins arrives at the lungs, it imbibes the vital air of the atmosphere, which changes its dark colour to a brilliant red, rendering it the spur to the action of the heart and arteries, the source of animal heat, and the cause of sensibility, irritability and motion. With regard to the nitrogen that is combined with atmospheric air, the greatest part of it is thrown out of the lungs at every respiration, and it rises above the head, that a fresh portion of air may be taken in, and that the same air may not be repeatedly breathed. The leaves of trees and other vegetables give out during the day a large portion of oxygen gas, which, uniting with the nitrogen thrown off by animal respiration, keeps up the equilibrium, and preserves the purity of the atmosphere. In the dark, plants absorb oxygen, but the proportion is small compared to what they exhale by day.

HYDROGEN GAS. Put a quantity of filings of zinc into a vessel which has a glass tube adapted to it, and pour upon them sulphuric acid, (oil of vitriol) diluted with six or eight times the quantity of water—an effervescence will immediately take place—the oxygen of it will immediately become united to the metal, and the hydrogen gas will be disengaged, and may be conveyed by the glass tube into any proper receiver. While it is rushing through the tube it may be kindled with a taper, and it will burn with a long flame like a candle.

Hydrogen gas is only one fourteenth the weight of atmospheric air, and occupies a space 1500 times greater than it possessed in its aqueous combination. It is continually emitting from vegetable and animal matter during their decay, and is evolved from various mines, volcanoes and other natural sources. From its great levity it has been used to fill air balloons. In the burning of the gas, the hydrogen unites with the oxygen of the atmosphere, and the result of the combination is flame and water. It has been supposed that torrents of rain, which generally accompany thunder storms may arise from a sudden combustion of hydrogen and oxygen gases by means of lightning. Hydrogen was the base of the gas which was formerly called inflammable air, and when in the aeriform state is the lightest of all ponderable things.

Hydrogen gas is procured by decomposing water by the galvanic battery; in this case it is extremely pure. It is also largely procured by decomposing the vapour of water made to pass over iron filings, or wire in a gun barrel.

NITROUS OXYDE GAS. (See chapter vi.)

PHOSPHURETTED HYDROGEN GAS. Take a tin quart basin—make an inch hole through the bottom—have a tin quart decanter with straight sides, let the mouth be soldered to the under side of the basin, so that it may fit the hole in the basin—now introduce through the hole in the basin, into the decanter, dry newly slacked lime, two parts mixed with one part of dry pearlashes, occasionally pouring in a little cold water, just sufficient for a thin paste, until it is nearly filled to the bottom of the basin—drop in two inches of a stick of phosphorus, cut into small pieces—stir the whole so as to mix all parts thoroughly

—set the decanter part on coals, or suspend it over a lamp—raise. a moderate heat: before the mass is to a boiling heat bubbles of the gas will appear in the neck and explode ;—now fill the neck with water, and lay on the mouth a piece of lead about two inches in diameter with a hole in the centre about the size of a pipe stem. Fill up the basin with cold water, which must be occasionally changed, by dipping out when it becomes too warm. Bubbles of gas will rise to the top of the water, explode, and form an ascending corona or wreath, but they will sometimes spread over the surface, appearing very small. Break off the foot of a wine-glass and use it as a receiver for collecting and turning up large bubbles, and for transferring gases into a cistern.

By this experiment we are furnished with an exhibition resembling what is sometimes called Jack o' the lantern, frequently seen in damp grounds, where animals are putrifying.

CARBONIC ACID GAS. This is more destructive of life than any other, and it extinguishes flame instantaneously. Water may be made by pressure, to absorb three times it bulk of this gas, by which it acquires an acidulous and not unpleasant taste. Soda water, cyder, and other fermented liquors owe their briskness and sparkling to the pressure of this gas. Fatal accidents often happen from the burning of charcoal in chambers, for wherever charcoal is burned, this gas is always formed. It so often occupies the bottom of wells that workmen ought not to venture into such places without prviously letting down a lighted candle—if the candle burns they may enter it with safety ; if not, a quantity of quicklime should be let down in buckets, and gradually sprinkled with water. As the lime slacks it will absorb the gas, and the workmen may afterwards descend in safety.

Pulverize a piece of marble—put a wine-glass full into a retort—pour on it a gill of water—when it has soaked a minute, pour in slowly half a wine-glass of sulphuric acid, diluted with about five times as much water : the carbonic acid will come over in the state of gas, and can be collected in any receiver placed on a shelf of the cistern. On this principle the carbonic acid for making acidulous waters, improperly called soda water, is obtained.

Pass some of the gas into a decanter of pure cold water, and agitate it until the water and gas are well mixed ; pour into a wine-glass of it some of the blue infusion of red cabbage, and it will become a very light red colour. The infusion ought rather to be greenish when put in, by having added to it an extremely small quantity of an alkali before it is used, otherwise the change in colour made by the acidulous water will hardly be perceived. Carbonated waters, called soda waters are made upon this principle. The waters, sold under the name of soda waters, as prepared generally, contain both sulphurous acid and muriatic acid. Chalk is commonly used, which contains generally a little of the muriate of soda—this being decomposed, furnishes muriatic acid—it is impossible to avoid a little mixture of sulphuric acid, used in the process. To cleanse the gas from these deleterious impurities, prepare the gas and force it through a condenser, containing a small quantity of water, before the water for use is introduced. Carbonated water, containing but about thrice its bulk of the gas, used with the syrups commonly employed makes an excellent table drink in hot weather.

C

SULPHUROUS ACID GAS.   Put into a glass retort, two parts of sulphuric acid, and one of mercury, and apply the heat of a lamp; the
mixture effervesces, and a gas issues from the beak of the retort,
which may be received in glass jars filled with mercury, and standing
in a mercurial trough.   In this process, the mercury in the retort combines with the oxygen of the sulphuric acid; and the sulphuric acid,
having lost a certain portion of its oxygen, is converted into *sulphurous* acid.   This gas is very abundant in the environs of volcanoes.
It was the vapour of sulphurous acid which suffocated Pliny, the natu-
ralist, in that eruption of Vesuvius by which Herculaneum was swal-
lowed up, in the year of Christ, 79.—It is composed of 68 parts sulphur and 32 parts oxygen.
    Sulphurous acid gas is produced by the slow combustion of sul-
phur.   If this gas be received in water the gas combines with it, and
sulphurous acid will be the result.   Water at 40° absorbs one third
of its weight of sulphurous acid gas.
    Sulphurous acid possesses very slight acid properties.   Instead of
changing vegetable blues to red, as acids generally do, it invariably
renders them white.   Suspend a red rose within a glass jar, and in
that situation expose it to the confined fumes of a brimstone match ;
this will soon produce a change in its colour, and at length the flower
will become quite white.
    MURIATIC ACID GAS.   Pour one part of sulphuric acid upon two
parts of dry muriate of soda, in a turbulated retort, and collect the gas
as it becomes disengaged, over mercury in a pneumatic apparatus.
Or, take some of the muriatic acid of commerce, heat it in a glass retort, and it may be collected as in the preceding method.   Proceed as
in the first experiment, but instead of collecting the gas over mercury,
receive it in a vessel containing a small portion of water.   By these
means liquid muriatic acid will be formed.   Take a small quantity of
silver, or a piece of an ore containing silver, and digest it in some *purified* nitric acid, which will dissolve the whole of the silver.   A single drop of muriatic acid will separate a portion of the silver in white
flakes, which will fall to the bottom of the glass in an insoluble precipitate.   Proceed as in the last experiment, but instead of using muriatic acid drop in a portion of common salt, which will as effectually
precipitate the silver. By these means any ore may be divested of
the silver it contains.
    To Remove Contagious Vapour arising from the Beds of the Sick.
Remove the sick and other persons from the room—set a tea-cup or
gallipot on the floor, half filled with table salt—pour into it strong
sulphuric acid, and the room will be filled with muriatic acid gas—
after a few minutes open the windows, and the air of the room will
be purified.
    To Neutralize Animal Effluvia arising from the Beds of the Sick.
Pour a tea-spoonful of muriatic acid upon a red hot iron shovel, and
then pouring a wine-glass of water upon it—the acid will rise up in
the state of a suffocating gas, and the water will follow it in the state
of vapour and absorb it almost instantaneously, so that the suffocating gas will wholly disappear.
    CHLORINE GAS.   Put into a retort a little black oxyde of manga-
nese in powder, and pour upon it double its weight of strong muri-

atic acid, connect the retort with the pneumatic trough, and receive the gas over water. When the ascension of the gas slackens, apply the heat of a lamp, and it will be disengaged in abundance. Its specific gravity is to that of hydrogen, nearly as 34 to 1.

If a small quantity of liquid oxymuriatic is wanted, it may readily be found with a little *euchlorine*, (a compound of chlorine and oxygen ; chlorous acid,) by dissolving a few grains of oxymuriate of potash, and adding the solution to an ounce of common muriatic acid. It is of a yellowish green colour, which was the cause of its being called *chlorine*. This gas cannot be breathed without great injury. It discharges vegetable colours—burns all the metals, and when combined with water, will dissolve gold and platinum : with various alkaline and earthy bases, it forms salts, called *chlorides*. Instead of changing blue vegetable colours red, as is the case with acids generally, chlorine destroys colours. Instead of distinguishing it as one of the acids, it would be more proper to call it an acidifying principle, for it possesses few properties which characterize that class of bodies. Its taste is astringent; and, unlike the acids, is combined very sparingly with water. It has not been decomposed either by electricity or galvanism ; which is presumptive proof of its being a simple substance. Its great use is in bleaching. The following experiment may be considered as a complete example of the process of bleaching coloured goods : if a few pieces of dyed linen cloth, of different colours be dipped into a phial of oxymuriatic acid, the colours will be quickly discharged ; for there are few colours which can resist its energetic effects.

Carburetted Hydrogen Gas. Take some pieces of coal from a coal pit bed, or some other place, where the coal has been exposed to the weather a long time, and has become intimately combined with water ; dry, pulverize, and heat it in a gun barrel ; the heat must be raised gradually, for a slow heat will evaporate the water, with but very little combination. Collect the gas into the cistern, and put some into a glass-holder and burn it, when will be produced a blue flame without giving much light.

Carburetted Hydrogen, united with Oxygen Gas. Mix the gases in equal volumes, in a bell glass, or tumbler, pour this into a narrow mouthed bottle or decanter, sink the bottle under the water of the cistern, holding the thumb over its mouth: wet a roll of paper in spirits turpentine, light it and hold it close to the water over the bottle and let up the gas in small bubbles—when they come in contact with the blaze of the taper they will explode, which produces a noise like the firing of musketry under the water.

Heavy Carburetted Hydrogen, or White Gas.—Take half a gill of alcohol, put it into a deep turbulated retort, pour upon it in a small steady stream, about twice as much by measure, of strong sulphuric acid—put in the stopper, and apply the candle to the retort, approaching it gradually. Let a little of the first escape, which consists of atmospheric air and ether, collect the gas over water ; if it contains considerable sulphuric acid, it will generally disappear soon, while standing over water; but lime water will purify it if necessary. Mix it with double its volume of oxygen and explode it, as directed with the carburetted hydrogen. Burn it pure in a stream, and it will give a very luminous blaze. Fill a glass cylinder, or eight ounce phial with liquid chlorine, pass this gas up into it, until about two-thirds of the liquid chlorine is displaced. The volume of the gas will be diminished on standing a few seconds, and water will ascend. On the surface of the water will be seen oily masses resembling small drops of tallow.

A Gas which will produce a luminous appearance. Take an ounce phial—fill it two-thirds full of sweet oil; now insert shavings of phosphorus, half an inch of a common stick will answer—hold the phial near the fire, until nearly as hot as can be borne by the hand; keep it at this temperature till the phosphorus is melted, then take out the cork, the upper part of the phial will become luminous in the dark; let every light be extinguished in the room, and pour two or three teaspoonfuls of it in your hand—rub it thoroughly over your face and hair—the face will become exceedingly luminous—the hair exhibiting undulating flames. The phial must be warm, not hot, that the oil may have a temperature equal to blood heat when applied.

Phosphorus, is obtained from animal bones. The process is too lengthy to show in this work; a very small quantity is sufficient for experiments—it can be purchased at $1 50, to $2 per oz.

To obtain the Oxyde of Phosphorus. Let a stick of phosphorus be exposed in water, for several days in a phial : the outside will be covered with a white substance—this is the oxyde, which is more inflammable than that which is free.

Application. 1. Scrape a little off, and expose it to the rays of the sun, and in a short time it will take fire.

2. By heating a phial moderately, with a piece of phosphorus attached to the end of a wire, and rubbing it about the inside in a half melted state, so as to coat it, we obtain the oxyde, or as it is sometimes called "Phosphoric coat match phial." If it is not very cold weather, by taking a little out and exposing it to the air, it will take fire and burn spontaneously. In preparing it there is danger of its taking fire, in which case the phial must be stopped until the flame is extinguished.

3. Rub a stick of phosphorus lightly on a board, and it will appear luminous in the dark. Blow on it, and undulating waves will be exhibited and vanish alternately.

4. *To produce brilliant sparks.* Place on a table, a pefectly dry earthen plate, in the centre of which lay a small piece of phosphorus; set it on fire and invert over it a half gallon turbulated bell glass, perfectly dry : raise one side of the glass a little, or place a chip under it; start the stopper of the turbulature a little, so as to permit the nitrogen gas to escape, as the oxygen of air in the glass becomes exhausted. We are thus furnished with the exhibition of a snow storm. Dry white phosphoric acid will fall on the plate; it strongly attracts water, like the other acids; it will become liquid, though corked very tight in a phial; therefore, much care is necessary to keep it perfectly tight in a phial. While the powder remains dry and undisturbed on the plate, dip a fine shaving brush into some cold water, and strike it across your finger, so as to sprinkle very fine drops of water on the powder, and very brilliant sparks will be exhibited.

Phosphorus Bottles. Phosphorus two drachms, lime one drachm, mixed together, put into a closely stopped phial, and heat it before the fire, or in a ladle of sand for about half an hour.

2. Phosphorus one drachm, cera alba fifteen grains, put it into a bottle under water, and melt them together; let the water cool, and as it begins to grow solid, turn the bottle round that the sides may be coated; then pour out the water and dry it in a cool place.

Matches for instantaneous light. Oxymuriate of potash, flour of sulphur, each half a scruple, vermilion two grains, a sufficient quantity of oil of turpentine to make a paste, with which coat the ends of slips of wood, previously dipped in oil of turpentine and dried; when these matches are plunged in oil of vitriol and immediately withdrawn, they take fire instantaneously. To prevent the oil of vitriol from spilling, if the bottle should accidentally fall on one side, pounded asbestos, or sand is put into the bottle to soak up the acid.

2. Oxymuriate of potash nine grains, sugar three grains, flour of sulphur two grains, a sufficient quantity of spirits of wine; the wood to be previously primed with camphire dissolved in spirits of wine.

CHAPTER X.

Glauber Salts. Put a tea spoonful of table salt into a wine glass, which has been previously dried on a plate; pour upon it a tea spoonful of sulphuric acid. Muriatic gas will escape into the atmosphere, and glauber salts will be formed in the wine glass. *By this experiment elective affinity is illustrated.*

Put some sulphuric acid into a tumbler, diluted with six times as much water; drop in some carbonate of soda until effervescence ceases; and the nauseous taste of glauber salts will be recognized. By slow evaporation it may be crystalized.

Silver Boiling Powder. White argol, common salt, of each a sufficient quantity; a small quantity of this powder is put into water, and plate is boiled in it, to which it gives a brilliant brightness.

Borax. Common borax dissolved in about sixteen times its bulk of hot water in a gallipot; then pour into it nearly half its weight of sulphuric acid; stir it on hot coals five or six minutes, then set it by to cool. Decomposition takes place; sulphate of soda is formed, which remains in solution; the boracic acid is disengaged and appears as shining solid scales; pour off the solution and rinse the scales several times in cold water; each time wait for them to separate from the water; when well washed they are nearly tasteless. Now dissolve some of the scales in alcohol on an earthen plate; set the alcohol on fire with a lighted roll of paper; as it burns the sides of the flame will be tinged with a beautiful green.

The salt which this acid forms in combustion with soda is much used in bronzing, under the name of borax. It brings brass to the liquid state, when thrown upon it at a temperature considerably lower than its fusing point.

Epsom Salts. Put sulphuric acid into a tumbler, diluted with about six times as much water; drop in carbonate of magnesia until effervescence ceases; thus epsom salts are formed in solution.

Pure Silex Powder. Heat a gun flint red hot and throw it into cold water in order to render it brittle; pulverize it very fine and mix the powder with about five times its bulk of pearlash, melt the mixture and keep it in a state of fusion fifteen minutes; now dissolve it in two or three times its bulk of water; pour in diluted sulphuric acid, a little at a time, as long as it continues to cause a precipitation. After it stands a little while to settle, pour off the liquid part, and wash or rinse the precipitate in hot water several times until the water poured off is tasteless.

This substance is the principal ingredient in gun flints, rock crystals, carnelian, &c. On this principle glass is manufactured.

Oxydated Tin. Put some tin in an iron ladle and heat it no higher than to melt it; the surface will immediately absorb oxygen from the atmosphere sufficient to form the *protoxid of tin,* called the yellow oxyde. This may be scraped off with an iron poker, when another similar pellicle will be formed; and the succession may be continued until the whole mass is an oxyd.

If the protoxid of tin be put into a crucible, heated to redness, and continually stirred with an iron rod for some time, it will absorb another definite proportion of oxygen. It then becomes *peroxyd of tin,* called the white oxyde, or putty of tin.

The white oxyde of tin is an excellent material for sharpening edge tools, as knives, razors, &c.—for polishing burnishes, glass lenses, &c. When melted with glass it forms the white enamel used for clock and watch faces, &c.

Acetate of Alumine. Dissolve equal parts of alum and sugar of lead in water, in separate wine glasses, and mix these solutions. The acids exchange bases; and the sulphate of lead falls down, while the acetate of alumine remains over it in a liquid state. This liquid may be poured off for use.

It is an important mordant much used in dying, and it is manufactured in this way by calico printers.

Explosive Powder. Scatter some thin shavings of phosphorus over the bottom of a broad iron mortar; sprinkle crystals of oxymuriate of potash among them. Now, putting a leather glove upon the hand, rub the iron pestle smartly around among the shavings and the phosphorus, and a succession of explosions will be made, resembling the irregular discharge of musketry.

All explosive powders are indebted for their powers to the same principle. Gun powder is composed of 75 per cent. of nitrate of potash, 15 per cent. of charcoal, and 10 per cent. of sulphur.

Lime. Put a little potter's clay paste into a crucible, and heat it in the forge as high as white heat of iron; now pour it out upon a brick on a table, and it will be perceived that it is not melted; mix some of the same kind of clay intimately with about an equal quantity of pulverized marble or chalk, and heat it again as hot as before; pour it out and the whole mass will spread on the brick in the state of melted cinder.

On this principle potters reject all clay which contains lime. When clay contains a very small per centum of carbonate of lime, it would be sufficient to cause a kiln of potter's ware to melt. The carbonate of lime can always be detected by pouring on a few drops of diluted muriatic acid. Ever so small a quantity of lime will cause an effervescence, and prove the mass to be clay-marl, unfit for pottery.

Bleaching Salt, used in manufactories. Pass into water, in which finely pulverized and newly slacked lime is suspended by continual agitation—a stream of oxymuriatic acid gas will come over. In the large way, a dry powder of newly slacked lime is agitated in a strong cask, which is absorbed by lime. Some prefer passing the gas into hogsheads of water, in which the lime is suspended by agitation; for an experiment it may be pressed from a bladder, as directed in making oxymuriate of potash; but the bladder may be held in the hand, and the receiver shaken continually.

Alkaline Salts. Dissolve in separate wine glasses a little copperas, blue vitriol, white vitriol, and sugar of lead; pour into each a small quantity of the solutions of either potash, soda, or ammonia, and the metallic oxyde of the salt will be precipitated, and an alkaline salt formed in each glass.

This principle is of much use in the manufacture of articles used in medicine and the arts, as will be evident by attending the daily business of the laboratory.

Cobalt, is sold in the shops in the state of an imperfect oxyde, called zaffre. The pure metal is reddish grey.

Mix finely pulverized flint and borax, and put in a small quantity of zaffre. Melt this mixture with pretty strong heat in a crucible, and a strong blue glass will be produced. Or, put a little zaffre in borax alone, or in pearlash, and melt the mixture.

The smalt sold in shops in powder is merely pulverized glass prepared as above.

Liver of Sulphur. Take some dry pearlash, and half as much sulphur, mix them and rub them well together: melt them in a crucible, covered with another. As soon as melted it must be poured out, and corked up tight in a phial to prevent its deliquencing. Sulphuretted hydrogen gas may be made with this equally as well as the sulphate of iron.

Artificial Volcanoes. Ram with force into a large pot, a paste, made of 100 pounds of iron filings, intimately mixed with 100 pounds of pulverized sulphur, and just water enough to make a dense paste. This pot is then buried to a considerable depth in the earth, and between ten and twenty hours afterwards it bursts and burns with great force. It is presumed this experiment was never tried in America. It requires a great quantity of the mixture to produce any effect. Lemery produced it with the quantity above specified.

Magnesia, is found pure, or merely combined with water: sometimes it forms one of the constituents of the soap stone or talcose rocks, of asbestos, and some other minerals. It is generally obtained from sea water, after it is separated from the common salt: it exists in the state of a muriate and sulphate in sea water, from which it is obtained by mixing with it a solution of common pearlash. A double decomposition takes place; and while the sulphate of potash remains in solution, the carbonate of magnesia falls down. This is the carbonated, or white magnesia of the shops.

Calcined Magnesia. Drop diluted sulphuric acid upon carbonate of magnesia of the shops, and it will effervesce violently; that is, a bubbling will be caused by the escape of carbonic acid in the state of gas: put a little of the same carbonate of magnesia into a crucible, and keep it about the white heat of iron fifteen minutes: now after it cools, drop on it diluted sulphuric acid, and it will scarcely effervesce, because the carbonic acid is driven out. If a little of it be dissolved in water it will give the alkaline test with red cabbage, much stronger than before heating.

It is difficult to drive off all the carbonic acid by heat, so that no effervescence can be produced by the application of sulphuric acid.

Tooth Powder.   Heat finely pulverized charcoal to redness in an iron skillet, and pouring it while hot into a bowl of clean water, is the best of all substances to preserve the teeth from decay, after it has commenced.   If kept in a bottle, it will remain under water, defended from gases, and if shaken up and a tea spoonful taken occasionally in the mouth, and the teeth rubbed with it, every thing impure will be absorbed.

Putrid meat will become purified by immersing it in a similar manner: putrid water is purified by pouring into it heated charcoal powder.

2.   Rad. irid. flor. four ounces; oss. sepiæ, two ounces; crem. tart. one ounce; ol. caryoph. sixteen drops; lake sixteen drops.

3.   Catechú, one ounce; cort. peruv. flav., crem. tart. cassia, bol. armen., of each 4 drahcms; sang. dracon. myrrh, of each two drachms.

4.   Rose pink, twenty ounces; bole armen. oss. sepiæ, crem. tart. of each eight ounces; myrrh four ounces; rad. irid. flor. two ounces; ess. bergam. half a drachm.

5.   Oss. sepiæ, four ounces; crem. tart. rad. irid. flor. of each two ounces; alum, ustri, rose pink, of each one ounce.

6.   Magnesia, rad. irid. flor., rose pink, cretæ ppæ, of each two ounces; natr. ppi. six drachms; ol. rhodii, two drops.

Ginger Beer Powders.   White sugar, one drachm two scruples; ginger, five grains; natr. pp. twenty-six grains in each blue paper : acid of tartar, one scruple and a half in each white paper.   These quantities are for half a pint of water.

Spruce Beer Powders.   White sugar, one drachm two scruples; natr. pp. twenty-six grains; essence of spruce, ten grains, in each blue paper: acid of tartar, half a drachm in each white paper; for half a pint of water.

Soda Powders.   Carbonate of soda, half a drachm in each blue paper: acid of tartar, twenty five grains, in each white paper; for half a pint of water—a very pleasant and cooling beverage in summer: sugar, if desirable, may be added to the paper containing the acid of tartar.

Portable Lemonade.   Acid of tartar, one ounce; sugar, six ounces; essence of lemon, one drachm: rub together, divide into twenty-four papers, for a tumbler of water each.

Copperas, Sulphate of Iron.   Put diluted sulphuric acid into a Florence flask, consisting of about five times as much water as acid.   Apply a very little heat, so as rather to warm than heat the acid.   Drop in iron filings until they will fall to the bottom quietly; pour off the limpid liquid into earthen plates.   This is copperas in solution; and by a slow evaporation it may be crystallized.   On this principle the copperas of commerce is manufactured; but the process is different. Iron pyrites is moistened and exposed to the atmosphere a considerable time in a shallow vat or box; after it becomes covered with a crust it is dissolved in water or leached, and evaporated.

Oxymuriate of Potash.   Mix common salt three pounds, manganese two pounds, and add oil of vitrol two pounds, previously diluted with a sufficient quantity of water, distil into a receiver containing prepared kali, six ounces; dissolved in water, three pounds: when the distillation is finished, evaporate the liquid in the receiver slowly in the dark; the oxymuriate will crystallize first in flakes; stimulant, from one to two grains; explodes when struck, or dropped into acid.

Salt of Sorrel. From the leaves of wood sorrel bruised and expressed; the juice is then left to settle, poured off clear, and crystallized by slow evaporation; one hundred weight of wood sorrel yields five or six ounces.

2. By dropping aqua kali into a saturated solution of oxalic acid in water, it will precipitate, and may be separated by filtration; if too much alkali is added, it is taken up, and will require an addition of the acid to throw it down again; cooling—used to make lemonade, and whey, as also salt of lemons.

Ammonia. Ammonia is serviceable in dying, and in staining ivory; but its principal use is in making the muriate of ammonia, of which it is the bases. It is formed by combining ammonia with muriatic acid. It is known in commerce by the name of *Sal Ammoniac.*

Convey some muriatic acid gas into a glass jar containing a portion of ammoniacal gas. From the mixture of these two invisible gases a solid substance will be produced; viz. the common sal ammoniac.

Sal ammoniac is used by some dyers in what they call composition, to prevent the tin from precipitating. In tinning metals it is of use to cleanse the surfaces, and to prevent them from oxydizing by the heat which is given to them in the operation. It is also employed in the assay of metals, to discover the presence of iron. Ammoniacal gas may be procured by heating strong liquid ammonia; this gas will be disengaged in abundance. On account of its affinity for water, it must be received over mercury, when it is intended to exhibit it in the state of gas. Pour a little caustic ammonia into a clear solution of sulphate of zinc. This will precipitate the metal in a white powder. If the phial be now shaken, the zinc will be immediately re-dissolved, thus serving as a test to distinguish zinc from iron and various metals. Drop as much nitrate of copper into water as will form a colourless solution; then add a little ammonia, equally colourless, and an intense blue color will arise from the mixture. Take the blue solution formed by the last experiment, add a little sulphuric acid, and the colour will *disappear;* pour in a little solution of caustic ammonia, and the blue colour will be restored. Thus may the liquor be alternately changed at pleasure. Dissolve some oxyde of cobalt in caustic ammonia; this will produce a *red* solution, different in colour from that of all other metallic solutions.

1. *Double elective affinity.* Take about four parts of muriate of lime, and five parts of sulphate of soda, weighing them after being well dried over coals, on plates. Dissolve them in water separately. Now mix them in a wine-glass, and a precipitate of lime (gypsum) will soon settle at the bottom, and a solution of the muriate of soda will stand over it. On testing the new compounds with red cabbage, they will be found to be neutral salts, exhibiting neither the acid or alkaline test. On tasting the liquid, it will be found a solution of table salt.

Corrosive sublimate of the shops is made upon this principle, by sulphate of mercury and muriate of soda.

Dr. Wallaston constructed a scale, by which the artist or chemist can at sight determine what proportions of any compounds are required for decomposing each other without loss. For example, if a given

E

quantity of sulphuric acid and muriatic acid would require three times as much potash as alumine for saturation: though all these acids would differ from each other in the absolute quantity required.

2. Put into two wine-glasses, half a spoonful of muriatic acid to each; weigh two equal parcels of carbonate of soda, about a teaspoonful to each glass. Drop the carbonate of soda from each parcel into its respective glass, till effervescence ceases. Now weigh what remains of each parcel, and they will be found equal. Try the two liquids with tasting rods, (pine sticks are as good for the purpose as tasting rods,) and the taste of common table salt will be recognized. From this experiment will be learned that the law of definite proportions, is of great importance in the arts. It regulates the uniformity of compound bodies, and prevents the evils which might arise from carelessness or mistake in the manufacture of many articles. For example, in the manafacture of copperas, 36 parts of protoxyde of iron will unite with precisely 40 parts of sulphuric acid. And in the manufacture of white vitriol, 42 parts of oxyde of zinc will unite with 40 parts of sulphuric acid. These are the uniform proportions in the dry state, and each take 63 parts of water for crystallization.

3. Mix alcohol and water, or sulphuric acid and water. The qualities and sensible proportions of both these liquids will remain unchanged, being diffused among the water, there will be less of them in a given measure, but they will remain unchanged. Thus, by affinity, some substances unite in indefinite proportions, and their properties and sensible qualities are not changed.

CHAPTER XI.
OF SOAP AND POMADES.

To make Soap. Melt a little common potash in an iron ladle, then put into it small bits of fresh meat and woollen rags, and boil them in a short time. The rags and meat will be dissolved, and soap will be formed. On this principle soap is made by boiling any animal substance with lye. It requires very strong lye, or rather potash, to convert rags and some other animal substances into soap.

White Soap. Into half a wineglass of water, pour a teaspoonful of olive oil—no combination takes place—drop in a piece of pearlash of the size of half a pigeon's egg: let it dissolve and stir the mixture, which effects a chemical combination, and produces white soap. This experiment illustrates simple affinity.

Hard Soap. Heat in a clean tin basin, good soft soap until dissolved, with about twice its measure of rain or river water—then put in about half a gill of fine common salt, to a quart of this solution. The muriatic acid of the salt will unite with the potash of the soap, and leave the soda of the salt to unite with the oil of the soap; this latter compound, after a little boiling, will become somewhat dense and float on the surface of the liquid. On draining off the liquid, which is chiefly muriate of potash, and drying the floating compound, we obtain common hard soap.

Soap boilers make common hard soap on this principle. The liquid muriate of potash, they call waste lye, or dead lye. The fine hard soap is made directly from the barilla or kelp, which is a rough sub-carbonate of soda, made from the leached ashes of sea-weeds.

White Wash Balls. One pound sap. alb. bisp.; three pints aqua rosar. album. ovor no. ij.; one ounce aq. kali ppi.: boil till hard again, add one scruple ol. lign. rhod., ten drops ol. caryoph. one drachm ess. jasmin. half a drachm of ess. neroli, and form into squares.

2. Five pounds of white soap, four ounces rad. irid. flor; three ounc. amyli; one ounce styræ calum. aq. rosar. q. s.

3. One pound sap. alb. hisp. almonds blanched, beat up into a paste with rose water and orange flower water, three ounces; one ounce magister. marcasitæ; two drachms of kali ppi.; six grains of musk. three grains of cive; one scruple ol. lign. rhodi; one drachm ess. jasmin.

Cream Balls. Seven pounds white curd soap; one pound amyli; water a sufficient quantity; beat it together, weigh it into ounce balls, and roll in pulverized amyli.

White soap, starch, of each one pound; ess. lemon four drachms; aq. rosar. eight ounces; make into balls of three ounces and a half each.

Red Mottled Wash Balls. Cut white soap into small square pieces, roll them in vermilion, and squeeze the pieces together into balls without mixing them more than is necessary.

Blue Mottled Wash Balls. In like manner rolling the pieces in powder blue.

Windsor Soap. Hard curd soap, melted and scented with ol. carui and ess. bergam.; an inferior sort is made with ol. carui only.

Starkey's Soap. Made by rubbing warm kali ppi. with ol. turpentine, adding a little water.

Macquer's Acid Soap. Four ounces sapon. ven.; ol. vitriol, q. s. add the acid by degrees to the soap, rendered soft by a little water, continually rubbing the mass in a mortar—detergent, used when alkalies would be prejudicial.

Shaving Liquid—Shaving Oil. Sap. Moll. four pounds; spirits wine rectified five pints.

Essence Royale pour fair la barbe. Sap. cast. eight ounces, proof spirits one pint.

Pomade de la jeunnesse. Pomatum mixed with pearl white, or magestery of bismuth; turns the hair black.

Pomade Divine. One pound eight ounces of beef's marrow; cinnamon, one ounce and a half; stor. calam. benzoini, rad. irid flor. of each one ounce; caryoph. nuc. myrist. of each one drachm.

2. Sevi. ovilli, one pound eight ounces; stor. calam, benzoini, rad. irid. flor., rad. cyperi, cinnam., caryoph. arom. nuc. mosch., of each nine drachms; keep melted in a gentle heat for some time, then strain.

3. Sevi. ovilli four pounds; cera alb. one pound; ess. bergam. ess. lemon, of each one ounce and a half; ol. lavend., ol. origani, of each four drachms.

CHAPTER XII.

PAINTING.

The art of painting gives the most direct and expressive representation of objects; and it was doubtless, for this reason employed by many nations, before the art of writing was invented, to communicate their thoughts, and to convey intelligence to distant places. The pencil may be said to write a universal language; for every one can instantly understand the meaning of a painter, provided he be faithful to the rules of his art. His skill enables him to display the various scenes of nature at one view; and by his delineation of the striking effects of passion, he instantaneously affects the soul of the spectator. Silent and uniform as is the address which a good picture makes to us, yet it penetrates so deeply into our affections, as to appear to exceed the power of eloquence. Painting is the most imitative of all the arts. It gives to us the very forms of those, whose works of genius and virtue, have commanded or won our admiration, and transmits them from age to age, as if not life merely, but immortality flowed in the colours of the artist's pencil; or to speak of its still happier use, it preserves to us the lineaments of those whom we love, when separated from us either by distance or the tomb. How many of the feelings, which we should most regret to lose, would be lost, but for this delightful art,—feelings that ennoble, by giving us the wish to imitate what was noble in the moral hero or sage, on whom we gaze, or that comfort us by the imaginary presence of those whose affection is the only thing dearer to us, than even our admiration of heroism or wisdom. The value of painting will, indeed, be best felt by those who have lost by death a parent or much loved friend, and who feel that they should not have lost every thing, if some pictured memorial had still remained.

Paintings, in regard to their subjects, are called historical, landscape or portrait; and in regard to the painters, they are divided into schools or countries; as the Italian, German, French, English, and other schools. Each of the schools has treated the practice of painting in its peculiar manner, and each with exquisite beauty and admirable effect. The great component parts of painting are, invention, or the power of conceiving the materials proper to be introduced into a picture; composition, or the power of arranging them; design, or the power of delineating them; the management of lights and shades; and the colouring. Invention consists principally in three things, the choice of a subject properly within the scope of the art; the seizure of the most striking and energetic moment of time for representation, and the discovery and selection of such objects, and such probable incidental circumstances, as, combined together, may best tend to develope the story, or augment the interest of the piece. In this part of the art, there is a cartoon of Raphael, which furnishes an example of genius and sagacity. It represents the inhabitants of Lystra about to offer sacrifice to Paul and Barnabas. It was necessary to let us into all the cause and hurry before us; accordingly, the cripple, whom they had miraculously healed, appears in the crowd: observe the means which the painter has used to distinguish this object, and of course to open the subject of his piece. His crutches, now useless, are thrown to the ground; his attitude is that of one accustomed to such support and still doubtful of his limbs: the eagerness, the impetuosity, with which he solicits his benefactors to accept the honours destined for them, points out his gratitude and the occasion of it. During the time he is thus busied, an elderly citizen of some consequence, by his appearance, draws near, and lifting up the corner of his vest, surveys with astonishment, the limb newly restored: whilst a man of middle age, and a youth, looking over the shoulder of the cripple, are intent on the same object. The wit of man could not devise means more certain of the end proposed. In the cartoon of Paul preaching at Athens, the elevated situation, and energetic action of the apostle, instantly denote him the hero of the piece, whilst the attentive but astonished circle gathered around him, receive as it were, light from him, their centre, and unequivocally declare him the resistless organ of divine truth.

Painting, as applied to purposes of building, is the application of artificial colours, compounded either with oil or water, in embellishing and preserving wood, &c. This branch of painting is termed *economical*, and applies more immediately to the power which oil and varnishes possess of preventing the action of the atmosphere upon wood, iron, and stucco, by interposing an artificial surface. But it is here intended to use the term more generally, in allusion to the decorative part, and as is employed by the architect, throughout every part of his work. In every branch of painting in oil, the general processes are very similar, and with such variation only, as readily occur to the workman.

The first coatings, or layers, if on wood or iron, ought always to be of white lead of the best quality, previously ground very fine in nut or linseed oil, either over a stone, with a muller, or passed through a mill. If used on shutters, doors, or wainscoting, made of fir or deal, it is very requisite to destroy the effects of the knots; which, generally, are so completely saturated with turpentine, as to render it perhaps, one of the most difficult processes in this business. The best mode, in common cases, is, to pass a brush over the knots, with lead ground in water, bound by a size made of parchment or glue; when that is dry, paint the knots with white lead ground in oil, to which add some powerful drier, as red lead, or litharge of lead; about one fourth part of the latter. These must be laid very smoothly in the direction of the grain of the wood. When the last coat is dry, smooth it with pumice stone, or give it the first coat of paint, prepared with nut or linseed oil; when dry, all nail holes or other irregularities must be stopped with a composition of oil and Spanish White. The work must then be again painted with white lead and oil, somewhat diluted with the essence of turpentine, which process should be repeated not less than three or four times, if a plain white or stone colour is intended; and if the latter colour, a small quantity of ivory or lamp black should be added. But if the work is to be finished of any other colour, either grey, green, &c. it will be requisite to provide for such color, after the third operation, particularly if it is to be finished flat, or as the painters style it, dead white, fawn, grey, &c. To finish a work flatted or dead, which is a preferable mode for all superior works, one coat of the flatted colour, or colour mixed with a considerable quantity of turpentine will be found sufficient, although it will be frequently requisite to give large surfaces two coats of the flatting colour. For stucco it will be almost a general rule. In all these operations, some sort of drier is necessary; a very general and useful one is made, by grinding in linseed, (or, perhaps, prepared oils boiled, are better,) about two parts of the best white copperas, well dried with one part of litharge.

The best drier for all fine whites, and other delicate tints is sugar of lead, ground in nut oil: about the size of a walnut will be sufficient for 20 lbs. of colour, when the basis is white lead. Painters' utensils should be always kept very clean. If the colour should become foul, it must be passed through a fine sieve or canvass, and the surface of the work carefully rubbed down with sand paper or pumice stone. The latter should be ground in water, if the paint is tender. In general cases, perhaps two or three years are not too long to suffer stucco to remain unpainted. When it is on battened work it may be painted much sooner than when prepared on brick. For priming and laying on the first coat on stucco, take linseed or nut oil, boiled with driers as before-mentioned; taking care in all cases not to lay on so much, as to render the surface rough, and no more than the stucco will absorb. It should be covered with three or four coats of white lead, prepared as described for painting on wainscoting, letting each coat dry hard. If it is wished to give the work a grey tint, light green, &c. about the third coat prepare the ground for such tint, by a slight advance towards it. Grey is made with white lead, Prussian blue, ivory black, and lake; sage green, pea and sea greens, with white, Prussian blue, and fine yellow; apricot and peach, with lake, white, and Chinese vermilion; fine yellow fawn colour, with burnt terra sienna, or umber and white; and olive greens with fine Prussian blues and Oxfordshire ochre.

Distemper, or painting in water colour, mixed with size, stucco or plaster, if not sufficiently dry to receive oil, may have a coating in water colours, of any given tint required. Straw colours may be made with French white and ceruse, or white lead and massicot, or Dutch pink. Grays, full, with some whites and refiner's verditure. An inferior grey may be made with blue black, or bone black and indigo. pea greens, with French green, Olympian green, &c. Fawn colour with burnt terra de sienna, or burnt umber and white, and so of any intermediate tint. Grind all the colours very fine, and mix with whiting and a size made with parchment, or some similar substance. Less than than two coats will not be sufficient to cover the plaster, and present a uniform appearance. If it should be desirable to have the stucco painted in oil, the whole of the water colours should be removed, which can be easily done by washing, and when quite dry, proceed with it after the directions given in painting on stucco. If old plastering has become disfigured by stains, or other blemishes, and if if it is desirable to paint in distemper, in this case, it is advisable to give the old plastering, when properly cleaned and prepared, one coat at least, of white lead ground in oil, and used with spirits of turpentine, which will generally fix old stains, and when quite dry, will take water colours very kindly.

Directions for Painting in oil on Canvass. After your cloth is nailed on the frame, pass over it a coat of size; when dry, rub it over with a pounce stone, to eat off all the knobs: the first size is intended to lay down all the threads, and fill up all the small holes, to prevent the colour from passing through. When the cloth is dry lay on a coat of simple colour, which may not destroy the others; for example, brown red, which is a natural earth, full of substance and lasting. If mixed with a little white lead it will dry sooner. In grinding this colour, use nut or linseed oil, and it should be prepared to lay on as thin as possible. When this colour is dry, rub it again with the pounce stone, which renders it smoother: lay another coat of white lead and charcoal black, to render the ground greyish, having care in putting on as little colour as possible, to prevent the cloth from cracking, and for the better preservation of the colours to be laid afterwards. We will observe, that if there was no ground laid on the canvass of a picture, previous to painting it, and if painted directly on the bare cloth without any preparation, the colours would appear much more to their advantage, and preserve their brightness much longer. Some of the first masters impregnate their canvass with water colours only, and paint afterwards in oil over that ground. This method renders pieces more lively and bright, because the ground in water colours draws and soaks the oil from the colours, rendering them finer; whereas, on the contrary, oil is the cause of their dulness, by its detention in their colours. It is desirable therefore, to use as little oil as possible; and in order to keep the colours stiff, mix with them a little of the oil of spike, which will evaporate very soon, but renders them more fluid and tractable in working. We cannot recommend too much care in keeping the colours (for the least tint might destroy the best design) unmixed, either with brush or pencil. When there is occasion to give more strength to some parts of a picture, let it be well dried before it is interrupted again. The custom prevails of grounding the canvass with oil colours; but when the canvass is good and very fine, the less colour which can be laid on for that purpose is preferable. Care is also requisite, that the colours and oils are good. The lead which some painters use to dry the sooner, soon destroys their brightness and beauty. In short, he shows his judgment in painting, who is not hasty in laying his colours, but lays them thick enough, and covers, at several times, his carnations, which, in terms of art is called *empater.*

Directions for Colouring Prints. All the colours used for this purpose are ground with gum water, excepting calcined green. For complexions, a mixture of white and vermilion.

For the lips, lake and vermilion.

For the shades, white and vermilion, and considerable umber.

For the hair, white with very little umber; if a carroty colour, yellow ochre and brown red; the shade with bistre and lake, mixed together; if light, mix black, white, and umber together.

For the clothes, if linen, white lead and a little blue; if stuffs, white lead alone, and the shades with a grey colour, made by means of a mixture of black and white lead together. If a white cloth, a mixture of white and umber together, and shade with a compound of umber and black. If a red cloth, use vermilion in the lighter parts of the folds; lake and vermilion, for the clear shades; lake alone laid on the vermilion, will form the dark shades.

Directions for mixing of Colours. Pale yellow for lights—white massicot. The chiaro ascuro, with the massicot and umber. The dark shade, with umber alone.

Orange. Black lead, for the lights; shade with the lake. The lake is used very clear for the lights, in drapery, and thicker for the shades.

Purple. Blue, white, and lake, for lights; blue, and lake, only, for the clear shades; and indigo and blue for the darker ones. The pale blue is used for the lights; and for the clear shades, a little thicker; but for the darker shades, mix the indigo and blue together.

The gold like yellow is made with yellow massicot for the lights—clear shades, a mixture of black lead and massicot—dark shade, lake, yellow ochre, and a very little black lead: and darkest of all, cologne earth and lake.

The green is of two sorts. The first—massicot and blue, or blue and white; for the shade, make the blue predominate in the mixture. The other is made with calcined green, and their shades may be formed by the addition of indigo.

For trees mix green and umber together. The grounds are made in the same way. For the distance, mix blue and green together. Mountains are always made with blue. The skies are made with blue, but add a little yellow when you come near the mountains, and to make the transition between that and the blue, mix a little lake and blue together to soften it.

Clouds are made with purple; if they be obscure, mix lake and indigo together. Stones are made with white and yellow mixed together; and their shades with black.

CHAPTER XIII.

OF PAINTS, COSMETICS, DYES, &c.

Patent Yellow. Pulverise common table salt very finely; put it into Wedgwood's mortar; add to it twice as much red lead, pulverised: rub them well together first; then add water a very little at a time, and continue rubbing until a paste is formed. The muriate of lead will now be formed, and the soda disengaged; pour in a large quantity of water and wash it several times; the soda will wash out and leave a white mass; dry this mass and then melt it in a crucible; and a beautiful substance will be formed, called patent yellow, which is one of the most durable pigments.

2. Common salt 100 lbs. litharge 400 lbs. ground together with water; keep for some time in a gentle heat, water being added to supply the loss by evaporation, the natron then washed out with more water, and the white residuum heated till it acquires a fine yellow colour.

Flake White. Made by suspending rolls of thin sheet lead over vinegar in close vessels; the evaporation from the vinegar being kept up by the vessels being placed in a heap of manure, or a steam bath.

2. By dissolving litharge in diluted nitrous acid, and adding prepared chalk to the solution; astringent, cooling; used externally: also employed as paint, mixed with nut oil.

Protóxid of Lead. Melt some lead in a ladle, and scrape off the pellicle which forms on its surface several times, or until a sufficient quantity is obtained; part of this is oxidated and part is not; now put this into a ladle by itself: and expose it to a low red heat, continually stirring it with a rod until it becomes of a yellow colour.

This is the *massicot* used in the arts; also for setting a fine edge to razors, for polishing burnishers, &c.

Red Lead. Put some *massicot* into a ladle; cover it over loosely with an earthen or iron plate, and raise the heat; raise up one side of the plate, and stir it often, until it becomes of a bright red; care must be taken not to raise the heat so high as to drive off the oxygen, previously acquired; thereby bringing it again to a state of pure melted lead; it is very difficult to succeed in this operation with small quantities.

This is the *red lead* used by painters; and it is on this principle, bút with a different apparatus, the lead of the shops is manufactured; but it is generally very impure.

Florence Lake. Pearlashes one ounce four drachms, water a sufficient quantity, dissolve; alum. Rom. two ounces four drachms, water a sufficient quantity, dissolve; filter both solutions and add the first to the alum solution while warm; strain: mix the sediment upon the strained with the first coarse residuum obtained in boiling cochineal with alum, for making carmine, and dry it.

Common Lake. Make a magestery of alum, as in making Florence lake; boil one ounce four drachms Brazil dust in three pints of water, strain; add the magestery, or sediment of alum, to the strained liquor; stir it well; let it settle, and dry the sediment in small lumps.

Fine Madder Lake. Dutch grappe madder (that-is, madder root ground between two mill stones, a small distance apart as in grinding pearl or French barley, so that only the bark, which contains the moist colour is reduced to powder, and the central woody part of the wood left) two ounces, tie it up in a cloth, beat it up in a pint of water in a stone mortar, repeat it with fresh water : in general five pints will take out all the colour; boil, add one ounce of alum, dissolved in a pint of water, then add one ounce and a half of oil of tartar; wash the sediment, and dry;—produces half an ounce.

Rose Pink. Whiting coloured with a decoction of brazil wood and alum.

Dutch Pink. Whiting coloured with a decoction of birch leaves, dyer's weed, or French berries, with alum.

Stone Blue. Starch coloured with indigo.

Litharge. Put some red lead into a ladle and heat it until it is partly melted, so that it begins to be agglutinated in a kind of scales. If not so bright a red it is a more durable colour.

White Lead. Make nitrate of lead as before directed, and dissolve it in water in a wine glass; pour into it a solution of pearlash, and a white insoluble precipitate will fall down. Let the liquid be poured off, and the powder washed several times. This is the *white lead* of painters in its purest state.

It is generally made by applying the vapour of vinegar to sheet lead, and contains some acetate of lead and other impurities.

Sugar of Lead. Put some white lead into a Florence flask; put in about ten times as much good sharp vinegar (distilled vinegar is best;) shake it up several times and let it stand until the vinegar tastes sweet. Add more vinegar, and continue adding by littles, until it will remain sour; evaporate and crystallize in the usual way. This is the acetate or sugar of lead used in medicine.

White Vitriol. Pour diluted sulphuric acid upon zinc; leaving the zinc in excess: after the action ceases, pour off the clear liquid, which is the white vitriol in solution, If this be evaporated slowly, crystals will be formed.

By a similar process the vitriol of the shops is manufactured.

Chrome. Chrome is found in the state of an acid, combined with iron, called chromate of iron, it is sometimes found in granular lime rocks. When chromate of iron is pulverized and mixed with nitrate of potash and heated to redness, a double decomposition takes place, and the chromate of potash is produced.

F

Dissolve chromate of potash in pure water, pour some of it in a so-lution of sugar of lead, and the beautiful yellow pigment, chromate of lead, will be precipitated; pour it into nitrate of mercury, cinnabar red is produced; into nitrate of silver, and common red is produced.

The chromate of lead is now in general use as a yellow paint; a very small quantity mixed with white lead, gives the whole a beautiful yellow colour.

Almond Bloom.   Brazil dust one ounce, water three pints, boil, strain; add of isinglass, six drachms; ground sylvestria, two ounces; (or cochineal, two drachms;) alum one ounce; borax three drachms; boil again, and strain through a fine cloth; used as a liquid cosmetic.

Pink Dye.   Tie safflower in a bag and wash it in water, until it no longer colours the water; then dry it:—of this take two drachms, salt of tartar, eighteen grains, spirits of wine, seven drachms; digest for two hours, add two ounces of distilled water, digest for two hours more, and add a sufficient quantity of distilled vinegar or lemon juice, to render it a fine rose colour, used as a cosmetic and to make French rouge.

Nankeen Dye.   Arnotto, prepared kali, of each equal parts, boiled in water;—the proportion of the kali is altered as the colour is required to be deeper or lighter; used to restore the colour of faded nankeen.

Blue Vitriol.   Boil copper filings in sulphuric acid, and the salt will be formed in the liquid state: this may be evaporated in the usual way.

On this principle the blue vitriol of the shops is made, though the operation is not similar; the native sulphuret is heated and exposed to air and moisture, and thereby the peroxyde is obtained; then the salt is readily formed by pouring sulphuric acid upon it.

Verdigris.   Cover a gallipot of boiling vinegar with a piece of polished sheet copper; after a short time it will be covered with a thin crust of verdigris.   Upon this principle, though with a very different apparatus, the verdigris of the shops is made.

Colours for Show Bottles.   Yellow.   Dissolve iron in spirit of salt, and dilute.

Red.   Spirits of hartshorn q. p. dilute with water and tinge with cochineal.

Dissolve sal. ammoniac in water and tinge with cochineal.

Blue.   Blue Vitriol and alum, of each 2 oz., water 24 oz. spirits of vitriol a sufficient quantity.

Blue vitriol, 4 oz. water 36 oz.

Green.   Rough verdigris 3 oz. dissolve in spt. vitriol, and add 48 oz. water.

Add distilled verdigris and blue vitriol to a strong decoction of turmeric.

Purple.   Verdigris two drachms; spts. hartshorn 4 oz. water 18 oz.

Sugar of lead one ounce; cochineal one scruple; water q. p.

Add a little spts. hartshorn to an infusion of logwood.

Scarlet Colour—Muriate of Tin.   Prepare the nitro-muriatic acid by mixing one part of muriatic acid with two of nitric acid, and put a very small quantity into a Florence flask.   Drop tin into it by small quantities, that it may not become too hot by the rapid union of the tin and acid.   After the acid is saturated, dissolve some of it in water. Dissolve in water in a wine-glass, a single cochineal insect of the shops, and drop in a little muriate of tin, and it will become a bright scarlet.

Wash Colours for Maps or Writing. Yellow. Gamboge dissolved in water a sufficient quantity; French berries steeped in water, the liquid strained, and gum Arabic added.

Red. Brazil dust steeped in vinegar and alum added.

Litmus dissolved in water, and spirits of wine added.

Cochineal steeped in water, strained, and gum added.

Blue. Saxon blue diluted with water q. p.

Litmus rendered blue by adding distilled vinegar to its solution.

Green. Distilled verdigris dissolved in water, and gum added.

Sap green dissolved in water, and alum added.

Litmus rendered green by adding kali ppm. to its solution.

To extinguish Vegetable Colours. Obtain chlorine as follows: fill a strong quart decanter one third full of water, put in a pulverized mixture, consisting of half a gill of red lead, and a gill of common table salt, well rubbed together; shake it up, then put in two thirds of a wine glass of sulphuric acid; put in the ground stopper loosely; shake the decanter half a minute; the atmospheric air and some gas will escape; now fix your stopper perfectly tight, then plunge the decanter into a tub or cistern of cold water, keeping the mouth a little above the water; briskly agitate it, keeping it under the water, once each minute for fifteen minutes. Now take it out and let the excess of red lead and salt settle; a yellowish green liquid is produced, nearly pure, but containing some muriatic acid; pour a little into a wine glass, and it is ready for use to wash out writing from paper, or extinguish the colour from calico.

The liquid chlorine obtained in this way, should be kept in a dark and cool place. It is used for taking spots out of linen, &c. It has been used for fraudulent purposes, to obliterate writing, that something different might be substituted.

English Verdigris. Blue vitriol 24 lbs. white vitriol 16 lbs. sugar of lead 12 lbs. alum 2 lbs. all coarsely powdered, put in a pot over the fire and stirred till they are united into a mass.

Venetian Ceruss. Flake white, cawk equal parts.

Hamburg White Lead. Flake white 100 lbs. cawk 200 lbs.

Best Dutch White Lead. Flake White 100 lbs. cawk 700 lbs.

English White Lead. Flake White reduced in price by chalk, inferior to the preceding.

Rouge. French chalk ppd. 4 oz. ol. amygd. 2 drachms, carmine one drachm.

2. Safflower, previously washed in water, until it no longer gives out any colour, and dried, 4 drachms, kali pp. one drachm, water one pint; infuse, strain; add French chalk, scraped fine with Dutch rushes four ounces, and precipitate the colour upon it with lemon juice a sufficient quantity.

Cologne Earth, Umber. Black or blackish brown, mixed with brownish red, fine grained, earthy, smooth to the touch, becomes polished by scraping, very light, burns with a disagreeable smell found near Cologne; used in painting both in water colours or in oil, used also in Holland, to render snuff fine and smooth: very different from the brown ochre—which is also called umber, and is not combustible.

Carmine. Boil one ounce of cochineal, finely powdered, in twelve or fourteen pounds of rain or distilled water, in a tinned copper vessel, for three minutes, then add twenty-five grains of alum and continue the boiling for two minutes longer, and let it cool; draw off the clear liquor as soon as it is only blood warm, very carefully, into shallow vessels, and put them by, laying a sheet of paper over them to keep out the dust, for a couple of days, by which time the carmine will have settled. In case the carmine does not settle properly, a few drops of a solution of tin, i. e. dyer's spirit, or a solution of green vitriol will throw it down immediately: the water being then drawn off, the carmine is dried in a warm stove. The first coarse sediment serves to make Florence'lake; the water drawn off is liquid rouge.

2. Boil 12 oz. of Cochineal powdered, six drachms of alum in 30 lbs. of water, strain the decoction, add half an ounce of dyer's spirit, and after the carmine has settled, decant the liquid and dry the carmine—yields about one and a half ounces, used as a paint by the ladies and by miniature painters.

Whiting. Prepared from the soft variety of chalk, by diffusion in water, letting the water settle for two hours, that the impurities and coarser particles may subside; then drawing off the still milky water, letting it deposite the finer sediment; is much finer than the prepared chalk of the apothecaries; but is principally used as a cheap paint.

Ultramarine Blue. Lapis lazuli—one pound is heated to redness, quenched in water, and ground to fine powder; to this is added yellow rosin six ounces; turpentine, beeswax, linseed oil, of each two ounces, previouly melted together, and the whole made into a mass: this is kneaded in successive portions of warm water, which it colours blue, and from whence it is deposited by standing, and sorted according to its qualities. It is a fine blue colour in oil.

Naples Yellow. Lead, one pound and a half; crude antimony, one pound; alum and common salt, of each one ounce, calcined together.

2. Flake white, twelve ounces; diaphoretic antimony, two ounces; calcined alum, half an oz. sal ammoniac, one ounce; calcine in a covered crucible with a moderate heat for three hours, so that at the end of that time it may be barely red hot: with a large portion of diaphoretic antimony and sal ammoniac, it verges to a gold colour.

Scheele's Green. Precipitate a solution of two pounds of blue vitriol in a sufficient quantity of cold water, by a solution of eleven ounces of white arsenic, and two ounces of kali ppm. in two gallons of boiling water, and wash the precipitate;—used as a paint.

Verditer Blue. Made by the refiners from the solution of copper, obtained in precipitating silver from nitric acid, by heating it in copper pans; this solution they heat and pour upon whiting moistened with water, stirring the mixture every day, till the liquor loses its colour, when it is poured off, and a fresh portion of the solution poured on, until the proper colour is obtained:—an uncertain process; the colour sometimes turning out a dirty green, instead of a fine blue.

French Verdigris. Blue vitriol, twenty-four ounces, dissolved in a sufficient quantity of water; sugar of lead, thirty ounces and a half, also dissolved in water; mix the solution; filter, and crystallize by evaporation. It yields about ten ounces of crystals;—a superior paint to common verdigris, and certainly ought to be used in medicine, instead of the common.

Pearl Powder. Magestery of bismuth; French chalk, scraped fine by Dutch rushes; of each a sufficient quantity—*cosmetic.*

Smalt—Powder Blue. Is made from roasted cobalt, melted with twice or thrice its weight of sand, and an equal weight of potash: the glass is poured out into cold water, ground to powder, washed over, and sorted by its fineness and the richness of its colour. It is used in painting and getting up linen.

Bleaching Liquid—Eau de Javelle. Common salt, two pounds; manganese, one pound; water, two pounds; put into a retort; and add gradually, oil of vitriol, two pounds: pass the vapour through a solution of prepared kali, four ounces, in twenty-nine ounces of water, applying heat towards the last. Specific gravity is 1,087. Stimulant, antisypilitic; used to bleach linen and take out spots, and to clean books from what has been scribbled on their margins.

Blackman's oil colour Cakes. Grind the colours first with oil of turpentine and a varnish made of gum mastic in powder, four ounces, dissolved without heat in a pint of oil of turpentine; let them dry; then heat a grinding stone by putting a charcoal fire under it; grind the colours upon it, and add an ointment, made by adding melted spermaceti, 3 lbs. to a pint of poppy oil; take a piece of the proper size, make it into a ball; put this into a mould and press it. When these cakes are used, rub them down with poppy oil, or oil of turpentine.

Brown Red. By recalcining green vitriol, previously calcined to whiteness, by an intense heat until it becomes very red, and washing the residuum.

Blackman's Colours in Bladders. Are prepared with the spermaceti mixture, like his oil colour cakes, but the proportion of oil is larger.

Kemp's White, for Water Colours. Cockscomb spar, q. p. spirits of salt, a sufficient quantity; dissolve—add carbonate of ammonia to precipitate the white; and dry in cakes for use.

Crayons. Spermaceti, three ounces, boiling water, one pint; add bone ashes finely ground, one pound, colouring matter, as ochre, &c. q. p. roll out the paste, and when half dry, cut it in pipes.

2. Pipe clay, coloured with ochre, &c. q. p.—make it a paste with alewort.

English Verdigris. Blue vitriol, twenty-four pounds, white vitriol, sixteen pounds, sugar of lead twelve pounds, alum, two pounds, all coarsely powdered, put into a pot over the fire and stirred till they are united into a mass.

Vanherman's Fish Oil Paints. The oil for grinding white, is made by putting litharge, and white vitriol, of each twelve pounds, into thirty-two gallons vinegar, adding after some time, a ton of whale, seal or cod oil; the next day the clear part is poured off, and twelve gallons of linseed oil and two gallons of oil of turpentine, are added.

2. The sediment, left when the clear oil is poured off, mixed with half its quantity of lime water, is also used under the name of prepared residue oil, for common colours.

3. *Pale Green.* Six gallons of lime water, whiting, and road dust, of each one hundred weight, thirty pounds of blue black, twenty-four pounds of yellow ochre, wet blue (previously ground in prepared res-

idue oil) twenty pounds—thin with a quart ppd. residue oil to each 8 pounds, and the same quantity linseed oil.

4. *Bright Green.*   100 lbs. yellow ochre, 150 lbs. of road dust, 100 lbs. of wet blue, 10 lbs. blue black, 6 galls. lime water, 4 galls. ppd. residue and linseed oil, seven and a half galls. of each.

5. *Lead Colour.*   100 lbs. whiting, 5 lbs. blue black, 28 lbs. white lead, ground in oil, 56 lbs. road dust, 5 galls. lime water, 2 1-2 galls. ppd. residue oil.

6. *Brown Red.*   8 galls. lime water, 100 lbs. Spanish brown, 200 lbs. road dust, 4 galls. ppd. fish oil, ppd. residue and linseed oil, of each four gallons.

7. *Yellow.*   Put in yellow ochre, instead of Spanish brown, as in the last.

8. *Black.*   Put in lamp black or blue black.

9. *Stone Colour.*   4 galls. lime water, 100 lbs. whiting, 28 lbs. white lead, ground in oil, 56 lbs. road dust, 2 galls. ppd. fish oil, ppd. residue, and linseed oil, of each, 3 1-2 gallons.

The cheapness of these paints, and the hardness and durability given to them by the road dust, or ground gravel, has brought them into great use, for common out door painting:

Saxon Blue, Scott's Liquid Blue.   Indigo, one pound, oil of vitriol four pounds—dissolve by keeping the bottle in boiling water; then add twelve pounds of water, or q. p.

Prussian Blue.   Red argol and salt petre of each two pounds, throw the powder by degrees into a red hot crucible; dry bullock's blood over the fire, and mix three pounds of this dry blood with the prepared salt, and calcine it in a crucible, till it no longer emits a flame; then dissolve six pounds of common alum in twenty-six pounds of water, and strain the solution; dissolve also two ounces and a half of dried green vitriol in two pounds of water, and strain while hot; mix the two solutions together, while boiling hot; dissolve the alkaline salt, calcined with blood, in twenty-seven pounds of water, and filter through paper, supported upon linen; mix this with the other solution, and strain through linen; put the sediment left upon linen, while moist, into an earthen pan, and add one pound and a half of spirit of salt,—stir the mass, and when the effervescence is over, dilute with plenty of water, and strain again—lastly, dry the sediment.

2. Mix one pound of kali ppd. with two pounds dried blood; put it into a crucible, or long pot, and keep it in a red heat till it no longer flames or smokes; then take out a small portion, dissolve it in water, and observe its colour and effects upon a solution of silver in aqua fortis, for when sufficiently calcined, it will neither look yellowish, nor precipitate silver of a brownish or blackish colour. It is then to be taken out of the fire; and when cool, dissolved in a pint and a half of water. Take green vitriol, one part, common alum, one to three parts; mix, and dissolve them in a good quantity of water, by boiling, and filter while hot: precipitate this solution by adding a sufficient quantity of the solution of ppd. alkali; and filter—the precipitate will be darker the less alum is added, but it will be greener from the greater admixture of the oxyde of iron, which is precipitated, and which must be got rid of, by adding while moist, spirit of salt, diluting the mixture with water, and straining.

3. Precipitate a solution of green vitriol, with a solution of ppd. al-

kali, and purify the precipitate with spirit of salt—precipitate a solution of common alum, with a solution of kali ppd.—mix the two sediments together, while diffused in warm water; strain and dry.

Vermilion. Cinnabar. Put quicksilver in a glazed dish, set it on a sand bath, let it be well surrounded with sand every way; pour some melted brimstone over it, and with an iron spatula keep constantly stirring till the whole is converted into a black powder. With this powder fill the quarter part of a retort, with a short and wide neck. Place it first on a fire of cinders,—increase it by degrees, and continue it for ten hours; after which, make a blasting one twelve hours.

By the first fire there will arise a black flame—by the second, a yellow,—and by the last, a red. As soon as this is the case let the vessel cool, and you will find in the receiver, and in the neck of the retort, a very fine cinnabar. Some, instead of a glass retort, use an earthen, or stone.

A Fine Azure. Boil and skim well, sixteen pounds of chamber lye; then, add one pound fine shellac, and five ounces of alum, in powder. Boil all together, till you observe the chamber lye is well changed with the colour, which is determined by steeping a white rag in it—if the the colour does not please, boil it longer, undergoing a repetition until satisfied. Now, put the liquor into a flannel bag—without suffering what runs into the pan under, to settle; re-pour it into the bag, and continue the process, till the liquor is quite clear and not tinged; then with a wooden spatula take off the lake, which is in the form of curd; make it into small cakes, and dry them in a shade on new tiles; then they are in a state to be kept for use.

To Marble Wood. Give it a coat of blacking varnish; repeat it as many times as you think necessary; then polish it.

2. Dilute some white varnish, lay it on the black ground, tracing with it, such imitations as you like; when dry, rub it lightly with rushes, then wipe it, and give a last coat of transparent white varnish, when dry, polish it.

To imitate White Marble. Break and calcine the finest white marble, grind it fine and dilute it with size; lay two coats of this on the wood, which, when dry, polish and varnish as before directed.

To imitate Black Marble. Burn lamp black in a ladle, red hot, then grind it with brandy. For the bulk of an egg of black, put the size of a pea in lead, in drops, as much of tallow, and the same quantity of soap—grind and mix; then dilute it with a very weak size water. Give four coats of this, and then polish.

To make Lamp Black for tinning. Burn some nut shells in an iron pan, and throw them into another full of water; then grind them on marble with either oil or varnish.

Blue. Whiting ground with verdigris will make a very good blue.

A Fine Green. Grind verdigris with vinegar, and a very small quantity of tartar; then add a little quicklime and sap green, which grind with the rest, and put it into shells for keeping. If it becomes too hard, dilute it with vinegar.

2. Grind on a marble stone, verdigris, and a third as much of tartar, with white wine vinegar.

Sap green. Express the blackberry juice, when full ripe; add some alum to it; put it in a bladder, and hang it in some place to dry.

To make Lake. Take three parts of an ounce of brazil wood, a pint of clear water, one and a half drachms alum, eighteen grains salt of tartar; the bulk of two filberts of mineral crystal; three quarters of a pound of the whitest sound fish bones, rasped; mix, boil till reduced to one third; strain three times through a coarse cloth; then set it in the sun under cover to dry.

A Liquid Lake.   On a quantity of alum and cochineal pounded and boiled together, pour drops of oil of tartar until it becomes a fine colour.

A Good Azure. Two ounces of quicksilver; sulphur and sal ammoniac, of each one ounce: grind all together, and put it to digest in a matrass over a slow heat; increase the fire a little; and when you see an azured fume arising, take the matrass off.   When cool, as beautiful an azure is produced as ultramarine.

To die Bones black.   Litharge and quicklime, of each six ounces; boil in common water, with the bones; stirring them till the water begins to boil; then take it from the fire, and continue stirring the mixture till the water is cold, when the bones will become dyed black.

To Dye Bones green.   Pound well together in a quart of strong vinegar, three ounces of verdigris, as much of brass filings, and a handful of rue.   When done put all in a glass vessel along with the bones you wish to dye, and stop it well.   Place this in a cold cellar; in a fortnight, the bones will be dyed green.

To dye Bones and Ivory a fine red.   Boil scarlet flocks in clear water, assisted with pearlashes to draw the colour; then clarify it with alum, and strain the tincture through a piece of linen.   To dye bones or ivory in red, you must first rub them with aqua fortis and then immediately with the tincture.

To whiten Bones.   Put a handful of bran and quick lime together into a new pipkin, with sufficient quantity of water, and boil it.   Boil the bones in this until freed from greasy particles.

To Dye Wood red.   Soak chopped Brazil wood in oil of tartar; (or boil it in common water;) give the wood a coat of yellow, made of saffron, diluted in water; when dry, give it several coats of the first preparation, till the hue becomes pleasing.   When dry burnish it, and lay on a coat of drying varnish with the palm of your hand.   If a very deep red is wanted, boil the brazil wood in water, by adding a small quantity of alum or quick lime.

To Dye Wood White and to produce a fine Polish.   Finest English white chalk ground in subtile powder on marble; then let it dry; set it in a pipkin on the fire, with a weak sized water, having great care not to let it turn brown,—when hot, give first a coat of size to your wood; let it dry; then give one or two coats of the white over it. These being dry also, polish with the rushes, and burnish.

To Dye in Polished Black.   Grind lamp black on marble with gum water; then put it into a pipkin, and with a brush give the wood a coat of this; when dry, polish.

To imitate Ebony.   Infuse nut galls in vinegar, in which you have soaked rusty nails: rub the wood with this, let it dry, polish and burnish.

To Dye in Gold, Silver, or Copper.   Rock crystal pulverised very fine, put into water, warm it in a new pipkin, with a little size; then give a coat of it on the wood with a brush.   When dry, rub a peice of gold, silver, or copper on the wood thus prepared, and it will assume the colour of the metal which you rub it with; after which burnish.

Ivory Black. Is made by burning ivory till it is quite black, which is usually done between two crucibles, well luted together; used either as an oil or water colour.

Bone Black. From bones burnt in the same manner, as ivory black; used by painters, &c. Burnt cork is also used.

An excellent dye, the basis of many colours. A decoction of the seeds of red Trefoil is mixed with different mineral substances; the dyes produced are very beautiful, and of a great variety. Among them are yellow and green of different shades, as also citron and orange colours. These dyes are well adapted to woollen and cotton manufactures: they resist the action of the substances, with which trials are usually made, much better than the common dyes.

Of the Colouring principle of Blood. After having drained the clots of blood through a hair sieve, tincture it in an earthen vessel, with four parts of sulphuric acid, previously diluted with eight parts of water, and heat the mixture at 70" (cent.—158° Fahrenheit.) for five or six hours: filter the liquor while hot, which contains the colouring principle of the blood, albumen, and probably some fibrin; wash the residuum with water, equal in quantity to that of the acid employed; evaporate the solutions to one half their bulk, then pour in ammonia sufficient to leave only a slight excess of acid; stir it, and we obtain a deposite of a purple red colour, principally consisting of the colouring matter, and containing neither albumen, nor fibrin; wash this deposite until the water contains no more sulphuric acid, or does not precipitate any longer the nitrate of barytes: it is then put on a filter, and dropped on blotting paper, from which it is taken by means of an ivory knife and dried on a capsule.

Prepared Ox Gall. The fresh gall is left for the night to settle; the clear fluid poured off, and evaporated in a water bath, to a proper consistence; used by painters in water colours, and thus enables them to form an even surface of colour; and also instead of soap to wash greasy cloth.

CHAPTER XIV.
GLUES, PASTES, &c.

Glue is made in Europe, of ears, feet, trimmings, sinews and scrapings of the skins of oxen, calves, sheep, &c. old leather, and fresh or raw hides mixed and manufactured together; and this mixture is said to yield one third of its weight in good strong glue. The best glue is from the hides of old animals; whole skins are seldom used, unless they are injured by the worm, rotted, or otherwise rendered unfit to make leather; but the smallest pieces are saved for that purpose. In making glue of fresh pieces of skin, let them be steeped in water for two or three days; dried hides may require longer time; and bits of leather much longer. While soaking they should be stirred occasionally, then put them to drain in hand barrows, with grated bottoms, or in boxes with sloping sides and grated bottoms: when drained let them be well washed in several waters. The ears and other dirty parts should be steeped and washed by themselves; after they are washed clean, put them in a weak limewater, in iron hooped

G

tubs.   Leather will require to be kept in weak limewater a considerable time, and a little fresh lime should be added occasionally; alumed skins, tallowed, greasy, bloody, or hairy skins, should be put into a stronger limewater, and kept longer in it. They sometimes require to be taken out, so as to permit the lime to dry on them, and to remain for a considerable time; after which they must be soaked and well stirred; then press them out as dry as possible, and put them in a copper kettle for boiling, at the bottom of which kettle, should be a wooden grate. The copper should be filled with the material pressed close, and as much water poured on as will run among the pieces: make a moderate fire, which increase by degrees, till it boils. As the materials melt into glue, some decrease the fire without stirring them, others stir them as they dissolve.   When the glue, on cooling, forms a pretty thick jelly, it is done: after this a box is made with wooden gratings for the bottom; the inside of the grating bottom is to be lined with horsehair cloth, and the box to be placed over a large tub.   The glue is to be passed through the horsehair cloth, or strainer, quickly, while it is very hot. The dregs are left to drain some time, and are called by the workmen glue-dreg; they make an excellent fuel mixed with wood.   The room should be kept warm while the glue is settling.   In the tubs there should be cocks to draw off the hot liquid glue: the first glue will be the brightest, but the last will be equally good.   Through the cocks it must run into flat moulds, previously wet.   When cool, cut it out with a wet knife into squares, and hang it on a line to dry and harden in a draught of air;—some place it on a net hung on four posts, turning it occasionally: ten days of dry weather, or fifteen days of wet (under cover) are required in Europe, but less time in America.   To polish the cakes, wet them and rub them with new lime. The best glue has few dark spots, and no bad smell; and shines when broken.   To try glue, put it into cool water for three or four days, where it must not dissolve, but when dried must preserve its weight.

The time of boiling is from twelve to fifteen hours, according to the fire.   Violent heat is to be avoided.

2. If bones are digested for seven or eight days, with weak hydrochloric acid, this acid disolves all the salts that enter into their composition: the bones are softened, become very flexible, and at length contain only animal matter. If, in this state, they are put for some moments, into boiling water, and after wiping them dry they are subjected to a stream of cold and fresh water, they may be regarded as pure gelatin, or at least, as a substance, which, being dissolved in boiling water, affords the handsomest size.

In order to prepare glue from the clippings of skins of parchment, or gloves; from the hoofs, the ears of oxen, horses, sheep, calves, &c. after taking off the hair and removing the fat from these substances, we boil them for a long time in a large quantity of water; the scum is separated, its formation being favoured by adding a little alum or lime; the liquor is strained, and suffered to rest; it is then poured off, and skimmed again, and then heated to concentrate it.   When sufficiently so, it is poured into moulds previously wetted, where, by cooling, it forms into soft plates; which at the end of twenty-four hours, are cut into tablets, and dried in a warm and airy situation.

A very Strong Glue.   Soak the finest isinglass twenty-four hours in spirits of wine or strong brandy, then boil all very gently together, continually stirring it, that it may not burn, until it becomes one liquor. Then strain it while hot through a coarse linen cloth, into a vessel when it should be kept close stopped; a gentle heat will melt this glue to use.

A Parchment Glue. Put two or three pounds of scrapings or cuttings of parchment into a bucket of water, boil the whole till it be reduced to half, pass it through an open linen, and then let the liquor cool, when it will be a parchment glue.

A Strong Paste. Common paste is made of wheat flour boiled in water, till it be of a viscid consistence, but when used by book binders and paper hangers, it is requisite to mix a fourth, fifth, or sixth of the weight of flour of powdered resin or rosin; and when it is wanted still more tenacious, gum Arabic, or any kind of size may be added. In order to prevent the paste used in papering rooms, &c. from being gnawed by rats &c. powdered glass is sometimes mixed with it; but the most effectual and easy remedy is to dissolve a little sublimate say one drachm to a quart of water, which not only prevents rats and mice, but all kinds of vermin being troublesome.

Of Fibrin. If blood is agitated with a handful of rods, immediately after having been drawn from the veins, the fibrin adheres to them; it is then only necessary to wash it repeatedly, in order to discolour it and obtain it pure.

Liquid Albumen. This constitutes the white of the egg; in truth this last, besides albumen, contains several salts, and some sub-carbonate of soda, of which it is impossible to divest it.

Solid Albumen. Pour alcohol on the white of an egg, dissolved in water, and filtered; the albumen immediately precipitates, and is to be washed.

Fish Glue—Isinglass. To procure this, the inner membrane of the *swimming bladders* of some kinds of sturgeon are washed; they are then slightly dried and rolled, and afterwards dried in the air. An inferior kind is prepared by digesting in boiling water, the head, the tail, and the jaws of certain whales, and almost all fish without scales.

Potatoe Starch—common Arrow Root: may be made from frozen potatoes in as large a quantity and as good, as those which have not been spoiled by the frost; very white, crimp to the fingers, and colours them; friable, heavy, sinking in water; when held to the light, it has shining particles in it: dissolves in boiling water as easily as the true arrow root: 100 pounds of potatoes yield 10 pounds of starch.

CHAPTER XV.

MINERALOGY.

The whole science of mineralogy has been created since the year 1770. All the solid materials of which this globe of ours is composed have received the name of minerals. But it is only very lately that the method of ascertaining the component parts of these substances was discovered, or that it was possible to describe them so as to be intelligible to others. Nothing at first appears easier to describe than a mineral, but in reality it is attended with a great deal of difficulty. The properties of minerals must be described in terms rigidly accurate, which convey precise ideas of the very properties intended, and of no other. The smallest deviation would lead to confusion and uncertainty. Mineralogy therefore must have a language of its own, that is to say, it must have a *term* to denote every mineralogical property, and each of these terms must be accurately defined. The language of mineralogy was invented by the celebrated Werner, of Fryburg, and first made known to the world by the publication of his treatise on the *External Characters of Minerals*. The object of this philosopher was to invent a method of describing minerals with such precision, that every species could readily be recognized by those who were unacquainted with the terms employed. For this purpose, it was necessary to make use of those properties only, which presented themselves to our senses on inspecting the mineral. These were called by Werner, external characters, because they may be ascertained without destroying the mineral examined. These constitute the first division of the characters of minerals. To the second belong those which are derived from a chemical composition, or discovered by any chemical change which the mineral suffers; to the third, are refered those properties which are afforded by certain physical characters, derived from circumstances frequently observed with regard to a mineral, as to the place where it is found, or the minerals by which it is usually accompanied.

Werner divides the external characters of minerals into two kinds, viz. *general* and *particular*. The general characters are the following: 1. Colour. 2. Cohesion. 3. Unctuosity. 4. Coldness. 5. Weight. 6. Smell. 7. Taste. The particular characters are: 1. Aspect of surface. 2. Aspect of the fracture. 3. Aspect of the distinct concretions. 4. General aspect. 5. Hardness. 6. Tenacity. 7. Frangibility. 8. Flexibility. 9. Adhesion to the tongue. 10. Sound.

General Characters. I. The *colours* of minerals are extremely various. Werner conceives eight fundamental colours, and describes all the rest as compounds of various proportions of these: The fundamental colours are, 1. Snow white. 2. Ash grey. 3. Velvet black. 4. Berlin, or Prussian blue. 5. Emerald green. 6. Lemon yellow. 7. Carmine red. 8. Chesnut brown. II. With respect to *cohesion*, minerals are either *solid, friable, or fluid.* III. With respect to *unctuosity*, minerals are distinguished into *greasy* and *meagre;* the first have a certain degree of greasiness in feeling; the second not. The other four general characters require no particular description.

Particular Characters. I. In the aspect of the surface of the mineral, three things claim attention. 1. The *shape* of the mineral. 2. The kind of *surface.* 3. The *lustre* of the surface, which is either splendent, shining, glistening, glimmering, or dull. II. When a mineral is broken, the new surface exposed is called the fracture. Three things claim attention: 1. The lustre of the fracture. 2. The kind of fracture. 3. The shape of the fragments. III. *Distinct concretions* are distinct masses, which may be separated from each other, without breaking through the solid part of the mineral, by natural seams. Three particulars in respect to them are, 1. Their *shape.* 2. Their *surface.* 3. Their *lustre.* IV. Under the head of *general aspect*, three particulars are comprehended. 1. The *transparency,*

2. The *streak*. 3. The *soiling*, or *stain* left when rubbed. V. Minerals are either, 1. *Hard*. 2. *Semi-hard*, or 3. *Soft*. VI. With respect to *tenacity*, minerals are, 1. *Brittle*, when on being cut with a knife the particles fly away with a noise. 2. *Sectile*, when the particles do not fly off but remain. 3. *Ductile*, when the mineral can be cut into slices. VII. By *frangibility* is meant the resistance which minerals make when we attempt to break them. The degrees are five, 1. *Very tough*. 2. *Tough*. 3. *Moderately tough*. 4. *Fragile*. 5. *Very fragile*. VIII. With respect to *flexibility*, some are, 1. *Elastic*. Others, 2. *Common*. Others, 3. *Inflexible*. IX. Some minerals *adhere* to the tongue, 1. *Very strongly*. 2. Others, *moderately*. 3. Others, *slightly*. 4. And others, *very slightly*. X. Some minerals give a *ringing* sound, others a *grating* sound, others a *creaking* sound, as tin. With respect to *electricity*, some minerals become electric when *heated*, others when *rubbed*, others cannot be rendered electric. The electricity of some is *positive*, of others *negative*.

CLASSIFICATION OF MINERALS.

Minerals are usually arranged under four classes; earthy, saline, inflammable and metallic. The *earthy* contain all such as derive their qualities from the earths; and they are divided into genera, according to the particular earth, which predominates in each, or more properly into families, according to their resemblance, in external characters, as the diamond family, the ruby family, tale family, and others. The diamond, of which there is only a single species, is the hardest and most beautiful of all the mineral productions. When heated to the temperature of melting copper, and exposed to a current of air, it is gradually but completely combustible. It is wholly converted into carbonic acid, and therefore consists of pure carbon. By means of diamond powder, this substance can be cut and polished on a wheel, in the same way as other gems are wrought by emery. It is manufactured by jewellers into brilliants and rose diamonds; employed by glaziers for cutting glass, by lapidaries for cutting and engraving on the hardest gems, and in the finer kinds of clock work. The ruby family is composed of seven species. They are all extremely hard, and several of them highly valued on account of their beauty. The saline minerals comprehend all the combinations of alkalies with acids, which exist in the mineral kingdom; such as salt petre or nitrate of potash, common rock salt, or muriate of soda, and sal ammoniac, or the muriate of ammonia.

The salt springs in some parts of the United States, owe their origin to beds of fossil salt. The rain water which penetrates to their surface, effects the solution of a certain portion of them, with which it comes in contact, and thus becomes in some cases, it is said, ten times salter than the water of the sea. The *inflammable* minerals, comprehend all combustible bodies, except metals, and the diamond, and include sulphur, resins, bitumens, and graphite. Among the bitumens are found the several varieties of mineral coal, that are used for fuel, gas lights, &c.

The *metallic* minerals comprehend all the mineral bodies that are composed either entirely of metals, or of which metals constitute the most considerable and important part. It is from the minerals of this class that all metals are extracted. The ores are found in a native state, either simple, consisting of only one substance, or compound, when composed of two or more substances. Of the metals, the first is *platina*, which is the heaviest. Platina is found among the gold ores of South America, in the form of small grains or scales. Its colour is between steel grey and silver white, and its ductility and malleability is very great. Gold is never found in a mineralized state, but it occurs native in many parts of the world, generally alloyed with a little silver or copper, and commonly in the form of grains. It is the heaviest of all metals except platina, and although its tenacity is such that a wire of one tenth of an inch in diameter, will support a weight of five hundred pounds without breaking, yet it possesses less tenacity than iron, copper, platina or silver. It is ductile and malleable beyond any known limits. The gold beaters extend it by hammering a number of thin rolled plates between skins or animal membranes, upon blocks of marble fixed in wooden frames. A grain of gold has been extended to more than forty-two square inches of leaf, and an ounce, which in the form of a cube, is not half an inch either high, broad, or long, is beaten under the hammer into a surface of 146 1-2 square feet. There are gold leaves, not thicker in some parts, than the three hundred and sixty thousandth part of an inch; but on wire used by lace makers it is still thinner. An ingot of silver, usually about thirty pounds. weight, is rounded into an inch and a half in diameter, and 22 inches long. Two ounces of gold leaf are sufficient to cover this cylinder, and frequently effected with a little more than one. The ingot is repeatedly drawn through the holes of several irons, each smaller than the other, till it becomes finer than a hair; and yet the gold covers it, and does not leave the minutest part of the silver bare, even to the microscope. It has been calculated that it would take 14 millions of filings of gold, such as are on some gilt wire, to make up the thickness of one inch. The ductility of it is such, that one ounce is sufficient to gild a silver wire more than thirteen hundred miles long.

Gold may be dissolved in nitro-muriatic acid and it thus becomes muriate of gold, which is obtained in small crystals, and is very soluble in water. If white satin ribbon, or silk, be moistened with a diluted solution of gold, and, while moist, exposed to a current of hydrogen, or sulphuric acid gas, the metal will be immediately reduced and the silk become gilt with a regular coat of gold. The potters dissolve gold to be applied to the common porcelain; and it is used in a state of solution for staining ivory and ornamental feathers. It gives a beautiful purple red; even marble may be stained with it.

Silver, is the most brilliant of metals. You may know when silver is pure, by heating it in a common fire, or in the flame of a candle; if it is alloyed it will become tarnished; but if it be pure silver, it will remain perfectly white. It is exceedingly ductile, of great malleability and tenacity.

Of the salts of silver, the nitrate is best known, and when melted and run into moulds, it forms the lunar caustic of the apothecary.

Mercury, in the temperature of our atmosphere, is a white fluid metal, having the appearance of melted silver. When submitted to a sufficient degree of cold, it is similar in appearance to other metals, and may be beaten into plates; at the poles it would probably be always solid.

The quicksilver mine of Guanea Velica, in Peru, is 170 fathoms in circumference, and 480 deep. In this profound abyss are seen streets, squares and a chapel: thousands of flambeaux are continually burning to enlighten it. Those who work in the mine are generally afflicted with convulsions. Notwithstanding this, the unfortunate victims of insatiable avarice are crowded together, and plunged naked into these abysses. Tyranny has invented this refinement in cruelty, to render it impossible for any thing to escape its restless vigilance.

Copper, is the most ductile of all the metals except gold. The salts of copper are numerous and much used in the arts connected with chemistry. All the salts are poisonous; therefore, great care should be taken not to taste wantonly the solutions.

Lead, is malleable and ductile, but possesses very little tenacity. It may be mixed with gold and silver in a moderate heat; but when the heat is much increased, the lead rises to the surface, combined with all heterogeneous matters. The ore of lead is so poisonous, that the steam arising from the furnaces where it is worked, infects the grass, in all the neighbouring places, and kills the animals which feed on it. Culinary vessels, lined with a mixture of tin and lead, which is the usual tinning, are apt to communicate to acid food, pernicious qualities, and require to be used with great caution. The same may be said of liquors, and other acid substances kept in glazed ware, and of wines adulterated with litharge, and such other preparations of lead as are sometimes used, for the purpose of rendering them sweet.

Iron. If utility were made the standard of estimation, iron would hold the first place in the class of metals, and would be counted more valuable than gold, as it appears indispensably necessary to the carrying on of every manufacture. There has never been an instance of a nation, acquainted with the art of manufacturing iron, which did not in time attain to a degree of civilization, greatly beyond the inhabitants of those countries where this metal was wanting, or its use unknown. It is plentifully and universally diffused throughout nature, pervading almost every thing, and is the chief cause of colour in earths and stones. It may be detected in plants and animal fluids.

Tin, must have been known very early, as it is mentioned by Homer, and also in the books of Moses. Tin enters into combination with many of the metals, and forms alloys with them, some of which are of great importance. It is not very ductile, but so malleable, that it may be beaten into leaves thinner than paper. Tin foil, as it is usually termed, is about one thousandth part of an inch thick. It is employed to give a brightness to several articles; used in forming reds and scarlets. Substances which produced to the ancients only faint and fleeting colours, give us such as are brilliant and durable, by the use of a solution of this metal.

Zinc, is one of the most abundant metals in nature, except iron. It is used in China for the current coin, and for that purpose it is employed in its utmost purity. Until recently it was used in Wales for mending roads. When zinc is heated, it readily attracts oxygen; and at a white heat the absorption of oxygen is so rapid and violent, that the oxyde immediately sublimes, and for this reason it has acquired the name of flowers of zinc. Combined with copper and tin, the mixtures constitute some of the most useful compound metals. It is used in medicine, is the base of white vitriol, and its carbonate or oxyde may be advantageously substituted for white lead in painting.

Manganese, is a brilliant metal, of a darkish white colour, inclining to grey, of considerable hardness, and of difficult fusibility. When exposed to the air it absorbs oxygen with rapidity, and falls into powder. Its oxydes are used in preparing the bleaching liquor, in purifying glass, and in glazing black earthen ware. By the application of a red heat the black oxyde produces oxygen gas in great abundance.

Antimony, is a brilliant, brittle metal, of a silvery colour, which has not much tenacity, and entirely destitute of ductility. It is wholly volatilized by heat; is susceptible of vitrification. Its oxydes are employed in medicine, and in colouring glass.

Arsenic, is generally found in combination with sulphur, oxygen and many of the metals. Its colour is bluish, or greenish white, becoming on exposure to the air, dark, almost black; it is extremely brittle, and the softest of all metals; and is one of the most active of mineral poisons. Beautiful shades of different colours may be given to different substances by solutions of arsenic; so that the substances which are most injurious to the animal economy, appear to be endowed with properties for embellishing the works of creation, and by imparting colour to other bodies, is made to minister in various ways to our gratification. How diversified are the means which the Creator has adopted for the promotion of his benevolent designs !

CHAPTER XVI.
THE ART OF ASSAYING ORES.

Before metallic ores are worked in the large way, we should know what sort of metal, and what portion of it, is to be found in a determined quantity of the ore, in order to ascertain whether it will be profitable to extract largely, and in what manner the process is to be performed.

The assaying may be performed in the dry or moist way; the first is the most ancient, and in many respects the most advantageous, and consequently continues to be mostly used. Assays are made either in crucibles, with the blast of the bellows, or in tests, under a muffle. The assay weights are always imaginary. Sometimes an ounce represents an hundred weight on the large scale, and is subdivided in the same number of parts, as that hundred weight is in the great; so that the contents of the ore obtained by the assay, shall accurately determine by such relative proportions, the quantity to be expected from any weight of the ore on a larger scale. In the lotting of the ore, care should be taken to have small portions, from different specimens, which should be pulverized and well mixed in an iron or brass mortar. The proper quantity of the ore is now taken, and if it contains either sulphur or arsenic, it is put into a crucible or test and exposed to a moderate degree of heat, till no vapour arises from it; to assist this volatilization, some add a small quantity of powdered charcoal.

FLUXES. To assist the fusion of the ores, and to convert the extraneous matters connected with them into scoria, assayers use different kinds of fluxes. The most usual and efficacious materials for the composition are borax, tartar, nitre, sal ammoniac, common salt, glass; flour-spar, charcoal powder, pitch, lime, litharge, &c. in different proportions.

Crude of White Flux. This consists of one part of nitre and two of tartar, well mixed.

Black Flux. The above crude flux detonates by means of kindled charcoal; and if it be effected in a mortar slightly covered, the smoke that rises unites with the alkalized nitre and the tartar, and renders it black.

Cornish Reducing Flux. Ten ounces of tartar, three ounces and six drachms of nitre, three ounces, and one drachm of borax; well mixed.

Cornish Refining Flux. Defflagrate, then pulverize, two parts of nitre, and one part of tartar.

In working at large, such expensive means cannot be applied to effect our purpose, as the inferior metals would be too much enhanced in value; consequently, where the object is the production of metals in the great way, in smelting works, cheaper additions are used; such as lime stone, felted-spar, flour-spar, quartz, sand, slate, and slugs, which are to be chosen according to the different views of the operator. The iron ores on account of the argillaceous earth they contain, require calcareous additions, and the copper ones, rather slugs, or vitrescent stones, than calcareous earth.

Humid assay of Metallic Ores. The mode of assaying ores for their particular metals by the dry way, is deficient, so far as relates to pointing out the different substances connected with them, because they are always destroyed by the process for obtaining the assay metal. The assay by the moist way is more correct, because the different substances can be accurately ascertained. The late celebrated Bergman first communicated this method. It depends upon a knowledge of the chemical affinities of different bodies for each other; and must be varied according to the nature of the ore; it is very extensive in its application, and requires great patience and address in its execution. To describe the treatment of each variety of metallic ores would take too much of our room; but to give a general idea, we shall describe the procedure, both in the dry and humid way, on one species of all the different ores.

To assay iron Ores. No. 1. The ore must be roasted till the vapour ceases to rise. Take two assay quintals of it, and triturate them with one of flour-spar; three-fourths of a quintal of powdered charcoal, and four quintals decrepitated sea-salt; this mixture is to be put into a crucible, and the crucible itself exposed to a violent fire for an hour, and when it is cool, broken. If the operation be well conducted, the iron will be found at the bottom of the crucible, to which must be added those metallic particles, which may adhere to the scoria. The metallic particles so adhering may be separated by pulverizing it in a paper, and then attracting them with a magnet.

No. 2. If the ore should be in a calciform state, mixed with earths, the roasting of it previous to assaying, if not detrimental, is at least superfluous; if the earths should be of the argillaceous and silicious kind, to half a quintal of them, add of dry quicklime and flour-spar, of each one-fourth of a quintal, reduced to powder, and mix them with

H

one-fourth of a quintal of powdered charcoal, covering the whole with one ounce of decrepitated common salt; and expose the luted crucible to a strong forge fire for an hour and a quarter, then let it gradually cool, and let the regulus be struck off and weighed. If the ore contain calcareous earth there will be no occasion to add quicklime; the preparations of the ingredients may be as follows: viz: one assay quintal of ore, one of decrepitated sea-salt, one half of powdered charcoal; and one of flour-spar, and the process conducted as above.

There is a great difference in the reguli of iron; when the cold regulus is struck with a hammer, and breaks, the iron is called cold short; when struck red hot, it is called red short; but if it resist the hammer, both in its cold and ignited state, it is good iron.

Humid assay of Iron Ore. To assay the calciform ores, which do not contain much earthy or stony matter, they must be reduced to a fine powder; dissolved in marine acid, and precipitated with the Prussian alkali. A determinate quantity of the alkali must be previously tried, to ascertain the portion of iron which it will precipitate, and the estimate made accordingly. If the iron contains a considerable portion of zinc or manganese, the precipitate must be calcined to redness, and the calx treated with dephlogistigated nitrous acid, which will then take up only the calx of the zinc; when this is separated, the calx should again be treated either with nitrous acid, with the addition of sugar, or with the acetous acid, which will dissolve the manganese, if any; the remaining calx of iron may then be dissolved by the marine acid, and precipitated by the mineral alkali, or it may be further calcined, and then weighed.

Zinc Ores. Take the assay weight of roasted ore, and mix it well with one-eighth part of charcoal dust, put it into a strong luted earthen retort, to which must be fitted a receiver; place the retort in a furnace and raise the fire, and continue it in a violent heat for two hours; then cool gradually, and the zinc will be found hanging to the neck of the retort in its metallic form.

In the humid way. Distil vitriolic acid over calamine to dryness; the residuum must be lixiviated in hot water; what remains undissolved is silicious earths; to the solution add caustic volatile alkali, which precipitates the iron and argil, but keeps the zinc in solution. The precipitate must be redissolved in vitriolic acid, and the iron and argil separated.

Tin Ores. Mix a quintal of tin ore, previously washed; pulverized and roast till no arsenical vapours arise, with half a quintal of calcined borax, and the same quantity of pitch, pulverized; put the whole into a crucible moistened with charcoal dust and water, and the crucible placed in an air furnace. After the pitch is burnt, give a violent heat for a quarter of an hour; and on withdrawing the crucible, the regulus will be found at the bottom. If the ore be not well washed from earthy matters, a larger quantity of borax will be requisite, with some powdered glass; and if the ore contains iron, some alkaline salt may be added.

In the humid way. Let the tin ore be well separated from its stony matrix, by well washing, and reduced to the most subtile powder; digest in concentrated oil of vitriol, in a strong heat for several hours; when cooled, add a small portion of concentrated marine acid, and let it stand one or two hours; then add water; and when the solution is clear, pour it off and precipitate it by fixed alkali.

One hundred grains of this precipitate, well washed and dried, are equivalent to one hundred of tin in its reguline state, if the precipitate consists of pure tin; but if it contain copper or iron, it must be calcined in a red heat for an hour, and then digested in nitrous acid, which will take up the copper; and afterwards in marine acid, which will separate the iron.

Lead Ores. As most of the lead ores contain either sulphur or arsenic, they should be well roasted. Take a quintal of roasted ore, and the same quantity of calcined borax; half a quintal of fine powdered glass; a quarter of a quintal of pitch, and as much clear iron filings. Line the crucible with wet charcoal dust, and put the mixture into the crucible; place it before the bellows of a forge fire. When it is red hot, raise the fire for twenty minutes, withdraw the crucible; when cold, break it.

In the humid way. Dissolve the ore by boiling it in diluted nitrous acid; the sulphur, insoluble stony parts, and calx of iron will remain. The iron may be separated by digestion in caustic fixed alkali. The nitrous solution contains the lead and and silver, which should be precipitated by the mineral fixed alkali, and the precipitate well washed in cold water, dried, and weighed. Digest it in caustic volatile alkali, which will take up the calx of silver; the residuum being again dried and weighed, gives the proportion of the calx of lead, 132 grains of which, are equal to 100 of lead in its metallic state. The difference of weight before and after the application of the volatile alkali, gives the quantity of silver; 129 grains of which are equal to 100 of silver in the metallic state.

Copper Ores. Take an exact ounce troy of the ore previously pulverized, and calcine it well; stir it all the time with an iron rod, without removing it from the crucible: after the calcination add an equal quantity of borax; half the quantity of fusible glass, one-fourth the quantity of pitch, and a little charcoal dust; rub the inner surface of the crucible with a paste composed of charcoal dust, a little fine powdered clay and water; cover the mass with common salt, and put a lid on the crucible, which place in a furnace; raise the fire gradually, till it burns briskly, and the crucible kept in it for half an hour; stir the metal often with an iron rod; and when the scoria adhering to the rod appears clear, take the crucible out and suffer it to cool, when it must be broken, and the regulus separated and weighed; this is called black copper, to refine which, equal parts of common salt and nitre are to be well mixed together. The black copper is brought into fusion, and a teaspoonful of flux is thrown on it, which repeat three or four times; then pour the metal into an ingot mould, and the button is found to be fine copper.

In the humid way. Make a solution of vitreous copper ore, in five times its weight of concentrated vitriolic acid, and boil it to dryness; add as much water as will dissolve the vitriol thus formed; to this solution add a clean bar of iron, which will precipitate the whole of the copper in its metallic form. If the solution be contaminated with iron, the copper must be redissolved in the same manner, and precipitated again. The sulphur may be separated by filtration.

Bismuth Ores. If it be mineralized by sulphur, or sulphur and iron, a previous roasting will be necessary. The strong ores require no roasting, only to be reduced to fine powder. Take the assay weight and mix it with half the quantity of calcined borax, and the same of pounded glass; line the crucible with charcoal; melt it as quickly as possible; when well done, take out the crucible, and let it cool gradually. The regulus will be found at the bottom.

In the humid way. Bismuth is easily soluble in nitrous acid, or aqua-regia. The solution is colourless, and is precipitable by the addition of pure water; 118 grains of the precipitate from nitrous acid, well washed and dried, are equal to 100 of bismuth in its metallic form.

Antimonial Ores. Bore a number of small holes in the bottom of a small crucible, place it in another, a size larger, lute them well together; then put the proper quantity of ore in small lumps in the upper crucible, lute thereon a cover; place the vessels on a hearth; surround them with stones six inches distant; fill with ashes the intermediate space, that the under crucible may be covered with them; but upon the upper, charcoal must be laid: the whole made red hot by the assistance of the hand bellows. The antimony runs through the holes of the upper vessel, being easy of fusion, into the other, where it is collected.

Humid assay of arseniated Antimony. Dissolve the ore in aquaregia, both the regulus and the arsenic remain in solution; the sulphur is separated by filtration. If the solution be boiled with twice its weight of strong nitrous acid; the regulus of antimony will be precipitated, and the arsenic converted into an acid, which may be obtained by evaporation to dryness.

Manganese Ore. To obtain the regulus, mix the calx or ore of manganese with pitch, made into a ball; put it into a crucible, lined with powdered charcoal, one-tenth of an inch on the sides, and one-fourth at the bottom; then fill the empty space with charcoal dust; cover the crucible with another inverted and luted on, and expose it to the strongest heat of a forge for an hour or more.

In the humid way. Roast the ore well to dephlogistigate the calx of manganese and iron, if any, and then treat with nitrous acid to dissolve the earths. Treat the residuum with nitrous acid and sugar, when a colourless solution of manganese is procured, and also of the iron, if any. Precipitate with Prussian alkali, digest the precipitate in pure water; the Prussiate of manganese will be dissolved, whilst the Prussiate of iron will remain undissolved.

Arsenical Ores—Made by sublimation in close vessels. Beat the ore into small pieces; put them into a matrass, which place in a sand pot, with a proper degree of heat; the arsenic sublimes, and adheres to the upper part of the vessel; collect it carefully, and ascertain its weight. A single sublimation will not be sufficient; sometimes, as in many cases, the arsenic will melt with the ore, and prevent its total volatilization; in which case, perform the first sublimation with a moderate heat; then bruise the remainder again, and expose it to a strong heat.

In the humid way. Digest the ore in marine acid, add the nitrous by degrees, to help the solution. The sulphur will be found on the filter; the arsenic will remain in the solution, and may be precipitated in its metallic form by zinc, adding spirits of wine to the solution.

Nickel Ore. Roast the ores well, to expel the sulphur and arsenic;

the greener the calx proves during this torrefaction, the more it abounds in the nickel; but the redder it is, the more iron it contains. Fuse in an open crucible, a proper quantity, with twice or thrice its weight of black flux, the whole covered with common salt. Expose the crucible to the strongest heat of a forge fire; make the fusion complete, and it will produce a regulus, though not pure. It contains a portion of arsenic, cobalt, and iron. Deprive the first by fresh calcination, adding powdered charcoal; the second, by scorification; but it is difficult to free it entirely from iron.

In the humid way. By solution in nitrous acid, it is freed from its sulphur; and by adding water to the solution, bismuth, if any, may be precipitated; silver, also, if contained in it, by the marine acid; and copper, when any, by iron.

To separate cobalt from nickel, when the cobalt is in considerable quantity, drop a saturated solution of the roasted ore in nitrous acid into liquid volatile alkali; the cobaltic part is instantly redissolved, and assumes a garnet colour; when filtered, a grey powder remains on the filter, which is the nickel. The cobalt may be precipitated from the volatile alkali, by any acid.

Cobalt Ores. Free them as much as possible from earthy matters, by washing, and from sulphur and arsenic by roasting. When prepared mix the ore with three parts of black flux, and a little decrepitated sea salt; put the mixture in a lined crucible, cover it, and place it in a forge fire, or hot furnace; for it is difficult of fusion. When well fused, a metallic regulus will be found at the bottom, covered with a scoria, of a deep blue colour: as almost all cobalt ores contain bismuth, this is reduced by the same operation as the regulus of cobalt; they are incapable of chemically uniting together, and are always found distinct from each other in the crucible. The regulus of bismuth having a greater specific gravity, is always at the bottom, and may be separated by a blow with a hammer.

In the humid way. Make a solution of the ore in nitrous acid, or aqua-regia, and evaporate to dryness; the residuum, treated with the acetous acid will yield to it the cobaltic part; the arsenic should be first precipitated, by the addition of water.

Mercurial Ores. The calciform ores of mercury are easily reduced without any addition. Put into the retort a quintal of ore, and a receiver luted on, containing some water—place the retort in a sand bath, give a sufficient degree of heat to force over the mercury which is condensed in the water of the receiver.

Sulphurated Mercurial Ores. They are assayed as above, by distillation; only, these ores require an equal weight of clean iron filings to be mixed with them; to disengage the sulphur, while the heat volatilizes the mercury, and forces it into the receiver. These ores should be tried for cinnabar, to know whether it will answer the purpose of extracting it from them; for this, take a determinate quantity finely powdered, put it into a glass vessel, expose to a gentle heat at first, gradually increased till nothing more is sublimed. By the quantity thus obtained, we may know whether the process will answer. Sometimes the cinnabar is not of so lively a colour, as that which is used in commerce; then, it may be refined by a second sublimation, and if then too dark, it may be brightened by the addition of mercury, and sublimed again.

Humid assay of Cinnabar. Dissolve the stony matrix in nitrous acid, the cinnabar being disengaged, should be boiled in eight or ten times its weight of aqua-regia, composed of three parts nitrous, and one of marine acid. The mercury may be precipitated in its running form by zinc.

Silver Ore. Take the assay quantity, finely pulverized; roast it well in a proper degree of heat; stir it often with an iron rod; then add about double the quantity of granulated lead, put it in a covered crucible, place it in a furnace, raise the fire gently at first, gradually increasing it, till the metal begins to work. If it appears too thick, add a little more lead; if it should boil too rapid, diminish the fire. By degrees the surface will be covered with a mass of scoria; then, carefully stir it with an iron hook heated, especially towards the border lest any of the ore should remain undissolved; and if what is adherent to the hook, when raised from the crucible, melts quickly again, and the extremity of the hook, after it is grown cold, is covered with a thin, shining, smooth crust, the scorification is perfect; but, on the contrary, if while stirring it, any considerable clamminess is perceived in the scoria, and when it adheres to the hook, though red hot, and appears unequally tinged, and seems dusty, or rough, with grains interspersed here and there, the scorification is incomplete; in consequence of which, the fire should be increased a little, and what adheres to the hook should be gently beaten off, and returned with a small ladle into the crucible. When the scorification is perfect, the metal should be poured into a cone, previously rubbed with a little tallow, and when it becomes cold, the scoria may be separated by a few strokes of a hammer.

In the humid way. Boil vitreous silver ore in diluted nitrous acid, using about twenty-five times its weight, until the sulphur is quite exhausted. Precipitate the silver from the solution by marine acid, or common salt; one hundred grains of this precipitate, contains seventy-five of real silver; if it contains any gold, it will remain undissolved. Fixed alkalies precipitate the earthy matters, and the Prussian alkali will show if any other metal is contained in the solution.

By cupellation. Take the assay quantity of ore, roast and grind it with an equal portion of litharge, divide it into two or three parts, and wrap each up in a small piece of paper; put a cupel previously seasoned under a muffle, with about six times the quantity of lead upon it. When the lead begins to work, carefully put one of the papers upon it, and after this is absorbed, put on a second, and so on till the whole is introduced; then raise the fire, and as the scoria is formed, it will be taken up by the cupel, and at last the silver will remain alone. This will be the produce of the assay, unless the lead contains a small portion of silver which may be discovered by putting an equal quantity of the same lead on another cupel, and working it off at the same time; if any silver be produced it must be deducted from the assay.

To assay the value of Silver. To ascertain the purity of silver, mix it with a quantity of lead proportionate to the supposed portion of alloy: test this mixture, and afterwards weigh the remaining button of silver. This is the same process as refining silver by cupellation.

Suppose the mass of silver to be examined, consists of twelve equal parts, called pennyweights; so that if an ingot weighs an ounce, each of the parts will be one-twelfth of an ounce. Thus, if the mass of silver be pure, it is called silver of twelve pennyweights; if it contains one-twelfth part of its weight of alloy, it is called silver of eleven pennyweights; if two-twelfths alloy, it is called ten pennyweights; which parts of pure silver are called fine pennyweights. Assayers give the name pennyweights, to a weight equal to twenty real. grains, which must not be confounded with the ideal weights. Assayer's grains are called fine. An ingot of fine silver, or silver of twelve pennyweights, contains, then, two hundred eighty-eight fine grains; if this ingot contains one-two hundred eighty-eighth of alloy, it is silver of eleven pennyweights, twenty-three grains; if four-two hundred eighty-eighths of alloy, eleven pennyweights, twenty grains, &c. A certain real weight must be taken to represent the assay weights: for example, thirty-six real grains reprresent twelve fine pennyweights, this subdivided into a number of other smaller weights, represent fractions of fine pennyweights, and grains. Thus, eighteen real grains represent six fine pennyweights; three real grains, one fine pennyweight, or twenty-four grains; a real grain and a half, represents twelve fine grains: one-thirty second of a real grain, represents a quarter of a fine grain, which is only one-seven en hundred fifty-second part of a mass of twelve pennyweights.

Double assay of Silver. The silver for the assay, should be taken from opposite sides of the ingot, and tried on a touchstone. Assayers know very nearly the value of silver by the look of the ingot; much better, by the test of the touchstone. The quantity of lead to be added is regulated by the portion of alloy, which is in general, copper: heat the cupel red hot for half an hour, before any metal is put upon it, which expels all moisture. When it is almost white by heat, put in the lead, increase the heat till the lead becomes red hot, smoking and agitated by a motion of all its parts, called its circulation. Then, put the silver on the cupel, and continue the fire, till the silver enters the lead. When the mass circulates well, diminish the heat by closing more or less the door of the assay furnace. Regulate the heat, that the metal on its surface may appear convex and ardent, while the cupel is less red, that the smoke shall rise to the roof of the muffle, that undulations shall be made in all directions, and that the middle of the metal shall appear smooth, with a small circle of litharge, which is continually imbibed by the cupel. When the lead and alloy is entirely absorbed by the cupel, the silver becomes bright and shining, when it is said to lighten; when, if the operation has been well performed, the silver will be covered with rainbow colours, which quickly undulate and cross each other, and then the buttons becomes fixed and solid.

The diminution of weight shews the quantity of alloy. As all lead contains a small portion of silver, an equal weight with that used in the assay, is tested off, and the product deducted from the assay weight. This portion is called the witness.

To assay plated metals. Take a determinate quantity of the plated metal; put it into an earthen vessel, with a sufficient quantity of the above menstruum, and place it in a gentle heat. When the silver is stripped, it must be collected with common salt; the calx tested with lead, and the estimate made according to the product of the silver.

Ores and Earths containing Gold. The general method is by amalgamation. Take a proper quantity, reduce it to powder, add about one-tenth of its weight of pure quicksilver, and triturate the whole in an iron mortar. The attraction which subsists between the gold and quicksilver, quickly unites them in the form of an amalgam, which is pressed through chamois leather; the gold is easily separated from this amalgam by exposure to a proper degree of heat, which evaporates the quicksilver, and leaves the gold.

This evaporation should be made with luted vessels; and this is the foundation of all operations by which gold is obtained from the rich mines of Peru.

2. Heat red hot, a quantity of gold sand, quench it in water; repeat two or three times, and the colour of the sand will become a reddish brown. Now mix it with twice its weight of litharge, and revive the litharge into lead, by adding a small portion of charcoal dust, exposing it to a proper degree of heat; when the lead revives, the gold is separated from the sand; and the freeing of the gold from the lead must afterwards be performed by cupellation.

Metallic ores containing gold are sometimes assayed as follows:—mix two parts of the ore, well pounded and washed, with one and a half of litharge, and three of glass: cover the whole with common salt; melt it in a smith's forge, in a covered crucible; then open the crucible, put a nail into it, and continue to do so till the iron is no longer attacked. The lead is thus precipitated which contains the gold, and is then separated by cupellation

Humid assay of Gold mixed with martial pyrites. Ore dissolved in twelve times its weight of diluted nitrous acid, gradually added; place it in a proper degree of heat; the soluble parts are taken up, and leaves the gold untouched, with the insoluble matrix, from which it is separated by aqua-regia. The gold is again separated from the aqua-regia by pouring ether upon it; the other takes up the gold, and by being burnt off, leaves it in its metallic state. The solution may contain iron, copper, manganese, calcareous earth, or argil; if evaporated to dryness, and the residuum heated to redness for half an hour, volatile alkali will extract the copper; dephlogisticated nitrous acid, the earths; acetous acid, the manganese; and marine acid, the calx of iron. The sulphur floats on the first solution, from which it is separated by filtration.

Parting of Gold and Silver. Gold and silver equally resisting the action of fire and lead, must therefore be separated by other means, which is effected by different menstrua. Nitrous acid, marine acid, and sulphur, which cannot attack gold, operate upon silver, and these are the principal agents employed in the process of *parting.* Parting by nitrous acid is the most convenient; this is called *simple parting,* and is generally the method preferred by goldsmiths. That made by the marine acid is by cementation, and called *concentrated parting;* that by sulphur, is made by fusion and called *dry parting.*

Parting by Aqua-Fortis. The following directions are to be regarded; first, must be in a proper proportion, viz. three parts of silver to one of gold, though a mass of silver containing two parts of silver to one of gold may be parted. The quality of the metal is determined by assayers, who make a comparison upon a touchstone, between it and needles composed of gold and silver in graduated proportions, and properly marked, which are called *proof needles.* If the silver is not to the gold, as three to one, the mass is improper for the operation, unless more silver is added; besides, the aqua-fortis must be very pure, containing neither vitriolic or marine acid. Granulate the metal previous to parting, by melting it in a crucible; then pour it into a vessel of water, giving the water a rapid circular motion with a stick. The vessels used are called *parting glasses*, free from flaws, and well annealed. The glasses are apt to crack on exposure to cold, or when even touched by the hand. The bottoms are secured by some operators, by a coating made of new slacked lime, with beer and white of eggs spread on a cloth, and wrapped round the bottom, over which they apply a composition of clay and hair. The glasses are placed in vessels containing water, supported by trivets, with a fire under them: thus if a glass breaks, the contents are caught in the vessel of water. If the heat communicated to the water is too great, regulate it by pouring cold water carefully down the side of the vessel into a parting glass fifteen inches high and ten or twelve inches wide at the bottom, placed in a copper pan twelve inches wide at bottom, fifteen inches wide at top, and ten inches high; assayers generally operate with about eighty ounces of metal, with twice as much aqua-fortis.

The aqua-fortis should be so strong as to act sensibly on silver, when cold, but not violently. Apply but little heat at first, as the liquor is apt to swell and rise over the vessel: when the acid is nearly saturated, increase the heat. When the solution ceases (which is known by the effervescence discontinuing) pour the liquor off; if any grains appear entire, add more aqua-fortis, till all the silver is dissolved. If the operation is performed slowly, the remaining gold will have distinct masses. The gold appears black after parting; its parts have no adhesion together; because the silver dissolved from it has left many interstices: to give them more solidity, and improve their colour, they are put into a test under a muffle, and made red hot; after which they contract and become more solid, and the gold resumes its colour and lustre. It is then called *grain gold*. If the operation has been hastily performed, the gold will have the appearance of black mud or powder, which must be melted after well washing.

Recover the silver, by precipitating it from aqua-fortis by means of pure copper. No precipitation will take place, if the solution is perfectly saturated, till a few drops of aqua-fortis are added. Wash the precipitate of silver well with boiling water, fuse with nitre and test off with lead.

Parting by Cementation. Bricks powdered and sifted, four parts, one part green vitriol, calcined till it becomes red, and one part of common salt; made into a firm paste, with a little water.

Reduce the gold to be cemented into plates as thin as money. Put at the bottom of the cementing pot, a stratum of the above paste, half an inch thick; cover with plates of gold; and so the strata are placed alternately: cover the whole with a lid, which is luted with a mixture of clay and sand. Place the pot in a furnace or oven, heat gradually, till it becomes red hot; keep it in the oven twenty-four hours; the heat must not melt the gold; then suffer the crucible to cool; separate carefully the gold from the cement, and boil at different times in a large quantity of pure water. Then assay upon a touchstone or otherwise; if not sufficiently pure, cement a second time.

In this process the vitriolic acid of the bricks, and the calcined vitriol, decomposes the common salt, during the cementation, by uniting to its alkaline base, while the marine acid becomes concentrated by the heat; and dissolves the silver alloyed with the gold. This is a very troublesome process, though it succeeds when the portion of silver is so small that it would be defended from the action of aqua-fortis by the superabundant gold; but is little used except to extract silver, or base metals, from the surface of gold, and thus giving to an alloyed metal, the colour and appearance of pure gold.

I

Dry Parting. As the dry parting is ever troublesome as well as expensive, it ought not to be undertaken, but on a considerable quantity of silver alloyed with gold. Granulate the metal; from one-eighth to one-fifth (as it is rich or poor in gold) reserve; mingle well the rest with an eighth of powdered sulphur; put into a crucible; keep a gentle fire, that the silver before melting, may be thoroughly penetrated by the sulphur; the sulphur will dissipate, if the fire is hastily urged. If to sulphuretted silver in fusion, pure silver is added, the latter falls to the bottom, and forms there a distinct fluid, not miscible with the other. The particles of gold having no affinity with the sulphuretted silver, are joined to the pure silver whenever they come in contact, and are thus transferred from the former into the latter, more or less perfectly, as the pure silver is more or less thoroughly diffused through the mixture. For this use a part of the granulated silver is reserved. Bring the sulphuretted mass into fusion, keep melting for nearly an hour in a covered crucible, throw in one-third of the reserved grains, which, when melted, stir the whole well, that the fresh silver may be distributed through the mixed, to collect the gold from it, which is performed by a wooden rod; which repeat, till the whole reserved metal is introduced. The sulphuretted silver appears in fusion, of a dark brown colour; after it has been in fusion for some time, a part of the sulphur having escaped from the top, the surface becomes white, and some bright drops of silver, about the size of a pea, are perceived on it. When this takes place, the fire must be immediately discontinued, or more and more of the silver, thus losing its sulphur, would subside and mingle with the part at the bottom, (perhaps as much as was unsulphuretted from the mass,) by a chisel or hammer, or more perfectly by placing the whole mass with its bottom upwards in a crucible, the sulphuretted part quickly melts, leaving unmelted that which contains the gold. The sulphuretted silver is assayed, by keeping a portion of it in fusion, till the sulphur is dissipated, and then by dissolving it in aqua-fortis.

If it should still be found to contain gold, it must be subjected to the same treatment as before. The gold thus collected may be concentrated into a smaller part, by repeating the whole process, when it may be parted by aqua-fortis, without too much expense.

To determine the quantity of gold. If its specific gravity is 17,157, it is lawful coin. The specific quality of pure gold is 19,3. Copper, silver, and most other metals which are alloyed with gold, may be easily separated from gold by nitric acid: for if the alloy be in fine filings, the nitric acid will dissolve the other metals, and leave the gold in a black powder. This powder may be separated and melted down in a pure mass; but the common method adopted by artists is, to melt the alloy with sulphuret of antimony. The other metals become sulphurets, and the gold will unite with the antimony, and all fall to the bottom of the crucible. After cooling it may be separated. Now melt the alloy of gold and antimony, boil it at a white heat, and the antimony will become volatilized, and fly off.

To obtain silver pure from alloy. Put some nitric acid in a wine glass diluted with an equal bulk of water; drop into it a six cent piece, and let it remain till action ceases. Now take out the undissolved silver, and put in a plate, or a coat of perfectly clean bright copper. The silver will be precipitated after a short time. Wash the powder several times; and put a little liquid ammonia into the water for the first washings. Now melt down the powder into a solid mass, which will be pure silver.

Silver coin is alloyed with copper as 12 1-3 to 1.

Weight of metals. Platina is twenty-three times heavier than water. Gold, nineteen; silver, eleven; quicksilver, fourteen; copper, nine; iron, eight; tin, seven; lead, eleven; nickel, nine; zinc, seven.

Method of ascertaining the specific gravity of bodies. The instrument generally used for obtaining the specific gravities, is called the hydrostatical balance; it does not differ much from the common balance. The way to find the specific gravity of a solid heavier than water, as a piece of metal, is this: weigh the body first in air, in the usual way, then weigh it when it is plunged in water, and observe how much it loses of its weight in this fluid, and dividing the former weight by the loss sustained, the quotient is the specific gravity of the body, compared with that of water. A piece of gold may be tried by weighing it first in air, and then in water, and, if upon dividing the weight in air, by the loss in water, the quotient comes to be about seventeen, the gold is good; if eighteen, or nearly nineteen, the gold is very fine; if less than seventeen, it is too much alloyed with other metal. The same principle is universal. Hence we see the reason why boats or other vessels float on water; they sink just so low, that the weight of the vessel, with its contents, is equal to the quantity of water which it displaces.

The method of ascertaining the specific gravity of bodies, was discovered by Archimedes. Hiero, king of Sicily, having given a workman a quantity of pure gold, to make a crown, suspected that the artist had kept part of the gold, and adulterated the crown with a base metal. The king applies to Archimedes, to discover the fraud. The philosopher long studied in vain, but at length he accidentally hit upon a method of verifying the king's suspicion. Going one day into a bath, he took notice that the water rose in the bath, and immediately reflected that any body of equal bulk with himself, would have raised the water just as much; though a body of equal weight, but not of equal bulk, would not raise it so much. From this idea he conceived a mode of finding out what he so much wished, and was so transported with joy, that he ran out of the bath crying out in the Greek tongue, "I have found it, I have found it." As gold was the heaviest of all metals then known, he therefore desired a mass of pure gold, equally heavy with the crown when weighed in air, should be weighed against it in water, conjecturing that if the crown was not alloyed it would counterpoise the mass of gold when they were both immersed in water, as well as it did when they were weighed in air. On making trial, the mass of gold weighed much heavier in water than the crown did, nor was this all; when the mass and crown were immersed separately in the same vessel of water, the crown raised the water much higher than the mass did, which showed it was alloyed with some other lighter metal which increased its bulk.

On this principle is founded the doctrine of the specific gravities of bodies.

Half of the civilized employments of man, consists in working the metals and minerals; civilization depends so much on the discovery of the useful metals, that little progress can be made from a savage state, without the useful trade of a blacksmith.

To avoid the inconveniences of exchanging or bartering, men, in early ages fixed on metals; as on gold, silver, copper, or iron, for a medium of value, so that if one man had too much corn and wanted wine, he was obliged to give corn for wine, but he might sell his corn for metal, and buy the wine with the metal, at his convenience. Hence the origin of money; as it was found inconvenient to weigh metal in every transaction, (as Abraham did when he bought the burying place for Sarah,) stamps were put on pieces of metal, to indicate that they might be safely received for a settled weight or value.

Viewing the metals in ordinary use, we consider them common productions; but no art is so curious as that of extracting metals from the earth, or ore, in which they are buried or concealed; and no discovery or invention was ever more wonderful. Workers of metal imitate nature, when they *beat* and *wash* their ores. No one on looking at most of the metallic ores, would suspect them to contain metals, as they are apparently the roughest, coarsest, and least desirable stones on earth. Research is on the wing of activity, and discoveries of minerals of the greatest utility are daily making. We are willing to believe there are still in reserve, beneath the surface of the earth, in our own country, *golden treasures* for the enterprising; if not near our most frequent walks, yet, in very many places which have never experienced the probing effects of a crobar, or the pressure of the foot of man.

CHAPTER XVII.
THE ART OF WORKING METALS, &c.

Method of reducing Iron Ore into malleable Iron. We proceed by stamping, washing, &c. the calcine and materials, to separate the ore from extraneous matter; then fusing the prepared ore in an open furnace, and instead of casting it, to suffer it to remain at the bottom of the furnace till it becomes cold.

New method of shingling and manufacturing Iron. The ore being fused in a reverberating furnace, is conveyed, whilst fluid, into an air furnace, where it is exposed to a strong heat, till a bluish flame is observed on the surface; it is then agitated on the surface, till it loses its fusibility, and is collected into lumps called *loops.* These loops are then put into another air furnace, brought to a white or welding heat, and then *shingled* into *half-blooms* or *slabs.* They are again exposed to the air furnace, and the half-blooms taken out and forged into *anconies, bars, half-flats,* and *rods* for *wire;* while the *slabs* are passed, when of a welding heat, through the grooved rollers. In this way of proceeding, it matters not, whether the iron is prepared from *cold* or *hot short* metal, nor is there any occasion for the use of finery, charcoal, coke, chafery, or hollow fire, or any blast by bellows, or otherwise: or the use of fluxes in any part of the process.

To weld Iron; an approved method. This consists in the skilful bundling of the iron to be welded; in the use of an extraordinary large forge hammer; in employing a *balling furnace,* instead of a *hollowfire* or *chafery;* and in passing the iron, reduced to a melting heat, through grooved mill-rollers of different shapes and sizes, as required.

Common hardening. Iron by being heated red hot, and plunged into cold water, acquires a great degree of hardness. This proceeds from the coldness of the water which contracts the particles of the iron into less space.

Case hardening. Is a superficial conversion of iron into steel, by cementation. It is performed on small pieces of iron, by enclosing them in an iron box, containing burnt leather, bone dust, or any other carbonic material, and exposing them for some time to a red heat. The surface of the iron thus becomes perfectly metallized. Iron thus treated is susceptible of the finest polish.

To convert Iron into Steel by Cementation. The iron is formed into bars of convenient size, and then placed in a cementing furnace,
with a sufficient quantity of cement which is composed of coals of animal or vegetable substances, mixed with calcined bones, &c. The
following are very excellent cements; 1. One part of powdered charcoal, one half a part of wood ashes, well mixed together. 2. Two
parts charcoal, moderately powdered, one part of bones, horn, hair or
skins of animals, burnt in close vessels to blackness and powdered;
and half a part of wood ashes; mix them well together. The bars of
iron to be converted into steel, are placed upon a stratum of cement,
and covered all over with the same; and the vessel which contains
them, closely luted, must be exposed to a red heat for eight or ten
hours, when the iron will be converted into steel.

Steel is prepared from bar iron by fusion; which consists in plunging a bar into melted iron,
and keeping it there for some time, by which process it is converted into good steel. All iron
which becomes harder by suddenly quenching in cold water, is called steel; and that steel
which in quenching acquires the greatest degree of hardness in the lowest degree of heat,
and retains the greatest strength in and after induration, ought to be considered as the best.

Improved process of hardening Steel. Articles manufactured of
steel, for the purpose of cutting, are, almost without an exception
hardened from the anvil; in other words, they are taken from the forger to the hardener, without undergoing any intermediate process; and
such is the accustomed routine, that the mischief arising has escaped
observation. The act of forging produces a strong scale or coating,
which is spread over the whole of the blade; and to make the evil still
more formidable, this scale or coating is unequal in substance, varying in proportion to the degree of heat communicated to the steel in
forging; it is, partially, almost impenetrable to the action of water
when immersed for the purpose of hardening. Hence it is that different degrees of hardness prevail in every razor manufactured; this is
evidently a positive defect; and so long as it continues to exist, great
difference of temperature must exist likewise. Razor blades not un-
frequently exhibit the fact here stated in a very striking manner; what
are termed clouds, or parts of unequal polish, derive their origin from
this cause; and clearly and distinctly, or rather *distinctly*, though not
clearly show how far this partial coating has extended, and when the
action of water has been yielded to, and when resisted. It cannot be
matter of astonishment, that so few improvements have been made in
the hardening of steel, when the evil here complained of, so universally obtains, as almost to warrant the supposition that no attempt has ever
been made to remove it. The remedy, however, is easy and simple
in the extreme, and so evidently efficient in its application, that it cannot but excite surprise, that in the present highly improved state of our
manufactures, such a communication should be made as a discovery
entirely new. Instead, therefore, of the customary mode of hardening the blade from the anvil, let it be passed immediately from the
hands of the forger to the grinder; a slight application of the stone
will remove the whole of the scale or coating, and the razor will then
be properly prepared to undergo the operation of hardening with advantage. It will be easily ascertained, that steel in this state, heats in
the fire with greater regularity, and that when immersed, the obstacles
being removed to the immediate action of the water on the body of the

steel, the latter becomes equally hard, from one extremity to the other. To this may be added, *that as the lowest possible heat at which steel becomes hard, is indubitably the best,* the mode here recommended will be found the only one by which the process of hardening can be effected with a less portion of fire than is or can be required in any other way. These observations are decisive, and will in all probability, tend to establish in general use, what cannot but be regarded as a very important improvement in the manufacturing of edged steel instruments.

English Cast Steel. The finest kind of steel, called *English cast steel,* is prepared by breaking to pieces blistered steel, and then melting it in a crucible with a flux composed of carbonaceous and vitrifiable ingredients. The vitrifiable ingredient is used only inasmuch as a fusible body, which flows over the surface of the metal in the crucible, and prevents the access of the oxygen of the atmosphere. Broken glass is sometimes used for this purpose.

When thoroughly fused it is cast into ingots, which by gentle heating and careful hammering, are tilted into bars. By this process the steel becomes more highly carbonized in proportion to the quantity of flux, and in consequence is more brittle and fusible than before. Hence, it surpasses all other steel in uniformity of texture, hardness, and closeness of grain, and is the material employed in all the finest articles of English cutlery.

To make edge tools from Cast Steel and Iron. This method consists in fixing a clean piece of wrought iron, brought to a welding heat, in the centre of a mould, and then pouring in melted steel, so as entirely to envelop the iron; and then forging the mass into the shape required.

To colour Steel blue. The steel must be finely polished on its surface, and then exposed to an uniform degree of heat. There are three ways of colouring: first, by a flame producing no soot, as spirit of wine; secondly, by a hot plate of iron; and thirdly, by wood ashes.

As a very regular degree of heat is necessary, wood ashes for fire work bears the preference. The work must be covered over with them, and carefully watched; when the colour is sufficiently heightened, the work is perfect. This colour is occasionally taken off with a very diluted marine acid.

Useful alloy of Gold and Platinum. Seven and a half dr. pure gold, and half dr. platinum. The platinum must be added when the gold is perfectly melted. The two metals will combine intimately, forming an alloy rather whiter than pure gold, but remarkably ductile and elastic; it is also less perishable than pure gold, or jeweller's gold, but more readily fusible than that metal.

These qualities must render this alloy an object of great interest to workers in metals. For *springs* when steel cannot be used, it will prove exceedingly advantageous.

It is a curious circumstance, that the alloy of gold and platina is soluble in nitric acid, which does not act on either of the metals in a separate state. It is remarkable, too, that the alloy has very nearly the colour of platinum, even when composed of eleven parts of gold to one of the former metal.

Ring Gold. Six dwts. twelve grs. Spanish copper, three dwts. sixteen grs. fine silver, and one ounce five pennyweights gold coin.

Tomback. Sixteen lbs. copper, one lb. tin, and one lb. zinc.

Red Tomback. Five and a half lbs. copper, and half a lb. zinc. The copper must be fused in a crucible before the zinc is added. This alloy is of a reddish colour, and possesses more lustre and is of greater durability, than copper.

White Tomback. Copper and arsenic put together in a crucible, and melted, covering the surface with muriate of soda, to prevent oxydation, will form a white brittle alloy.

Gun Metal. 1. One hundred twelve pounds Bristol brass, fourteen pounds zinc, and seven pounds blocktin. 2. Nine parts copper, and one part tin. The above compounds are those used in the manufacture of small and great brass guns, swivels, &c.

Specula of Telescopes. Seven lbs. copper, and when fused, add three lbs. of zinc, and four lbs. of tin. These metals will combine and form a beautiful alloy of great lustre, and of a light yellow colour, fitted to be made into specula for telescopes. Some use only copper and grain tin in the proportion of two lbs. to fourteen and a half ounces.

To distinguish Steel from Iron. Let fall one drop of nitric acid upon a piece of polished iron, and another upon a piece of polished steel. The acid on the iron will be limpid or whitish, that on the steel will become dark brown or black.

It is not necessary to polish the iron or steel to try its hardening qualities—if a spot on a coarse bar of iron or steel be filed bright it will be sufficient.

Compounds of Metals. Four ounces of bismuth; two ounces and a half lead; and one ounce and a half tin. Put the bismuth into a crucible, and when it is melted, add the lead and tin. This will form an alloy fusible at the temperature of boiling water.

2. Zinc, bismuth, lead; of each one ounce.

This alloy is so very fusible, that it will remain in a state of fusion if put on a sheet of paper and held over the flame of a candle or lamp.

3. Lead, three parts; tin, two parts; bismuth, five parts; will form an alloy fusible at 197° Fahrenheit, peculiarly applicable to casting, or the taking of impressions from gems, seals, &c. In making casts with this and similar alloys, it is necessary to use the metal at as low a temperature as possible; otherwise the water adhering to the things from which the casts are to be taken, forms vapour, and produces bubbles. The fused metal should be poured into a teacup, and allowed to cool, till just ready to set at the edges, when it must be poured into the mould. In taking impressions from gems, seals, &c. the fused alloy should be placed on paper or pasteboard, and stirred about till it has, by cooling, attained the consistence of paste, at which moment the die, gem, or seal should be stamped on it, and a very sharp impression will be obtained.

Bath Metal, is a mixture of four ounces and a half of zinc, and one pound of brass.

Brass, is composed of four and a half pounds copper; one and a half pounds of zinc.

Brass that is to be cast into plates from which pans and kettles are to be made and wire is to be drawn, must, instead of using the zinc in a pure state, be composed of fifty-six pounds of the finest calamine, or ore of zinc; and thirty-four pounds of copper. Old brass which has been frequently exposed to the action of fire, when mixed with copper and calamine, renders the brass far more ductile, and fitter for making fine wire, than it would be without it; but the German brass, particularly that of Nuremburgh, is, when drawn into wire, said to be far preferable to any made in England, for the strings of musical instruments.

Pinchback. Three ounces of pure copper; and one ounce of zinc. The zinc must not be added till the copper is in a state of fusion. Some use only half this quantity of zinc, in which proportion the alloy is more easily worked, especially in the making of jewelry.

2. One ounce of brass; and two ounces of copper, fused together under a coat of charcoal dust.

Prince's Metal. 1. Three ounces of copper, and one ounce of zinc; or eight ounces of brass, and one of zinc.

2. Four ounces of copper, and two ounces of zinc. In this last the copper must be fused before the zinc is added; when they have combined, a very beautiful and useful alloy is formed called Prince Rupert's Metal.

Bell Metal. Six parts of copper, and two parts of tin.

These preparations are the most approved for bells, throughout Europe and in China. In the union of the two metals, the combination is so complete, that the specific gravity of the alloy is greater than that of the two metals in an uncombined state.

2. Ten parts of copper, and two parts of tin. It may in general be observed, that a less proportion of tin is used for making churchbells, than clockbells; and that a little zinc is added for the bells of repeating watches, and other small bells.

Tutania, or Britannia Metal. Four ounces of plate brass, and four ounces of tin; when in fusion, add four ounces bismuth, and four ounces regulus of antimony. This is the composition, or hardening that is to be added at discretion, to melted tin, until it has acquired the requisite degree of colour and hardness.

2. Melt together, two pounds of plate brass; two pounds of tin; two pounds of bismuth; two pounds of regulus of antimony; two pounds of a mixture of copper and arsenic, either by cementation or melting. This composition is to be added at discretion, to melted tin.

3. One pound copper, one pound tin, and two pounds regulus of antimony, with or without a little bismuth.

4. Eight ounces of shruff brass; two pounds regulus of antimony; and twelve ounces of tin.

German Tutania. Two drachms of copper; one ounce regulus of antimony; and twelve ounces of tin.

Spanish Tutania. Eight ounces scrap iron, or steel; one pound antimony; and three ounces nitre. The iron or steel must be heated to a white heat, and the antimony and nitre must be added in small portions. Melt and harden one pound tin with two ounces of this compound.

2. Melt together four ounces antimony, one ounce of arsenic, and two pounds tin. The first of these Spanish alloys would be a beautiful metal, if arsenic were added.

Engestroom Tutania. Four parts copper, eight parts regulus of antimony, and one part bismuth: when added to one hundred parts tin, the compound will be ready for use.

Queen's Metal. Four and a half pounds tin, half a pound bismuth, half a pound antimony, half a pound lead. This alloy is used for making tea-pots and other vessels which are required to imitate silver. It retains its lustre to the last.

2. One hundred pounds tin, eight pounds regulus of antimony, one pound bismuth, and four pounds copper.

White Metal. Ten ounces lead, six ounces bismuth, and four drachms regulus of antimony.

2. Two pounds regulus of antimony; eight ounces brass; and ten ounces tin.

Common Hard White Metal. One pound brass, one and a half ounces zinc, and half an ounce of tin.

Metal for Tinning. To one pound malleable iron, at white heat, add five ounces regulus of antimony; and twenty-four pounds of the purest Molucca tin. This alloy polishes without the blue tint, and is free from lead or arsenic.

Metal for Flute Key Valves. Four ounces lead, and two ounces antimony, fused in a crucible and cast into a bar. It is used by flute manufacturers (when turned into small buttons in a lathe) for making valves to stop the key holes of flutes.

To burn metals. Procure a glass jar, such as is generally used for defflagrating the gases, and fill it with oxymuriatic acid gas. If nickel, arsenic, or bismuth in powder, be thrown into this gas; and the temperature of the atmosphere be not lower than 70° the metal will inflame, and continue to burn with the most brilliant combustion.

Prepare a jar of chlorine, (oxymuriatic gas) and suspend in it a piece of copper foil; it will immediately inflame, and afford a very striking spectacle. When subsided, it it will form a substance exactly similar to the native muriate of copper, brought from Peru.

2. Make a hole in the side of a large piece of charcoal; put into it some iron filings, iron wire, zinc shavings, lead shavings, &c.; fill a glass-holder with oxygen, provided with a tin or lead tube, terminating in a pipe stem: hold the charcoal in a suitable position to receive the current of oxygen upon the metals. Let an assistant hold the flame of a candle between the metals and the pipe, till the current of oxygen drives the flame into the coal; then remove the candle and continue the current of oxygen, enlarging or contracting it at pleasure, by turning the stop. The metals will burn very brilliantly, each exhibiting its own peculiar flame.

3. Coil up a piece of fine iron wire about the size of sowing thread; wind it spirally and closely around a pipe stem; let the coil be three or four inches long; the upper end fitted into a cork, which suits the mouth of an eight ounce phial. Fill the phial nearly with oxygen, leaving water in it to cover the bottom an inch thick, in order to defend it from being broken with the globules of hot oxyde of iron which fall upon it: set the phial on the table, well stopped with another cork: now tie a small knot of silk thread on the lower end of the coil; hold a piece of brimstone in a candle till it melts a small spot; blow out the blaze of brimstone, and dip in the knot of thread. Be certain that the thread and melted brimstone which adheres to it, do not exceed in

size a large pin head.   Now pull out the cork; hold the thumb over the mouth, and let an assistant steady the phial; light the brimstone match; put the coil of wire quickly into the phial, fitting in the cork to which it is attached: the phial will soon send off brilliant sparks, and make a beautiful exhibition.

4. If a piece of wire, about twice as large as the wire of the coil, be flattened with a hammer, and fitted into the cork, so as to extend down through the centre of the coil, and set on fire at the same time, in the same manner with the coil, it will present a very curious appearance: the central wire will burn with a large globular flame, while a smaller globular flame will perform evolutions around it, resembling the motion of a planet while revolving around the sun. We are taught by the foregoing experiment, if the oxygen of the air was not reduced in power by hydrogen, iron itself would not resist combustion.

To refine Pewter.   Take fine pewter, melt it in a crucible.   When done, project over it at several times some nitre, till you see it calcined.   Then pound it into powder, and mix it with an equal quantity of charcoal pulverized very fine.   If in this condition you melt it again, it will resume its form of pewter, only refined in a much superior degree.

Common Pewter.   Seven pounds tin, one pound lead, six ounces copper; and two ounces zinc.   The copper must be fused before the other ingredients are added.

Best Pewter.   One hundred parts tin, and seventeen parts regulus of antimony.

Hard Pewter.   Twelve pounds tin, one pound regulus of antimony, and four ounces copper.

Common Solder.   Two pounds lead, and one pound tin.   The lead must be melted before the tin is added.   This alloy, when heated by a hot iron, and applied to tinned iron with powdered rosin, acts as a cement or solder; it is also used to join loaden pipes.

Soft Solder.   Two pounds tin, and one pound lead.

Solder for Steel Joints.   Nineteen pennyweights fine silver, one pennyweight copper, and two pennyweights brass, melted together under a coat of charcoal dust.   This solder has several advantages over the usual zinc solder, or brass, when employed in soldering cast steel, &c. as it fuses with less heat, and its whiteness has a better appearance than brass.

Silver Solder for Jewellers.   Nineteen pennyweights fine silver, one pennyweight copper, and ten pennyweights brass.

Silver Solder for Plating.   Ten pennyweights brass, and one ounce pure silver.

Gold Solder.   Twelve pennyweights pure gold, two pennyweights pure silver, and four pennyweights copper.

Brass Solder for Iron.   Thin plates of brass are to be melted between the pieces that are to be joined.   If the work be very fine, as when two leaves of a broken saw are to be brazed together, cover it with pulverized borax, melted with water, that it may incorporate with the brass powder, which is added to it; the piece must then be exposed to the fire, without touching the coals, and heated till the brass is seen to run.

Bronze.   Seven pounds pure copper, three pounds zinc, and two pounds tin. The copper must be fused before the other ingredients are added. These metals, when combined, form the bronze so much used, both in ancient and modern times.

Mock Platina. Melt together, eight ounces brass, and five ounces zinc.

Powder Gold. Verdigris, eight ounces, tutty, four ounces, borax, nitre, of each two ounces, corrosive sublimate, two drachms, made into a paste with oil, and melted together: used in japan work, as a gold colour.

True Gold Powder. Grain gold, one ounce, quicksilver nearly boiling, six ounces; rub together; then either distil off the quicksilver, or corrode it away with spirits of nitre, and heat the black powder that is left red hot.

2. Grain gold, one ounce, dissolve in a mixture of spirit of nitre, sixteen ounces, with common salt, four ounces; add to the clear solution, green vitriol, four ounces; dissolve in water; wash the precipitate, and heat it red hot.

3. Dissolve gold in aqua-regia, and draw off the acid by distillation; used in painting, gilding, &c.

Tutenag. Bismuth, one pound, tin, two pounds; melt together: used for buttons and vessels.

Zaffre. One part of roasted cobalt, ground with two or three parts of very pure quartzose sand; is either in a cake or reduced to powder: used as a blue colour for painting glass.

Purple Precipitate; Cassin's Purple. Solution of gold in aqua-regia, one ounce, distilled water, one pound and a half; hang it in the liquid slips of tin.

2. By precipitating the diluted solution of gold, by dyer's spirit, will communicate a purple colour to glass, when melted in an open vessel. In a close vessel the glass receives no colour.

Tin and Copper. Scrape a piece of copper well with a knife, and rub it over with sal ammoniac; then heat the copper over clean coals, which will not emit any smoke; at the same time rubbing it over with rosin. While hot and thus cleansed with the sal ammoniac and rosin, rub tin upon it in its solid state, which being melted by the heat of the copper, will adhere to it, giving it a silvery white surface.

Copper vessels are tinned inside by a similar process; and any ingenious person may repair them in this way when the tin has rubbed off.

Method of tempering edge tools that are of too brittle a quality. Plunge them into boiling fat for two hours, then take them out, and let them cool gradually. They will retain their hardness without being brittle.

Transmutation of Iron into the finest German Steel. Take clean soot, one pound, oak wood ashes, twelve ounces, and four ounces of pounded garlics. Boil all together in twelve pounds common water, till reduced to four pounds. Strain this, and dip in it the iron pigs, which you will afterwards stratify with the following cement, viz: Take burnt wood coals, otherwise called *cokes*, and quick lime of each three pounds, soot dried and calcinated in an iron pan, one pound, decrepitate salt, four ounces. Make of this and your iron several beds alternately, one over another; and having well luted the vessel in which you shall have made those beds of iron and cement, give them a reverberating fire, for three times twenty-four hours, and the operation is done.

Of Zinc or Spelter, and its various uses. Zinc combined with gold in equal proportions, forms a hard white compound metal, that admits of a fine polish, and may be advantageously manufactured into specula for optical instruments.

Zinc and tin melted together form a kind of pewter.

Spelter and copper readily unite in the fire, provided the combustion of the former be carefully prevented during the process. In this state it forms a metal distinguished by the name of yellow copper; but which is divided into several sorts according to the respective proportions contained in the alloy. Thus three parts of copper and one of zinc, constitute brass; five or six of copper and one of one zinc, form pinchback. Tombac is composed of a still larger proportion of copper than pinchback; is of a deep red, and bears the name of its inventor. Prince's metal requires a still larger proportion of zinc than either of the preceding compositions.

Test for Metals. Let a stream of sulphuretted hydrogen gas pass into a phial of liquid ammonia; the best method is to put the ammonia into a broad mouthed phial, filling it about half full; turn the phial in an oblique position, and extend the beak of the retort to the bottom of it. Wet tow may be wound about the neck of the retort when it enters the mouth of the phial to prevent the escape of the gas; or if a little does escape it is immaterial, for we should become sufficiently acquainted with this gas to detect it by its smell; now pour some of the liquid into a solution of copperas and another of blue vitriol.

For many metals this is a perfect test; it precipitates all metallic solutions with such different colours, when applied as a test, that, with collateral tests, almost any metal may be detected.

To give tools such a temper as will enable them to saw marble. Make the tool hot in the fire, and when red cherry colour, take it off from the fire, rub it with a piece of candle, and steep it immediately in good strong vinegar, in which some soot must be diluted.

The transmutation of Iron into Damask Steel. You must at first purge it of its usual brittleness; and after having reduced it into filings, make it red hot in a crucible; steep it several times in oil of olives, in which you shall have before thrown melted lead. Take care to cover the vessel in which the oil is contained, every time you throw the steel into it, for fear the oil should catch fire.

To whiten Brass. Brass, copper, iron, or steel may be easily whitened, by means of the Cornwall tin, or pewter, prepared with sublimate, proceeding as follows: Take Cornwall pewter, about one pound, add to it half that quantity of sublimate. Set it on a strong fire and sublime. Throw away the first water; the second is good, which you know by its white colour. Now if you make a piece of copper, brass, steel or iron, it is not material which, red hot and steep it in that water it will become as white as silver.

To calcine Pewter, and render it as white and as hard as silver. Melt well your pewter in a crucible, so that it may be very fine and clear; pour it afterwards into a very strong vinegar, then into mercurial water; repeat that operation as many times as you please, you will each time give it an additional degree of hardness and whiteness drawing near to silver, so much that it will at last be very difficult to distinguish from silver.

To render Iron as white and as beautiful as Silver. Take ammoniac salt in powder, and mix it with an equal quantity of quicklime. Put them all together in cold water and mix well; when done, any iron piece which you shall have made hot, will if you steep it in that prepared water, become as white as silver.

To prevent Iron from rusting. Warm your iron till you cannot touch it without burning yourself. Then rub it with new and clean white wax. Put it again to the fire till it has soaked in the wax. When done, rub it over with a piece of serge, and the iron will never rust.

To soften Iron and harden it more than it was before. Make a little chink lengthways in an iron bar, in which pour melted lead. Then make it evaporate by a strong fire, as that of copelling; renew this operation four or five times, and the bar will become very soft. You harden it afterwards by steeping it, when red hot, in mere forge water, and it will be of so good a temper as to be fit for lancets, razors and knives, with which you will be able to cut other iron without its splitting or denting.

It has been found by experience that an armour can never be good proof against fire arms, if it has not first been softened with oils, gums, wax, and other incerative things, and afterwards hardened by steeping them several times over in binding waters.

Method of giving a lustre to Silver. Dissolve any quantity of alum in water so as to make a pretty strong brine, which you must scim carefully, add some soap to it, and when you want to use it, dip a piece of linen rag into it, and daub it over your plates. This process will add much to their lustre.

To preserve the brightness of Arms. Rub them with hart's marrow, or else dissolve some alum powder, with the strongest vinegar you can find, and rub your arms with it. By this means they keep for ever bright.

To coat Copper with Silver. Take a few grains of silver in powder as precipitated by copper in a preceding experiment, after it is washed and before melting; about an equal weight of alum or a little more; six times as much table salt; also six times as much tartrite of potash; pulverize all these articles and rub them well together; rub the clean bright surface of a piece of copper with this powder and it will be silvered.

This silvering is not very durable, though it may be easily renewed. Plating copper is much preferable. This is done by brazing on a thin bar of silver upon a thick bar of copper. Then both are rolled out into the proper thickness for use.

Tin alloyed with Copper. Scour a very thin slip of iron bright, which while doing, dip it several times in very dilute sulphuric acid; bend one end of it so that it will fit the bottom of a crucible. Melt some tin in the crucible and dip the bent end of the slip of iron into it; the tin will combine with the surface of the iron, and if very thin will penetrate entirely through it.

On this principle sheet tin is manufactured.

Chinese Sheet Lead. The operation is carried on by two men; the one is seated on the floor, with a large flat stone before him, and with a moveable flat stone stand, at his side. His fellow workman stands by his side with a crucible filled with melted lead; and having poured a certain quantity upon the stone, the other lifts the moveable stone, and dashing it on the fluid lead, presses it out into a flat and thin plate, which he instantly removes from the stone. A second quantity of lead is poured in a similar manner, and a similar plate formed, the process being carried on with singular rapidity. The rough edges of the plates are then cut off, and are soldered together for use.

This method has been applied with great success to the formation of thin plates of zinc, for galvanic purposes.

To cover bars of Copper, &c. with Gold, so as to be rolled out into sheets. Prepare ingots or pieces of copper or brass, in convenient lengths and sizes—clean them from impurity, making their surfaces level: now prepare plates of pure gold, or gold mixed with a portion of alloy, of the same size of the ingots of metal, and of suitable thickness. Having placed a piece of gold upon an ingot intended to be plated, hammer and compress them together, so that they may have their surfaces as nearly equal to each other as possible: now bind them together with wire, in order to keep them in the same position during the process required to attach them: now take silver filings, and mix with borax, to assist the fusion of silver; lay the mixture upon the edge of the plate of gold, and next to the ingot of metal. Having thus prepared the two bodies, place them on a fire in a stove or furnace, and let them remain until the silver and borax placed along the edges of the metals melt, and until the adhesion of the gold with the metal is perfect; then take the ingot carefully out of the stove, and by this process it is plated with gold, and prepared ready for rolling into sheets.

Metallic Watering, or for Blanc Moire. This article of Parisian invention, which is much employed to cover cabinet ornamental work, dressing boxes, telescopes, &c. is prepared as follows: dilute sulphuric acid, with from 7 to 9 parts of water; then dip a sponge or rag into it, and wash the surface of a sheet of tin; this will speedily exhibit the appearance of crystallization, which is the moire. This effect is not easily produced upon every sort of sheet tin; for if much hardened by hammering and rolling, then the moire cannot be effected until the sheet has been heated so a to produce an incipient fusion on the surface, after which the acid will act upon it, and produce the moire. Almost any acid will do as well as the sulphuric, and it is said the citric acid, dissolved in a sufficient quantity of water, answers better than any other. The moire can be much improved by employing the blow-pipe, to form small and beautiful specks on the surface of the tin, previous to the application of the acid. When the moire has been formed, the plate is to be varnished and polished, the varnish being tinted with any glazing colour, and thus the red, green, yellow, and pearl coloured moires are manufactured.

To plate Iron. 1. Polish the surface very clean and level with a burnisher; and afterwards by exposing it to a bluing heat, a silver leaf is properly placed, and carefully burnished down. This is repeated till a sufficient number of leaves are applied to give the silver a proper body.

2. By the use of solder; slips of thin solder are placed between the iron and silver, with a little flux, and secured together by binding wire.

It is then placed in a clean vessel, and continued in it till the solder melts; when it is taken out, and on cooling is found to adhere firmly.

3. By tinning the iron first, and uniting the silver by the intermedia of slips of rolled tin, brought into fusion in a gentle heat.

To tin Copper and Brass. Boil six pounds cream tartar, four gallons water, and eight pounds grain tin, or tin shavings. After they have boiled a sufficient time, the substance to be tinned is put therein, and the boiling continued, when the tin is precipitated in its metallic form.

To tin Iron and Copper Vessels. The iron to be tinned must be previously steeped in acid materials, such as sour whey, distiller's wash, &c. then scoured and dipped in melted tin, having been first rubbed over with a solution of sal ammoniac. The surface of the tin is prevented from calcining, by covering it with a coat of fat. Copper vessels must be well cleansed; and then a sufficient quantity of tin, with sal ammoniac, is put therein, and brought into fusion, and the copper vessel moved about. A little resin is sometimes added. The sal ammoniac prevents the copper from scaling, and causes the tin to be fixed wherever it touches. Lately, zinc has been proposed for lining vessels, instead of tin, to avoid the consequences which are unjustly apprehended.

To Dye in Gold, Silver Medals through. Take some saltpetre, pour over it a sufficient quantity of oil of vitriol, to swim over. When the ebullitions, arising from that mixture shall be ended, distil to dryness—there remains a white salt. Dissolve in what quantity of warm water you think proper, or may be in need of, which you know when you see the water can dissolve no more of it—put into this a drachm of calx or magister of gold. Then put in digestion, in it, laminas cut small and thin, for twenty-four hours, over a very gentle fire. At the end of that time, you will find them thoroughly dyed gold colour, inside and out.

Silvering Powder. Silver dust from fifteen to twenty grains, cream tartar, common salt, each two drachms, alum half a drachm.

2. Silver dust, half an ounce, common salt, sal ammoniac, of each two ounces, corrosive sublimate, one drachm; make into a paste with water, used to silver copper, which is to be cleaned by boiling with argol and alum, then rub it with either of these powders, and polish with soft leather.

White Metal. Ten oz. lead, six oz. bismuth, and four oz. regulus of antimony.

2. Two lbs. regulus of antimony, eight oz. brass, and ten oz. tin.

Common hard White Metal. Eight oz. copper, and half an oz. neutral arsenical salt, fused together, under a flux composed of calcined borax, charcoal dust, and fine powdered glass.

Manheim Gold. Three and a half oz. copper, one and a half oz. brass, and fifteen grs. pure tin.

Imitation of Silver. Three-fourths oz. tin, and one lb. copper, will make a pale bell metal which will roll and ring very near to sterling silver.

Yellow dipping Metal. Two parts Cheadle brass, one part copper, with a little Bristol old brass, and one-fourth of an oz. of tin to every pound of copper. This alloy is almost of the colour of gold coin.   Cheadle brass is the darkest, and gives the metal a greenish hue.   Old Bristol brass, is pale and yellow.

Gilding Metal.   Four parts copper, one part Bristol old brass, and fourteen oz. of tin to every pound of copper.

Common Jewelry.   Three parts copper, one part Bristol old brass, and four oz. of tin, to every pound of copper.

If this alloy is for fine polishing, the tin may be omitted, and a mixture of lead and antimony substituted.   Paler polishing metal, by reducing the copper to two, or to one part.

CHAPTER XVIII.
SCULPTURE AND PRINTING.

To ascertain when the art of sculpture was first practised, and by what nation, is beyond human research; we may safely conjecture, however, that it was one of the original propensities of man.   This will still appear in the ardent and irresistible impulse of youth to make representations of objects in wood; and the attempts of savages to embody their conceptions of their idols; a command from the Author of our being, was necessary to prevent the ancient Israelites from making graven images; and the inhabitants of the rest of the earth possessed similar propensities.   The descriptions in the Scriptures demonstrate that the art had been brought to great perfection at the period of which they treat.   It is necessary to make a distinction between carving and sculpture; the former belongs exclusively to wood, and the latter to stone or marble.   The acknowledged masters of this sublime art, were the ancient Greeks.   Such have been the excellence and correctness of their imitations of nature, and the refined elegance of their taste, that many of their works are mentioned, as efforts never to be exceeded or perhaps imitated.   Statuary is a branch of sculpture, employed in the making of statues.   The term is also used for the artificer himself.   Phidias was the greatest statuary among the ancients, and Michael Angelo, among the moderns.   Statues are not only formed with the chisel from marble, and carved in wood, but they are cast in plaster of Paris, or other matters of the same nature, and in several metals, as lead, brass, silver, and gold.

The Process of Casting in Plaster of Paris.   Mix the plaster with water, and stir it until it attains a proper consistence; then pour on any figure, for instance, a human hand or foot, previously oiled in the slightest manner possible, which prevents the adhesion of the plaster; in a few minutes the plaster will be dry to the hardness of soft stone, taking the exact impression of every part, even the minutest pores of the skin.   This impression is called the mould.   When taken from the figure that produced it, and slightly oiled, plaster mixed with water as before, may be poured into it, where it must remain until hardened; if it be then taken from the mould, it will be an exact image of the original figure.   When the figure is flat, having no hollows, or high projections, it may be moulded in one piece, but when its surface is varied, it must be moulded in many pieces fitted together, and held in one or more outside, or containing piece.

This useful art supplies the painter and sculptor with exact representations from nature, and multiplies models of all kinds.   It is practised in such perfection, that casts of the antique statues are made so precisely like the originals in proportion, outline, and surface, that no difference is discoverable, excepting in colour, and materials.

Composition of Ancient Statues. According to Pliny, the metal used by the Romans, for their statues, and for the plates on which they engraved inscriptions, was composed in the following manner. They first melted a quantity of copper, into which they put one-third of its weight of old copper which had been long in use—to every hundred lbs. weight of this mixture, they added twelve and a half lbs. of alloy composed of equal parts of lead and tin.

Metallic Casts from Engravings on Copper. A most important discovery has lately been made, which promises to be of considerable utility in the fine arts; some beautiful specimens of metallic plates of a peculiar composition, have lately appeared—under the name of "cast engravings." This invention consists in taking moulds from every kind of engravings, with lime, mezzotinto, or aqua-tinta, and pouring on this mould an alloy, in a state of fusion, capable of taking the finest impression. The obvious utility of this invention, as applicable to engravings, which meet with a ready sale, and of which great numbers are required, will be incalculable, as it will wholly prevent the expense of retracing, which forms so prominent a charge in all works of an extended sale. No sooner is one cast worn out, than another may be immediately procured from the original plate, so that every impression will be a proof. Thus, the works of our most celebrated artists, may be handed down, *ad infinitum*, for the improvement and delight of future ages, and will afford at the same time, the greatest satisfaction to every lover of the fine arts.

The art of Printing, deserves to be considered with attention and respect. From the ingenuity of its contrivance, it has ever excited mechanical curiosity; from its intimate connexion with learning, it has justly claimed historical notice; and from its extensive influence on morality, politics, and religion, is now become a very important speculation. Coining and taking impressions in wax, are of great antiquity, and the principle is precisely that of printing. The application of this principle to the multiplication of books, constituted the discovery of the art of printing. The Chinese have for many ages, printed with blocks, or whole pages engraved on wood. But the application of single letters or moveable types forms the merit of the European art. The honour of giving rise to this method has been claimed by the cities of Harlaem, Mentz, and Strasburg; and to each of these it may be ascribed in some degree, as printers resident in each, made successive improvements in the art. It is recorded by a reputable author, that Laurens Foster, of Harlaem, walking in a wood near that city, cut some letters upon the rind of a beech tree, which for fancy's sake, being impressed upon paper he printed one or two lines for his grandchildren; and having thus succeeded, he invented a more glutinous ink, because he found that the common ink sunk and spread; and then formed whole pages of wood, with letters cut upon them, and, (as nothing is complete, in its first invention,) the backsides of the pages were pasted together, that they might have the appearance of manuscripts, written on both sides of the paper. These beechen letters, he afterwards exchanged for leaden ones, and these again for tin and lead, as a flexible, and more solid and durable substance. He died in 1440; and by some, his first attempt is supposed to have been made about 1430, but by others, as early as 1423.

From this period, printing has made a rapid progress in most of the principal towns of Europe, superseded the trade of copying, which, till that time, was very considerable, and was in many places considered as a species of magic.   In 1490, it reached Constantinople, and was extended by the middle of the following century to Africa and America.

During the period since its invention, what has not the art of printing effected?   It has blunted the edge of persecution's sword, laid open to man his own heart, struck the sceptre from the hand of tyranny, and awakened from its slumbers, a spirit of knowledge, cultivation and liberty.   It has gone forth like an angel, scattering blessings in its path, solacing the wounded mind, and silently pointing out the triumphs of morality, and the truths of revelation to the gaze of those, whom the want of precept or good example had debased, and whom ignorance had made sceptical.

The fourth centennial anniversary of the invention of printing, was observed at Harleem in Holland, on the 10th and 11th of July, 1823, with great rejoicing, and a splendid festival.

Printer's Types.   Ten pounds of lead, and two pounds of antimony.   The antimony must be thrown into the crucible, when the lead is in a state of fusion.   The antimony gives a hardness to the lead, without which, the type would speedily be rendered useless, in a printing press.   Different proportions of lead, copper, brass and antimony, frequently constitute this metal.   Every artist has his own proportions, so that the same composition cannot be obtained from different foundries; each boasts of the superiority of his own mixture.

Small Types and Stereotype Plates.   Nine pounds of lead, and when melted, add two pounds of antimony, and one pound of bismuth.

This alloy expands as it cools, and is, therefore, well suited for the formation of small printing types (particularly, when many are cast together, to form stereotype plates,) as the whole of the mould is accurately filled with the alloy; consequently, there can be no blemish in the letters.   2. Eight parts of lead, two parts of antimony, and one-third part of tin.   For the manufacture of stereotype plates, plaster of Paris, of the consistence of a batter pudding before baking, is poured over the letter-press page, and worked into the interstices of the types, with a brush.   It is then collected from the sides, by a slip of iron or wood, so as to lie smooth and compact.   In about two minutes, the whole mass, is hardened into a solid cake.   This cake, which is to serve as the matrix of the stereotype plate, is now put upon a rack in an oven, where it undergoes great heat, so as to drive off the superfluous moisture.   When ready for use, these moulds, according to their size, are placed in flat cast iron pots, and are covered over with another piece of cast iron, perforated at each end, to admit the metallic composition intended for the preparation of stereotype plates.   The flat cast iron pots are now fastened in a crane, which carries them steadily to the metallic bath, or melting pot, where they are immersed, and kept for a considerable time, until all the pores and crevices of the mould are completely and accurately filled.   When this has taken place, the pots are elevated from the bath, by working the crane, and are placed over a water trough, to cool gradually.   When cold, the whole is turned out of the pots, and the plaster being separated, by hammering, and washing, the plates are ready for use, having received the most exact and perfect impression.

CHAPTER XIX.
ENGRAVING, ETCHING, &c.

Engraving is the art of cutting metals and precious stones, and representing on them whatever device the artist pleases, and that great numbers of an impression from the same engraving may be taken, in a short time, and at a small price.

The French divide the art into several branches, according to the different materials wrought upon, and the manner of execution.

Among us, the first method is distinguished, as cutting in wood; that on metals, with aqua-fortis, is named *etching;* that by the knife, burnisher, or scraper, mezzotinto; that on stones, carving, or stone cutting; and that performed with a graver on metals or precious stones, which we shall now attempt more immediately to illustrate. The principle on which this art is grounded, are the same with those of painting, viz. *design,* which an engraver ought to make his peculiar study, for without that he will neither be able to imitate the performances of the greatest masters in painting, or design any thing beautiful of his own. In imitating the paintings of eminent masters, the engraver should studiously conform himself to the taste and beauty of the copy, in order to preserve that elegance of character which distinguishes the style of one master from another; and in doing which to any tolerable degree of perfection, it is necessary that an engraver should understand perspective, and architecture. The former enables him with ease to throw backwards, by the natural degradations of strong and faint, the figures and other objects of the picture, or design he would execute; the latter will capacitate him to preserve the due proportion of its order. To execute in this art, as well as every other, the materials which are used should be duly regarded. The best workmen prefer the red copper, which is the toughest. His plates should be well polished when he commences to trace any thing on them; his graver should be of the purest steel, well tempered and never blunt.

In conducting the strokes of the graver, care ought always to be taken that they flow freely and naturally. The graver should be conducted according to the various risings and cavities of the muscles, which in some measure depends upon a knowledge in anatomy, as well as design. In sculpture the work should never be made dark; as statues, &c. are commonly made of white marble, or stone, the colour reflecting on all sides, does not produce dark shades. In regard to drapery of every kind, if the diversity of stuffs can be represented, it generally adds to the beauty of the piece; when there is a necessity of crossing the strokes, it must be observed that the first should be finer than the second and the third than the second which makes the work appear more soft and mellow. Stuffs that have a lustre should be imitated, by striking with stronger and straighter strokes than others; being generally silk, producing flat and broken folds, should be expressed by one or two strokes, as their colours vary, with finer ones between them. Velvet and plush are represented in the same manner, by fine strokes between others, with this difference; the first strokes should be much stronger than for stuffs, and the finer ones proportionate. Metals, or vessels of gold and copper, or armour of polished steel, are to be engraved with fine strokes, between the strong ones, it being the opposition of light and shade, that occasions the lustre. With respect to architecture, perspective shows us, that the strokes which form receding objects tend to the point of view; when the piece is to contain entire columns, they are to be represented by perpendicular lines; for in crossing them according to their roundness, those strokes which are near their capitals, being opposed to those near their base, produce a disagreeable effect; unless supposed to be at a great distance, which renders the object near parallel.

For landscapes, the practisers of etching may form the outlines by it, particularly of the leaves of trees, which is more expeditious than engraving, and does as well. In this case, care should be taken in finishing it well with the graver, that the etching be imperceptible, because it has not the softness of engraving. In representing steep objects, the first strokes should be frequently interrupted and broken off, the second straight, cutting the others with acute angles, accompanied with long points. To represent rocks, the second strokes should not form the angles so acute as in representing other objects. Objects receding towards the horizon should be touched very lightly, and charged with little shade, though the mass should appear dark, as from some shade supposed to proceed from the clouds intercepting the rays of the sun. Calms are represented by straight strokes, running parallel with the horizon, with finer ones between them, and are to be omitted in some places, to make their shining reflection which proceeds from the water. By the second strokes also, made more or less strong, and sometimes by perpendicular ones, the forms of objects, either reflected on the surface of the water, or advanced at a distance on its banks, are represented.

The waves of the sea, are represented by strokes, bending according to the agitation of the water, with finer ones between them, cutting them with very acute angles. To represent water falling with rapidity from rocks or precipices, must be expressed by first strokes according to the nature of their fall, with finer ones between them, leaving the lights formed by the beams of the sun, falling directly on them very bright, and the more so as they approach the fore part of the piece. When the clouds appear thick and agitated, the graver should be turned about according to their form and agitation; and if they produce dark shades, which require double strokes, the second should cut the first in more acute angles than in figures. Flat clouds, losing themselves insensibly with the sky, must be formed by strokes parallel with the horizon, waved a little, as they appear more or less thick. A calm serene sky should be expressed by parallel strokes, very straight without any winding. Though all the parts of a piece of engraving may be executed according to the rules of art, yet, unless there be a general proportion and harmony diffused throughout it will not appear beautiful. The principal objects of a piece should be wholly sketched out before any part of them are finished. Engraving seems to be in one respect, the same in relation to printing, as painting is to hand writing; this art being capable of multiplying copies ad infinitum.

No art, perhaps, can have a happier or more influential tendency to the advancement of virtue, religion and industry; nothing has a more familiar efficacy to form an universal good taste than prints, though it may be prostituted to the vilest, most debauched and detestable purposes. When this admirable art is thus abused, we see no reason why the authors should not be as liable to punishment by the laws, as others, who are the promoters and perpetrators of vice and immorality.

As this art is applicable to most others, so, to arrive at any excellence in it, requires a knowledge in various other arts, as geometry, perspective, anatomy, drawing, painting, sculpture, and above all things, *designing*. What is ordinarily called genius, is certainly an innate discernment, and a strong impulse and propensity to excel in any peculiar art; without which, nature seems to be unnaturally constrained; and when that is the case, the performances of such persons will also appear forced, uncouth, and unnatural also, like the disposition of the performer; for as some poet says,

> No art without a genius can prevail,
> And parts without the help of art will fail;
> But both ingredients jointly must unite,
> To make the happy character complete.

When Marius, being driven from Rome, by Sylla, and was a prisoner at Minturnæ, a soldier was sent to murder him. Upon his coming into the room with his sword drawn for the purpose, Marius said aloud, "durst thou, man, kill Caius Marius?" which so terrified the ruffian that he retired without effecting his purpose. "This story, or one glance of the eye upon his statue that I have seen," says an English writer, "gives me a greater idea of him than all that Plutarch has wrote." And further remarks, "the Odyssey cannot give a greater idea of Ulysses, than a drawing I have of Polydore, when he is discovering himself to Penelope and Telemachus, by bending the bow. And I conceive as highly of St. Paul, by once walking through the the gallery of Raphael at Hampton Court, as by reading the whole book of the Acts of the Apostles, though written by divine inspiration. Finally, in regard to history, nothing can be more useful than an attempt to excel in this art, in order to fix in remembrance memorable events. And as it is considered to be but in its infancy, it is to be greatly desired, that every meritorious performance, made in this country, will meet with public encouragement, not only for the honour of the nation, and rising artists, but for the benefit of traffic; so that, instead of importing immense quantities of foreign prints, we may not only supply ourselves, but become exporters of a commodity that is universally vendible.

Floric Acid, with which etchings of any device, name or stanza, &c. on glass, common flint, cornelian, &c. can be performed. Put into the etching box a tea spoonful of coarsely pulverized flour-spar, and set the box into a pan of coals, placed on bricks upon a table; pour in strong sulphuric acid, sufficiently to moisten or moderately wet it; the acid will immediately rise up out of the cup, which may be known by its attracting so much vapour from the air as to exhibit the appearance of common steam. As soon as it begins to appear, which will be in a few seconds, lay over the cup a piece of common window glass, large enough to cover its mouth, which had been previously waxed and written upon; let an assistant immediately apply snow, ice, or cold water to the upper side of the glass, in order to keep it so cool as to prevent the wax which is on the under side from melting; take off the glass in ten seconds, and apply another and so on; two or three may be applied before the flour-spar and sulphuric acid are renewed. The writing made in wax will appear beautifully etched upon the glass, on scraping off the wax. The best method of preparing the glass is to warm, or rather heat moderately, the face of a smoothing iron or piece of polished marble; so that white wax or very fine beeswax will melt on being applied to it. Lay the glass flint upon the melted wax, and on sliding it off it will be very evenly waxed; a dozen pieces may be prepared in succession; the writing may be made with the end of a hard stick, &c. Care must be taken to lay the glass perfectly bare through all the strokes, or there will be interruptions in the etching.

A Wax to lay on Iron and Steel. Take the bulk of a nut of white wax, melt it, and add the size of a musket ball of ceruse of Venice. When both are incorporated, form this composition into small sticks. With them rub your piece of iron or steel, after having previously warmed it sufficiently to melt the wax, which spread well over it with a feather. When the wax is cold, trace whatever you will on it, and pass afterwards on the lines you have drawn, the following water.

A Mordant Water to engrave on Steel. Take the strongest ver-juice you can find; alum in powder, and a little dried salt, pulverized: mix until perfectly dissolved; then pass some of that water on the lines of your drawing, repeating the same till it is engraved: Or else take verdigris, strong vinegar, ammoniac and common salts, and cop-peras, equal parts. Set the compound a boiling for a quarter of an hour; then strain it through a rag, and run some of that water on your plate. In about half an hour afterwards it will be perfectly engraved.

See Callot's varnish, which is an admirable composition to lay on the plate you propose to engrave.

To engrave with aqua-fortis, so that the work may appear like basso relievo. Take equal parts of vermilion and black lead, two or three grains of mastic in drops, mix and grind them on marble, with linseed oil: then put the composition into a shell; then cut some soft quills, and let your steel or iron be well polished; try first whether your col-our runs sufficiently with your pens; and if it should not, you must add a little more oil to it, so as to have your pen mark freely, as if you intended writing with ink on paper; then rub well your plate of steel with wood ashes, to clean it; after which wipe it with a clean rag, and draw your design upon it with your pen, prepared as before. If you wish to draw birds or other animals, you must only draw the out-lines of them with your pen, then fill up the inside of those lines with a hair pencil; that is, you must cover all the space contained between the first outlines drawn with the pen, the same colour, which you must lay with a brush to preserve all that part against the mordacity of the aqua-fortis. When that is done, let your work dry for a day or two; and when dried, take some fire made with charcoal into a chafing dish, and bake over it your colour by degrees, till it becomes quite brown. Take care, notwithstanding, not to burn it, for fear you should scale it, when you come to scratch, with the point of a needle, those etchings or pla-ces which you wish to engrave with the following aqua-fortis.

Aqua-Fortis for engraving. Take verdigris, alum, rom. vitriol, and common salt, each, three ounces, pounded finely; put a little more than a quart of water into a new pipkin, and the articles mentioned; infuse two hours, then place them over a charcoal fire, and when the water has in some degree evaporated, take the pipkin from the fire, let it cool, so as to bear your hand without scalding. Then take an earthen cup, and pour over the work intended to be engraven, the liquid; and continue to do so for nearly three quarters of an hour. Then pour on it clean water, to wash off every impurity. Try the depth of the lines of your engraving with a needle, and if not sufficiently prepared, the process of wetting it with the mixture, must be again repeated; care should be taken, that the liquid is not too warm, as it will spoil the work.

To engrave on Brass or Copper with Aqua-Fortis. Add more mastic in drops to your colour, and bake the plate until it becomes nearly black; if a flat work, raise round it a border of wax, to prevent the aqua-fortis from running off, which is to be a separating aqua-fortis, with which, cover the plate to the thickness of a crown; after it has been thus covered for a little while, it becomes green; then throw it away, and pour in its place some clear water, now examine the lines; if not of sufficient depth, put on some more aqua-fortis.

To engrave prints by Aqua-Fortis. Grind some ceruse with clear water; size with isinglass. Lay this on the plate with a coarse brush, or pencil. When dry, draw on it your design. Or, if you wish to counterproof a copperplate print, blacken the back of the print, and place that part on the plate, prepared as before; go over all the strokes of the print, with a smooth ivory or wooden point, which stamps the back of the print, in all those places, on the plate; then go over the black strokes on the plate, with a pen and ink; afterwards take a steel point, very fine and well tempered, etch the plate with it, in following all the strokes marked on it, and pour aqua-fortis as heretofore directed.

Directions to be observed in engraving with Aqua-Fortis. The plate must be well polished and perfectly clean; warm it over a chafing dish, in which there is a charcoal fire. While over the fire, cover it with varnish; then blacken it with the smoke of a candle; then chalk your design. The artists generally prefer drawing the outlines of their work, that the spirit and beauty of the design may be preserved. And for this purpose aqua-fortis is often employed to sketch lightly the outlines of the figures, and to have them more correct. It is necessary to touch a little occasionally with the graver, certain parts where the aqua-fortis has not eaten in sufficiently. In putting the aqua-fortis on the plate, care should be taken, that it does not eat too much; to prevent which, oil and tallow mixed, must be dropped on the work from the blaze of a candle. The artist should have a framed wooden board, overlaid with wax, on which the plate should be fixed a little slanting, that the aqua-fortis may pass over, and run into a pan placed there to receive it.

Thus covering at several times, and as much as is necessary, such places of the plate, as should not be kept so strong as others, rendering the figures which are forward in the picture, constantly every time, washed with the aqua-fortis which eats in them, till they are sufficiently engraved, and according to the strength which is necessary to give them.

To engrave on wood, prepare a board, of the size and thickness wanted, and polish it on the side to be engraved. Pear tree or box-wood is generally preferred. Draw first your design, as you wish to have it appear after printing. Care should be taken, that all the strokes of the drawing should touch well, and stick on the wood; and when the paper is very dry, (which is pasted on the board, by its right side, with a paste made of good flour, water, and a little vinegar, in case there is wanting a talent of drawing extemporaneously,) wet it gently, and with the top of your finger, rub it off by degrees, leaving only the strokes of the drawing on the board, as if it had been drawn with pen and ink. These strokes or lines show all that are to be spared or preserved; the rest should be cut off, and sunk down with delicacy, by means of a sharp and well pointed penknife, small chisel, &c. according to the size and delicacy of the work.

To engrave on Copper with the graver. The plate should be red copper, well polished; then draw your design on it with either the black lead stone, or a steel point. When that is done, you must be furnished with a sharp and well tempered graver to cut, in order to give more or less strength to certain parts, (as has heretofore been observed,) according to the subject; a tool of six inches in length is necessary, one end of which, is called a *scraper*, is made in the form of a triangle, sharp on each edge, for the purpose of scraping on the copper, when necessary; the other end is called a burnisher, nearly the shape of a fowl's heart, a little prolonged by the point, round and slender. This serves to polish the copper, to mend the faults, and soften the strokes. In order to form a better judgment of your work, you must occasionally, make use of a stump, made with the piece of an old hat, rolled up and blackened, to rub the plate, which fills the strokes with black, and which enables you to discover imperfections. A leather cushion is also necessary to be provided with, to lay the plate on while engraving.

Etching may be performed by dipping a clean copper cent into melted white wax. On taking it out, the wax will immediately harden upon it. Mark out the form of a letter or figure upon it. Then immerse the cent in nitric acid, and let it remain fifteen minutes. Now take it out, scrape off the wax, and wash the whole clean, and the letter will be etched upon the cent.

On this principle the etching upon razors, sword blades, &c. is performed. Artists have various methods for preparing compositions for applying to the metals before the acid is applied; they generally make use of something for writing the letters, which will flow from the pen like ink. Then they surround the whole space to be acted upon, by an edging to confine the acid, and, pour on the acid, instead of immersing the metal in it, as is more particularly described in this chapter. This is called etching in basso-relievo.

To make Blue Letters on Sword Blades. Take a well polished sword blade and hold it over a charcoal fire, till it is blue, then with oil colour, write such letters, (or make such figures) as you wish should appear and remain, and let them dry; then warm some strong vinegar, and pour all over the blade, which will infallibly take off the blue colour. After this process, a little common warm water will take off the oil colour, and the letters or figures will appear and remain of a curious and indelible blue; the same may be done on any polished steel.

Method to detect false Gems. Let the gems be divided into four classes, the diamond, sapphire, rock crystal, and glass imitation: look out a smooth face upon it with a magnifying glass; apply to that face a point or angle of a quartz crystal, and attempt to scratch it; if any scratch is made, attempt to scratch the quartz with the gem; if the quartz cannot be scratched with it, it is glass; if it can, it is quartz. Minerals of equal hardness, will scratch each other, therefore quartz will scratch quartz, &c. if it cannot be scratched with a quartz crystal, it may be considered as belonging either to the sapphire, or the diamond class. Select a large smooth grain of unground emery, and apply it to the gem as before directed; if it can be scratched with emery, but with great difficulty, and not by the quartz crystal, it may be considered as belonging to the sapphire class; but if it cannot possibly be scratched with the emery, after the most careful trials, and with severe pressure, it is a diamond. If an imitation gem be put into the hydro-sulphuret of ammonia it will soon become tarnished.

CHAPTER XX.

GLASS.

It is controverted among naturalists, to what class of bodies glass should be referred; some make it a concrete juice, others a stone, and others again rank it among semi-metals; but Dr. Merret observes, that these are all natural productions; whereas glass is a factitious compound, produced by fire, and never found in the earth, but only the sand and stones that form it; but metals are perfectly formed by nature into certain species, and fire only produces them by its faculty of separating heterogeneous and uniting homogeneous bodies; whereas it produces glass by uniting heterogeneous matters, viz. salt and sand, of which it evidently consists. The chief characters or properties of glass are, that it fuses in a vehement fire; when fused, adheres to iron; does not waste in the fire, is ductile, but not malleable; and while red hot can be cast into any shape. It is friable when cold; diaphanous, either hot or cold; flexible and elastic; disunited and broke by cold and moisture; and especially by saline liquors; is only cut by the diamond or emery; acid or other juices extract no quality from it; it does not wear by the longest use, nor will any liquor make it musty, change its colour, or rust; it softens metals and makes them fusible; receives all metallic colours externally and internally; will not calcine, and may be cemented like stones and metals. It is said 100 weight of sand in the compositions, yields 150 of glass. The salt is procured from the ashes of a water plant called kali.

There are many other plants besides kali, which produces a salt fit for glass. The sand or stones is the second ingredient, and what gives it the body; they must be such as will fuse; the whitest are the best; consequently, crystals are preferred to all others. Sometimes manufacturers use a sort of pebble resembling white marble. Flints make a pure crystalline metal. When stones cannot be had conveniently, sand is used. The glass houses in England are furnished with a fine white sand, which is frequently used for sand boxes, with a coarser kind for green glass. For crystal glass, 200 pounds sand or stone are mixed, finely pulverized, with 130 of salt; they are then calcined in a reverberatory furnace for several hours. When the process is completed, it is called *frit*, or *ballito*. This frit is set off in melt-

M

ing pots in the working furnace, with some manganese added, which destroys the greenish cast natural to all glass. While it is in fusion the workman mixes the metal well together; skimming off the sand, over which is a white salt, called sandiver, which, if suffered to remain, would render the glass brittle and unfit to work. When the vitrification is completed, and the metal sufficiently clear, it is formed into the articles required, by dipping a hollow iron into the melting pot, with which a sufficient quantity is taken out for the intended work: while red hot, it is rolled on a marble to unite its parts more firmly, then blowing moderately swells it, repeating it until of sufficient size, then the artist, by whirling it about, lengthens and cools the glass; moulds it in the stamp irons, and flats the bottom, by pressing it on the marble; after which it is fashioned as occasion requires, after being broken from the blowing iron. As the workman finishes them, another takes them up with an iron fork, and places them in a tower over the melting furnace to anneal, where, after remaining some time, they are put into pans, which are gradually withdrawn to cool. There is scarcely a branch of manufacture, which deserves more attention than that of glass; and although the art has excited the astonisment of the world, still it is highly probable, that in order to bring it to the highest state of perfection, there is abundant room for much improvement.

Pliny relates that "glass was first discovered by accident in Syria, at the mouth of the river Belus, by certain merchants driven thither by the fortune of the sea, and obliged to continue there, and dress their victuals by making a fire on the ground; where there was an abundance of the herb kali: the plant burning to ashes, its salt incorporating with the sand and stones, became vitrified."

Some writers assert that the discovery of glass is as ancient as the art of pottery, or making brick; for that a kiln of brick cannot be burnt, or a batch of pottery made, but some of the brick or ware will be at least superficially turned to glass; so that it must have been known at the building of Babel, and likewise by the Egyptians, among whom the Iraelites were many years employed in making bricks. Of this kind no doubt, was that fossil glass mentioned by Ferrant, Imperat. to be found under ground in many places where great fires had been.

A writer of eminence, makes a distinction between glass contained in its own mine or stone, and true glass that is extracted from the same; that the latter is more artificial than a metal is, when extracted from the ore; and as to the former, he urges, that as metal, by having its existence in the ore, so glass, by having it in the stone out of which it is produced, is a natural production. After what has been advanced, the supposition arises, if glass is procured from "stone alone, the weight of the metal must be less than the substance from which it is extracted, whereas it far exceeds, as 100 pounds of sand yield 150 pounds of glass. Considering also, that the salts made use of are of the most fixed kind, therefore, we cannot suppose them to be carried off by the fire; besides, as a proof, in the coarser glasses one may discern, or even pick out pieces of salt, furnishing a test by the taste. Flint, sand, and stone afford different species of glass, and the ashes, as they are variable in quality, will proportionately alter the glass. A fixed alkaline salt, sharp and well purified, mixed with a pure calx of flint, yields a glass clearer than amber itself. Our representation of the manufacture of glass, no doubt, is imperfect, though we are flattered it may not be wholly uninteresting.

CHAPTER XXI.

GILDING, SILVERING, &c.

Grecian Gilding. Equal parts of sal ammoniac and corrosive sublimate, are dissolved in spirit of nitre, and a solution of gold made with this menstruum. The silver is brushed over with it, which is turned black, but on exposure to a red heat, it assumes the colour of gold.

To dissolve Gold in Aqua-Regia. Take an aqua-regia, composed of two parts of nitrous acid, and one of marine acid, or of one part of sal ammoniac, and four parts of aqua-fortis; let the gold be granulated, put into a sufficient quantity of this menstruum, and expose to a moderate degree of heat. During the solution an effervescence takes place, and it acquires a beautiful yellow colour, which becomes more and more intense, till it has a golden or even orange colour. When the menstruum is saturated, it is very clear and transparent.

To gild Iron or Steel with a solution of Gold. Make a solution of eight ounces of nitre and common salt, with five ounces crude alum, in a sufficient quantity of water; dissolve half an ounce of gold, thinly plated and cut; and afterwards evaporate to dryness, digest the residuum in rectified spirit of wine or ether, which will perfectly abstract the gold. The iron is brushed over with this solution, and becomes immediately gilt.

2. Pour into a saturated solution of muriate of gold (that is, when there is no excess of acid) about twice as much sulphuric ether: now brush upon a clear polished surface of iron or steel, some of this liquid. The ether will soon evaporate and leave the gold covering the surface. To gild silver or copper, heat gold and mercury together in a crucible, one part of gold to about eight of mercury, until they are completely alloyed; then throw the hot alloy into cold water. Having wet the silver or copper with diluted nitric acid, brush on the alloy with a fine brush (a wire brush is best) as uniformly as possible. Then drive off the mercury with heat, placing the gilded metal over the hot coals: afterwards the surface must be polished with a burnisher. The only objection made to this method by artists is, that it is very difficult to lay on the alloy evenly. But old artists learn to brush over the bare spots while it is heating, being careful to avoid inhaling the mercurial fumes.

This method of gilding iron is undoubtedly very perfect; but it is desirable some better method should be discovered for gilding the other metals.

To gild by dissolving gold in Aqua-Regia. Fine linen rags are soaked in a saturated solution of gold in aqua-regia, gently dried, and afterwards burnt to tinder. The substance to be gilt must be well polished; a piece of cork is first dipped into a solution of common salt in water, and afterwards into the tinder, which is well rubbed on the surface of the metal to be gilt, and the gold appears in all its metallic lustre.

To gild Ivory, Silk, &c. with Hydrogen Gas. Immerse a piece of white silk or ivory into a solution of nitro-muriate of gold, in the proportion of one part of the acid to three of distilled water; whilst the substance to be gilded is still wet, immerse it in a jar of hydrogen gas; it will soon be covered by a complete coat of gold. The foregoing experiment may be advantageously varied as follows: Paint flowers or other ornaments with a very fine camel's hair pencil, dipped in the above mentioned solution, on pieces of silk, satin, &c. hold them over a Florence flask, from which hydrogen gas is evolved, during the decomposition of the water by sulphuric acid, and iron filings. The painted flowers, in a few minutes, will shine in all the splendour of the purest gold, which will not tarnish on exposure to the air or in washing.

Oil gilding on Wood. Cover and prime the wood with two or three coatings of boiled linseed oil, and carbonate of lead, in order to fill up the pores, and conceal the irregularities of the surface, occasioned by the veins in the wood. When dry, lay on a thin coat of gold size, which is prepared by grinding some of the red oxyde of lead with the thickest drying oil procurable, and mixed previously to using with a little oil of turpentine, till brought to a proper consistence. If the gold size is good, it will dry in twelve hours, more or less. Then spread a leaf of gold on a cushion, formed by a few folds of flannel, secured on a piece of wood, eight inches square, by a tight covering of leather, and cut into strips of a proper size by a blunt pallet knife; then take each strip upon the point of a fine brush, and apply it to the part intended to be gilded, which gently press down with a ball of soft cotton; in a few minutes sweep away the loose particles with a large camel's hair brush. In a day or two the size will be completely dried, and the operation finished.

To gild by Burnishing. This operation is chiefly performed on picture frames, mouldings, &c. Cover the surface to be gilt carefully with a strong size, made by boiling down pieces of white leather, or clippings of parchment, till they become a stiff jelly; this coating being dry, eight or ten more must be applied, consisting of the same size, mixed with fine plaster of Paris, or washed chalk. When a sufficient number of layers are put on, as the nature of the work requires, and become quite dry, apply a moderately thick layer, composed of size and armenia bole or yellow oxyde of lead. While this last is yet moist, put on the gold leaf in the usual manner; pressing it with the cotton ball; and before the size is become perfectly dry, the parts intended to be most brilliant, should be carefully burnished by an agate or dogs tooth fixed in a handle.

It is sometimes common, in order to save labour, but a bad practice, slightly to burnish the brilliant parts, and to deaden the rest, by drawing a brush over them dipped in size. This kind of gilding can only be applied on in-door work, as rain, or even a considerable degree of dampness will occasion the gold to peel off. When dirty, it may be cleansed by a soft brush, with hot spirit of wine, or oil of turpentine.

To gild Copper, &c. by Amalgamation. Immerse a very clean bright piece of copper in a diluted solution of nitrate of mercury. By the affinity of copper for the nitric acid, the mercury will be precipitated; now spread the amalgam of gold rather thinly over the coat of copper just given to the mercury. This coat unites with the amalgam, but will remain on the copper. Now place the piece thus operated upon, in a clean oven or furnace, where there is no smoke. If the heat is a little greater than 600° the mercury of the amalgam will be volatilized, and the copper will be beautifully gilt.

In the large way of gilding, the furnaces are so constructed, that the volatilized mercury is again condensed, and preserved for further use, so that there is no loss in the operation. There is also a contrivance by which the volatile particles of mercury are prevented from injuring the gilders.

To Gild Steel. Pour some of the etherial solution of gold into a wine glass, and slip therein the blade of a new penknife, lancet or razor; withdraw the instrument and allow the ether to evaporate. The blade will be found to be covered with a very beautiful coat of gold. A clean rag, or a small piece of very dry sponge may be dipped in the ether, and used to moisten the blade, and used with the same result. In this case there is no occasion to pour the liquid into a glass, which would lose by evaporation; but the rag or sponge may moistened with it by applying either to the mouth of the phial. This coating of gold will remain on the steel for a great length of time, and will preserve it from rusting. This is the way in which swords and other cutlery are ornamented. Lancets too are in this way gilded with great advantage, to secure them from rust.

To heighten the colour of Yellow Gold. Six ounces saltpetre, two ounces copperas, one ounce white vitriol and one ounce alum. If it be wanted redder, a small portion of blue vitriol must be added. These are to be well mixed and dissolved in water as the colour is wanted.

To heighten the colour of Green Gold. One ounce ten pennyweights saltpetre, one oz. four pennyweights sal ammoniac, one oz. four pennyweights Roman vitriol, and eighteen pennyweights verdigris. Mix them well together, and dissolve a portion in water, as occasion requires. The work must then be dipped in these compositions, applied to a proper heat to burn them off, and then quenched in water or vinegar.

To heighten the colour of Red Gold. Four oz. yellow melted wax; add 1 1-2 oz. red ochre, in fine powder, 1 1-2 oz. verdigris, calcined till it yields no fumes, and half an oz. calcined borax. It is necessary to calcine the verdigris, or else, by the heat applied in burning the wax, the vinegar becomes so concentrated as to corrode the surfaces, and make it appear speckled.

To separate Gold from gilt Copper or Silver. Apply a solution of borax, in water, to the gilt surface with a fine brush, and sprinkle over it some fine powdered sulphur. Make the piece red hot, and quench it in water. The gold may be easily wiped off with a scratch brush, and recovered by testing it with lead. Gold is taken from the surface of the silver, by spreading it over a paste, made of powdered sal ammoniac, with aqua-fortis, and heating it till the matter smokes, and is nearly dry, when the gold may be separated by rubbing it with a scratch brush.

To Silver by heat. Dissolve an ounce of pure silver in aqua-fortis, and precipitate it with common salt; to which add one pound of sal ammoniac, sandiver, and white vitriol, and one ounce of sublimate. 2. Dissolve an ounce of pure silver in aqua-fortis, precipitate it with common salt, and add after washing, six oz. common salt, three oz. each of sandiver and white vitriol, and one fourth of an ounce of sublimate. These are to be ground into a paste upon a fine stone with a muller; the substance to be silvered must be rubbed over with a sufficient quantity of the paste, and exposed to a proper degree of heat. When the silver runs, it is taken from the fire, and dipped into a weak spirit of salt to clean it.

Silvering on Gilt Work by Amalgamation. Silver will not attach itself to any metal by amalgamation, unless it be first gilt; the process is the same as gilding in colours, only no acid should be used.

To Silver in the Cold Way. Two drachms tartar, two drachms common salt, one-half drachm alum and twenty grains silver, precipitated from the nitrous acid by copper. Make them into a paste with a little water. This is to be rubbed on the surface to be silvered with a cork, &c. 2. Dissolve pure silver in aqua-fortis, and precipitate the silver with common salt; make this precipitate into a paste, by adding a little more salt and cream of tartar.

To silver Copper Ingots. The surface of the copper on which the silver is to be fixed must be made flat by foiling, and should be left rough. The silver is first annealed, and afterwards pickled in weak spirit of salt; it is planished, and then scraped on the surface to be fitted on the copper. These prepared surfaces are anointed with a solution of borax, or strewed with fine powdered borax itself, and then confined in contact with each other, by binding wire. When they are exposed to a sufficient degree of heat, the flux causes the surfaces to fuse at the same time, and after they become cold, they are found finely united. Copper may likewise be plated by heating it, and burnishing leaf silver upon it; so may iron and brass.

The principal difficulties in plating copper are to bring the surfaces of the copper and silver into fusion at the same time, and to prevent the copper from scaling; for which purpose fluxes are used.

To separate Silver from Plated Copper. This process is applied to recover the silver from the plated metal, which has been rolled down for buttons, toys, &c. without destroying any large proportion of the copper. For this purpose a menstruum is composed of three pounds oil vitriol, one and a half ounces nitre, and a pound of water. The plated metal is boiled in it, till the silver is dissolved, and then the silver is recovered by throwing common salt into the solution.

Amalgam of Gold in the large way. A quantity of quicksilver is put into a crucible or iron ladle which is lined with clay, and exposed to heat till it begins to smoke. The gold to be mixed should be previously granulated, and heated red hot, when it should be added to the quicksilver, and stirred about with an iron rod, till it is perfectly dissolved. If there should be any superfluous mercury, it may be separated by passing it through clean soft leather, and the remaining amalgam will have the consistence of butter, and contain about three parts of mercury to one of gold.

To gild by Amalgamation. The metal to be gilt is to be previously cleansed on its surface, by boiling in a weak pickle, which is a very dilute nitrous acid. A quantity of aqua-fortis is poured into an earthen vessel, and quicksilver put therein, when a sufficient quantity of mercury is dissolved, the articles to be gilt are put into the solution, and stirred about with a brush till they become white. This is called quicking; but, as during quicking by this mode, a noxious vapour continually arises, which proves very injurious to the health of the workmen, they have adopted another method, by which they in a great measure, avoid that danger. They now dissolve the quicksilver in a bottle containing aqua-fortis, and leave it in the open air during the solution, so·that the noxious vapours escape into the air. Then a little of this solution is poured into a basin, and with a brush dipped therein, they stroke over the surface of the metal to be gilt, which immediately becomes quickened. The amalgam is now applied by one of the following methods:

1. By proportioning it to the quantity of articles to be gilt, and putting them into a white heat together, working them about with a soft brush, till the amalgam is uniformly spread. Or, 2. By applying a portion of the amalgam upon one part, and spreading it on the surface, if flat, by working it about with a harder brush. The work thus managed is put into a pan, and exposed to a gentle degree of heat; when it becomes hot, it is frequently put into a heat and worked about with a painter's large brush, to prevent an irregular dissipation of the mercury, till, at last, the quicksilver is entirely dissipated, by a repetition of the heat, and the gold is attached to the surface of the metal. This gilt surface is well cleansed by a wire brush, and the artists heighten the colour of the gold by the application of various compositions; this part of the process is called colouring.

To Gild Glass and Porcelain. Drinking and other glasses are sometimes gilt on their edges. This is done, either by an adhesive varnish, or by heat. The varnish is prepared by dissolving in boiled linseed oil an equal weight, either of copal or amber. This is to be diluted by a proper quantity of oil of turpentine, so as to be applied as thin as possible to the part of the glass, intended to be gilt. When this is done, which will be in about twenty-four hours, the glass must be placed in a stove, till so warm as almost to burn the fingers when handled. At this temperature the varnish will become adhesive, and a piece of leaf gold applied in the usual way, will immediately stick. Sweep off the superfluous portions of the leaf, and when quite cold it may be burnished, taking care to interpose a piece of very thin paper, between the gold and burnisher. If the varnish is very good, this is the best method of gilding glass, as the gold is thus fixed on more evenly.

It often happens that the varnish is but indifferent, and that by repeated washing the gold wears off; on this account the practice of burning it, is sometimes had recourse to. For this purpose, some gold powder is ground with borax, and applied to clean glass, by a camel's hair pencil; when quite dry, the glass is put into a stove heated to about the temperature of an annealing oven: the gum burns off, and the borax, by vitrifying, cements the gold with great firmness to the glass; when it may be burnished. Porcelain and other wares may be platinized, silvered, tinned, and bronzed, in a similar manner.

To gild Leather. Dust the leather over with very fine powdered yellow resin or mastic gum. The iron tools should be arranged (if letters alphabetically) on a rack before a clear fire; to be well heated without becoming red hot. Each letter or stamp must be tried as to its heat, on the raw side of a piece of waste leather. Now, press the tool downward on the leaf, if it has acquired a proper heat; which will become indented and show the figure imprinted on it—the next letter is taken and stamped in like manner; and so on with the others: the superfluous gold may be rubbed off by a cloth.   The cloth should be slightly greased, to retain the gold wiped off.   The cloth will soon become saturated with gold, and is generally sold to refiners to recover the gold.   Some afford as much gold by burning as to be worth a guinea and a half.

Gold Powder for Gilding.   Gold powder may be prepared in three different ways: 1. Put into an earthen mortar some gold leaf, with a little honey, or thick gum water, and grind the mixture till the gold is reduced to extremely minute particles.   When this is done, a little warm water will wash out the honey or gum leaving the gold behind in a pulverulent state.

2. Dissolve pure gold, (or the leaf,) in nitro-muriatic acid, and then precipitate it by a piece of copper, or by a solution of sulphate of iron.   The precipitate, (if by copper,) must be digested in distilled vinegar, and then washed, (by pouring water over it repeatedly,) and dried.   This precipitate will be in the form of a very fine powder; it works better, and is more easily burnished than gold leaf ground with honey as above.

3. Or the best method is, by heating a prepared amalgam of gold, in an open clean crucible, and continuing the strong heat until the whole of the mercury is evaporated; at the same time constantly stirring the amalgam with a glass rod.   When the mercury has completely left the gold, the remaining powder is to be ground in a wedgewood mortar, with a little water, and afterwards dried.   It is then fit for use. Although the last mode of operating has been here given, the operator cannot be too much reminded of the danger attending the sublimation of mercury.   In the small way here described it is impossible to operate without danger; it is therefore better to prepare it according to the former directions, than to risk the health by the latter.

To Gild Writings, Drawings, &c.   Letters written on vellum or paper are gilded in three ways; for the first, mix size with the ink, and the letters are written as usual; when dry a slight degree of stickiness is produced, by breathing on them; then apply the gold leaf, making a little pressure, that it may adhere with firmness.   The second method is, some white lead or chalk is ground up with strong size, and the letters are made by this means with a brush; when dry, the gold leaf may be laid on, and afterwards burnished.   The last process is to mix up some gold powder with size, and to form the letters by means of a brush.   It is supposed this last method was used by the monks in illuminating their missals, psalters, and rubrics.

To Gild on the Edges of Paper.   Leaves of books and letter paper should be gilded while in a horizontal position in the book binder's press.   Apply a composition formed of four parts of Armenian bole, and one of candied sugar, ground to a proper consistence in water, and laid on by a brush with the white of an egg.   When nearly dry, smooth the coating by a burnisher; which is generally a crooked piece of agate, very smooth, and fixed in a handle.   Then slightly moisten it by a sponge dipped in clean water, and squeezed in the hand.   Take up the leaf on a piece of cotton, from the leather cushion, and apply it to the moistened surface.   When dry, burnish it by rubbing over it the agate repeatedly from end to end, taking care not to wound the surface by the point of the burnisher. A piece of silk or India paper is usually interposed between the gold and burnisher.

To gild in Colours. The principal colours of gold for gilding are red, green, and yellow. These should be kept in different amalgams. The part which is to remain of the first colour is to be stopped off with a composition of chalk and glue; the variety required is produced by gilding the unstopped parts with the proper amalgam, according to the usual mode of gilding. Sometimes the amalgam is applied to the surface to be gilt without any quicking, by spreading it with aqua-fortis; but this depends on the same principle as a previous quicking.

To plate Looking-glasses. On tin foil fitly disposed on a flat table, mercury is to be rubbed with a hare's foot; it soon unites itself with the tin. A plate of glass is then cautiously to be slid upon the tin leaf, in such a manner as to sweep off the redundant mercury, not incorporated with the tin. Lead weights are then placed on the glass, and in a little time, the quicksilver tin foil, adheres so firmly to the glass, that the weights may be removed without danger of its falling off. About two ounces of mercury is sufficient for covering three square feet of glass. The glass should be perfectly clean: the least dirt or dust on the surface will prevent the adhesion of the amalgam.

Put a drop of mercury into a wine glass, and drop into it small pieces of tin foil, which will become liquified and unite with the mercury. Continue these additions until the amalgam contains about half as much tin as mercury. Next spread a small piece of tin foil very evenly on the face of a smoothing iron or a piece of polished marble; pour the amalgam upon it and rub it over the tin foil with the finger for about two minutes. Now press upon it a piece of dry clean glass; press it down with such force as to press out all the uncombined mercury; lay a weight upon the glass and leave it half an hour, when it may be taken up, and it will be found to be a mirror.

All looking glasses are made in this way, upon a large scale; the slab is placed in an inclined position, so that the excess of mercury runs, and is saved for the next, &c.

To silver Glass Globes. One ounce clean lead, one ounce fine tin, one ounce bismuth, and ten ounces of quicksilver. Put the tin and lead into the ladle first; when melted, add the bismuth. Scim off the dross, remove the ladle from the fire, and before it sets, add the quicksilver; stir the whole carefully together, taking care not to breathe over it as the fumes of the mercury are very pernicious. Pour this through an earthen pipe, into the glass globe, which turn repeatedly round. 2. Two parts mercury, one part tin, one part lead, and one part bismuth; or four ounces of quicksilver and tin foil. The quantity of tin foil to be added, is so much as will become barely fluid when mixed. Let the globe be clean and warm, and inject the quicksilver by means of a pipe at the aperture, turning it about till it is silvered all over. Let the remainder run out, and hang the globe up.

A Gold coloured Ink. Pulverize very fine one ounce of orpine, and as much crystal; put this powder in five or six whites of eggs, well beaten, then turned into water. Mix all well, and it will be prepared to write or paint, producing a gold colour.

A Silver coloured Ink. Finest of pewter, one ounce, quicksilver, two ounces. They should be mixed until quite fluid. Then grind it

N

on porphyry with some gum water, when it is fit to use.   The writing will appear as if it had been done with silver.

To prepare the Silver Tree.   Pour into a glass globe or decanter, four drachms nitrate of silver, dissolved in a pound or more of distilled water, and lay the vessel on the chimney piece; or where it may not be disturbed.   Now pour in four drachms of mercury.   The silver will become precipitated in the most beautiful arborescent form; resembling real vegetation.

To prepare the Tin Tree.   Into a vessel similar to that used in the last experiment, with the same quantity of water put in three drachms of muriate of tin, adding ten drops nitric acid.   Shake the vessel until the salt be completely dissolved.   Replace the zinc (which must be cleared of the effects of the former experiment,) as before, and set the whole aside to precipitate without disturbance.   In a few hours the effects will be similar to the last, only that the tree will have more lustre.   In these experiments it is surprising to observe the laminæ shoot out as it were from nothing; but this phenomenon seems to proceed from a galvanic action of the metals and the water.

To prepare the Lead Tree.   Put one half an ounce of the superacetate of lead in powder, into a clear glass globe or decanter, filled to the bottom of the neck, with distilled water, and ten drops nitric acid, and shake the mixture well.   Prepare a rod of zinc with a hammer and file, a quarter of an inch thick and one inch long.   Form notches in each side for a thread, by which it is to be suspended; tie the thread so that the knot may be uppermost, when the metal hangs quite perpendicular.   When tied, pass the two ends of the thread thro' a perforation in the cork and let them be again tied over a small splinter of wood, which may pass between them and the cork.   When the string is tied, let the length between the cork and zinc be such that the zinc may be at equal distances from the side, bottom and top of the vessel when immersed in it.   Now put the vessel in a place where it may be undisturbed; introduce the zinc, at the same time fitting in the cork.   The zinc will assume the form of a tree or bush, whose leaves and branches are laminal, or plates of a metallic lustre.

Glazing the Clay Cake.   Lay a sun dried plastic or refractory clay cake obliquely across a crucible of such a length as to go entirely into the crucible, but not let it reach the bottom.   Heat the crucible until the clay cake is at a white heat, then throw a little common salt, (muriate of soda) into the crucible and continue to raise the heat.   On taking out the clay cake, its surface will be found covered with a glazing, made of the soda and alumine fused together.   Dip a dried cake into mortar, sufficiently diluted with water to become a free liquid, which is made of marly clay.   Then heat it as before, and it will become glazed.   Upon this principle potter bakers glaze their wares.

To prepare Copper Foils.   When coloured foils are wanted, copper may therefore be best used, and may be prepared for the purpose as follows.   Take copper plates, beaten to a proper thickness, and pass them between a pair of fine steel rollers, very close set, and draw them as thin as is possible to retain a proper tenacity.   Polish them with very fine whiting or rotten stone, till they shine, and have as much brightness as can be given them, and they will then be fit to receive the colour.

To whiten Foils. When the yellow, or rather orange colour of the ground would be injurious to the effect, as in the case of purple or crimson red, the foils should be whitened, which may be done in the following manner.

Take a small quantity of silver and dissolve in *aqua-fortis;* then put bits of copper into the solution, and precipitate the silver; which being done, the fluid must be poured off, and fresh water added to it, to wash away all the remainder of the first fluid; after which the silver must be dried, an equal weight of cream of tartar and common salt must then be ground with it, till the whole is reduced to a fine powder; and with this mixture the foils, being first slightly moistened, must be rubbed by the finger or a bit of linen rag, till they be of the degree of whiteness desired; after which, if it appear to be wanting, the polish must be refreshed. Tin foils are only used in the case of colourless stones, when quicksilver is employed; and they may be drawn out by the same rollers, but need not be further polished, so that the effect is produced by other means in this case.

Foils for Crystals, Pebbles, or Paste, to give the lustre of Diamonds. The manner of preparing foils to give colourless stones the greatest degree of play and lustre, is by raising so high a polish or smoothness on the surface, as to give them the effect of a mirror, which can only be done, in a perfect manner, by the use of quicksilver, applied in the same general way as in the case of looking-glasses. The method is as follows: Take leaves of tin, prepared in the same manner as for silvering looking-glasses, and cut them into small pieces of such size as to cover the surface of the sockets of the stones that are to be set. Lay three of these, then, one upon another, and having moistened the inside of the socket with this gum water, and suffered it to become again so dry, that only a slight stickiness remains, put the three pieces of leaves, lying on each other, into it, and adapt them to the surface in as even a manner as possible. When this is done, heat the socket, and fill it with warm quicksilver, which must be suffered to continue in it three or four minutes, and then gently poured out. Then thrust the stone into the socket, which must be closed with it, care having been taken to give such room for it, that it may enter without stripping off the tin and quicksilver from any part of the surface. The work should be well closed round the stone to prevent the tin and quicksilver contained in the socket from being shaken out by any violence.

The lustre of stones, set in this way, will continue longer, than when they are set in the common way, as the cavity round them being filled, there will be no passage found for moisture, which is so injurious to the wear of stones treated in any other way. This kind of foil gives some lustre.

To colour Foils. For colouring foils two methods have been invented. The first by tinging the surface of the copper with the colour required, by means of smoke, the other by staining or painting it with some pigment, or other colouring substance. The colours used for painting foils may be tempered with either oil, water rendered duly viscid by gum Arabic, size, or vanish. If deep colours are wanted, oil is most proper, as some pigments become wholly transparent in it, as lake or Prussian blue; the yellow and green may be laid on in varnish, as these colours may be had in perfection, from a tinge wholly dissolved in spirit of wine, in the same manner as in the case of lacquers; and the most beautiful green is to be produced by distilled verdigris, which is apt to lose its colour and turn black with oil. In common cases, any of the colours may be laid on with the least trouble, in the same manner as the glazing colours used in miniature painting.

Ruby Colours. For red, where the ruby is to be imitated, a little lake is used with isinglass size; carmine, or shell-lac varnish, should be used if the glass or paste is of a full crimson, verging towards the purple; but if the glass incline to the scarlet or orange, very bright lake, that is, not purple, may be used alone in oil.

Garnet Red. Dragon's blood dissolved in seed-lac varnish, may be used; for the vinegar garnet, the orange lake tempered with shell-lac varnish will be found excellent.

Amethyst. Lake, with a little Prussian blue, used with oil, and thinly spread on the foil.

Blue. When a deep colour or the effect of the sapphire is wanted, Prussian blue, that is not too deep, used in oil, and spread more or less thinly on the foil, according to the lightness or deepness of the colour required.

Eagle Marine. Common verdigris, with a little Prussian blue, tempered in shell-lac varnish.

Yellow. Colour the foil with a yellow lacquer; if a full yellow is desired, lay it on as for other purposes. For the slighter colour of topazes, the burnish and foil itself will be sufficiently strong without any addition.

Green. If a deep hue is required, the crystals of verdigris tempered in shell-lac should be used. But if the emerald is to be imitated, a little yellow lacquer should be added, to produce a truer green, less verging to the blue.

Other Colours. Stones of more diluted colour, such as the amethyst, topaz, vinegar garnet, &c. may be very cheaply imitated by transparent white glass or paste, even without foils. This is done by tempering the colours above enumerated with turpentine and mastic, and painting the socket in which the counterfeit stone is to be set with the mixture, the socket and stone being previously heated. The stone should be immediately set, and the socket closed upon it before the mixture cools and grows hard. The orange lake was invented for this purpose. The colour it produces is that of the vinegar garnet, and has been used with great success by a manufacturer. The colour before directed to be used in oil should be extremely well ground in oil of turpentine, and tempered with old nut or poppy oil; or, if time can be given to dry, with strong fat oil diluted with spirits of turpentine, which gives a fine polish of itself. The colours used in varnish, should also be well ground and mixed—when dragon's blood in the seed-lac varnish and the lacquer, the foils should be warmed before they are laid out. All the mixtures should be laid on the foil with a broad soft brush, passed from one end to the other; no part crossed or gone over twice, or at least, until the first coat is dry. When the colours are not strong enough another coat may be given.

Lacquer for Brass. Six ounces of seed-lac, two ounces of amber or copal, ground on porphyry, forty grains dragon's blood, thirty grains extract of red sandal wood, obtained by water, thirty-six grains orient-tal saffron, four ounces pounded glass, and forty ounces very pure alcohol.

To apply this varnish to articles or ornaments of brass, expose them to a gentle heat, and dip them into varnish. Two or three coatings may be applied in this manner, if necessary. The varnish is durable, and has a beautiful colour. Articles varnished in this manner, may be cleaned with water, and a bit of dry rag.

Lacquer for Philosophical Instruments. This lacquer is destined to change, or to modify the colour of those bodies to which it is applied. Three-fourths of an ounce of gum guttæ, two ounces of gum sandarac, two ounces of gum elemi, one ounce of dragon's blood, opt. one ounce of seed lac, three-fourths of an ounce terra merita, two grains oriental saffron, three ounces of pounded glass, and twenty ounces of pure alcohol. The tincture of saffron and terra merita, is first obtained by infusing them in alcohol for twenty-four hours, or exposing them to the heat of the sun in summer. The tincture must be strained through a piece of clean linen cloth, and ought to be strongly squeezed. This tincture is poured over the articles which do not compose the tincture, all pounded and mixed with the glass. The varnish is then made according to the directions before given. It may be applied with great advantage to philosophical instruments: the use of it might be extended also, to various, or moulded articles with which furniture is ornamented. If the dragon's blood be of the best quality, it may give too high a colour; in this case the dose may be lessened at pleasure, as well as that of the other colouring matters.

It is with similar varnish that the artists of Geneva, give a golden orange colour, produced by certain compositions, the preparation of which has no relation to that of varnish, and which has been successfully imitated by saline mixtures, in which orpiment is a principal ingredient. The nails are heated before they are immersed in the varnish, and they are then spread out on sheets of dry paper.

Gold Coloured Lacquer for Brass Watch Cases, Watch Keys, &c. Six ounces of seed-lac, two ounces of amber, two ounces of gum guttæ, twenty-four grains extract of red sandal wood in water, sixty grains of dragon's blood, thirty-six grains of oriental saffron, four ounces of pounded glass and thirty-six ounces of pure alcohol, grind the three first articles and the dragon's blood on a piece of porphyry; then mix them with the pounded glass, and add the alcohol, after forming with it an infusion of the saffron, and the extract of the sandal wood. The varnish must be completed as before. The metal articles destined to be covered by this varnish, are heated, and those which will admit of it are immersed in packets. The tint of the varnish may be varied, by modifying the doses of the colouring substances.

Lacquer of a less drying quality. Four ounces of seed-lac, four ounces of sandarac or mastic, one-half an ounce of dragon's blood, thirty-six grains of terra merita, thirty-six grains of gum guttæ, three ounces of pounded glass, two ounces of clear turpentine, thirty-two ounces of essence of turpentine.

Extract by infusion the tincture of the colouring substances, and then add the resinous bodies according to the directions for compound mastic varnish. Lacquer or varnishes of this kind are called changing, because, when applied to metals, such as copper, brass, or hammered tin, or to wooden boxes and other furniture, they communicate to them a more agreeable colour.   Besides, by their contact with the common metals, they acquire a lustre which approaches that of the precious metals, and to which, in consequence of peculiar intrinsic qualities or certain laws of convention, a much greater value is attached.   It is by means of these changing varnishes, that artists are able to communicate to their leaves of silver and copper, those shining colours observed in foils.   This product of industry becomes a source of prosperity to the manufacturers of buttons and works formed with foil, which in the hands of the jeweller, contributes with so much success to produce that reflection of the rays of the light, which doubles the lustre and sparkling quality of precious stones.

It is to varnish of this kind that we are indebted for the manufacture of gilt leather, which, taking refuge in England, has given place to that of papier mache, which is employed for the decoration of palaces, theatres, &c.

In the last place it is by the effect of a foreign tint obtained from the colouring part of saffron, that the scales of silver disseminated in *confection de hyacynth*, reflect a beautiful gold colour.   The colours transmitted by different colouring substances, require tones suited to the objects for which they are destined.   The artist has it in his own power to vary them at pleasure.   The addition of arnotto to the mixture of dragon's blood, saffron, &c. or some changes in the doses of the mode intended to be made in colours.   It is therefore impossible to give limited formulae.

To make Lacquer of various Tints.   Four ounces gum guttæ in thirty-two ounces of essence of turpentine, one ounce arnotto, and four ounces dragon's blood; also in separate doses of essence.

These infusions may be easily made in the sun.   After fifteen days exposure, pour a certain quantity of these liquors into a flask, and by varying the doses, different shades of colours will be obtained.   These infusions may also be employed for changing alcoholic varnishes; but in this case, the use of saffron, as well as that of red sandal wood, which does not succeed with essence, will soon give the tone necessary for imitating, with other tinctures, the colour of gold.

To brown Gun Barrels   After the barrel is finished, rub it over with aqua-fortis, or spirit of salt diluted with water, then lay it by a for a week, till a complete coat of rust is formed. A little oil is then to be applied, and after rubbing the surface dry, polish it with a hard brush and a little beeswax.

CHAPTER XXII.

VARNISHES.

To make white Copal Varnish. 1. White oxyde of lead, cerused, Spanish white, white clay.   Such of these substances as are preferred ought to be carefully dried. Ceruse and clays obstinately retain a great deal of humidity, which would oppose their adhesion to drying oil or varnish.   The cement then crumbles under the fingers, and does not assume a body.

2. On sixteen ounces melted copal, pour four, six, or eight ounces of linseed oil, boiled and quite free from grease; when well mixed by

repeated stirrings, and after they are pretty cool, pour on sixteen ounces of the essence of Venice turpentine. Pass the varnish through a cloth.

Amber Varnish, is made in the same way.

Black. Lampblack made of burnt vine twigs, and black of peach stones. The lampblack must be carefully washed, and afterwards dried. Washing carries off a great many of its impurities.

Yellow. Yellow oxyde of lead of Naples and Montpelier, both reduced to impalpable powder. These yellows are hurt by the contact of iron and steel; in mixing them up, therefore, a horn spatula, with a glass mortar and pestle must be employed. Gum guttæ, yellow ochre, or Dutch pink, according to the nature and tone of the colour to be imitated.

Blue. Indigo, Prussian blue, blue verditure, and ultra-marine. All these substances must be very much divided.

Green. Verdigris, crystallized verdigris, compound green (a mixture of blue and yellow.) The first two require a mixture of white in proper proportions, from a fourth to two-thirds, according to the tint intended to be given. The white used for this purpose is the ceruse, or the white oxyde of lead, or Spanish white, which is less solid.

Red. Red sulphuretted oxyde of mercury, (cinnabar vermilion,) red oxyde of lead, (minium,) different red ochres, or Prussian reds, &c.

Purple. Cochineal, carmine, and carminated lakes, with ceruse, and boiled oil.

Brick. Dragon's blood.

Chamois Colour. Dragon's blood, with a paste composed of flowers of zinc, or, what is still better, a litte red vermilion.

Violet. Red sulphuretted oxyde of mercury, mixed with lampblack, washed very dry, or with the black of burnt vine twigs; and to render it more mellow, a proper mixture of red, blue and white.

Pearl Grey. White and black, white and blue; for example, ceruse and lampblack; ceruse and indigo.

Flaxen Grey. Ceruse, which forms the ground of the paste, mixed with a small quantity of Cologne earth, as much English red, or carminated lake, which is not so durable, and a particle of Prussiate of iron, (Prussian blue.)

For Violins, &c. To a gallon of rectified spirit of wine, add six ounces of gum sandarac, three ounces of gum mastic, and half a pint turpentine varnish. Put the whole into a tin can, which keep in a warm place, frequently shaking it, for twelve days, until it is dissolved. Then strain and keep it for use.

To make a colourless Copal Varnish. In selecting such pieces as are good, as all copal is not fit for this purpose, each piece must be taken separately;—let fall on it, a drop of pure essential oil of rosemary, not altered by keeping. The pieces which soften at the part that imbibes the oil are good: reduce them to powder, which sift through a very fine hair sieve, and put it into a glass, on the bottom of which it must not lie more than a finger's breadth thick. Pour upon it essence of rosemary to a similar height; stir the whole for a few minutes, when the copal will dissolve into a viscous fluid; let it stand for two hours, then pour on to it gently, two or three drops of very pure alcohol, which distribute over the oily mass by inclining the bottle in different directions with a very gentle motion: repeat this operation by little and lit-

tle till the incorporation is effected, and the varnish reduced to a proper degree of fluidity.   It must then be left to stand a few days, and
when very clear, be decanted off.   This varnish thus made without
heat, may be applied with equal success, to pasteboard, wood, and
metals, and takes a better polish than any other.   It may be used on
paintings, the beauty of which it greatly heightens.

Gold coloured Copal Varnish.   One ounce copal in powder, two
ounces essential oil of lavender, and six ounces essence of turpentine.   Put the oil of lavender into a matrass of proper size, placed
on a sand bath, heated by a lamp, or over a moderate coal fire; add to
the oil while very warm, and at several times, the copal powder, stir
the mixture with a stick of white wood, rounded at the end; when the
copal has entirely disappeared, add at three different times, the essence almost in a state of ebullition, and keep continually stirring the
mixture.   When the solution is completed, the result will be a varnish
of gold colour, exceedingly durable and brilliant, but less drying than
the preceding.

2.   To obtain this varnish colourless, it will be proper to rectify the
essence of the shops, which is often highly coloured, and to give it
the necessary density by exposure to the sun in bottles closed with
cork stoppers, leaving an interval of some inches between the stopper
and the surface of the liquid; a few months are thus sufficient to communicate to it the required qualities; besides, the essence of the shops
is rarely possessed of that state of consistence, without having at the
same time a strong amber colour.

The varnish resulting from the solution of copal in oil of turpentine
brought to such a state as to produce a maximum of solution, is exceeding durable and brilliant.   It resists the shock of hard bodies
much better than the enamel of toys, which often becomes scratched
and whitened by the impression of repeated friction; it is applied with
greater success to philosophical instruments; and the paintings with
which vessels and other utensils of metal are decorated.

3.   Four ounces copal, and one ounce clear turpentine.   Put the copal, coarsely pulverized, into a varnish pot, and give it the form of a
pyramid, which must be covered with turpentine.   Shut the vessel
closely, and placing it over a gentle fire, increase the heat gradually,
that it may not attack the copal; as soon as the matter is well liquified,
pour it upon a plate of copper, and when it has resumed its consistence reduce it to powder.   Put half an ounce of this powder into a
matrass with four ounces of the essence of turpentine, and stir the
mixture till the solid matter is entirely dissolved.

Camphorated Copal Varnish, is designed for articles which require
durability, pliableness, and transparency.   Two ounces pulverized
copal, six ounces essential oil of lavender, one-eighth of an ounce
camphor, and essence of turpentine, a sufficient quantity, according
to the consistence required to be given to the varnish.   Put into a phial of thin glass, or into a small matrass, the oil of lavender
and the camphor, and place the mixture on a moderately open fire, to
bring them to a slight state of ebullition; then add the copal powder
in small quantities, which must be renewed as they disappear in the
liquid.   Favour the solution by continually stirring it with a stick of
white wood; and when the copal is incorporated with the oil, add the

turpentine boiling; but care must be taken to pour in, at first, only a small portion. This varnish is little coloured, and by rest it acquires a transparency, which, united to the solidity observed in almost every kind of copal varnish, renders it fit to be applied with great success in many cases, and particularly in the ingenious invention substit:ting varnished metallic gauze, used for the cabin windows of ships, as presenting more resistance to the concussion of air, during the firing of guns, in the room of Muscovy tale, a kind of mica, in large laminæ.

Fat Amber or Copal Varnish. Four ounces of amber or copal of one fusion, fourteen ounces essence of turpentine, and ten ounces of drying linseed oil. Put the whole into a pretty large matrass, and expose to the heat of balneum mariæ, or move it over the surface of an uncovered chafing dish, but without flame, and at the distance from it of two or three inches. When the solution is completed, add still a little copal or amber to saturate the liquid: then pour the whole on a filter prepared with cotton; and leave it to clarify by rest. If the varnish is too thick, add a little warm essence to prevent the separation of any of the amber.

This varnish is coloured, but far less so than those composed by the usual methods. When spread over white wood, without any preparation, it forms a solid glazing, and communicates a slight tint to the wood.

If it be required to charge this varnish with more copal, or prepared amber, the liquid must be composed of two parts of essence for one of oil.

Compound Mastic Varnish. Thirty-two ounces of pure alcohol, six ounces of purified mastic, three ounces of gum sandarac, three ounces of very clear Venice turpentine, and four ounces of glass, coarsely pounded.

Reduce the mastic and sandarac to fine powder; mix with white glass, from which the finest parts have been separated by a hair sieve; put all the ingredients, with alcohol, into a short necked matrass, adapted to a stick of white wood rounded at the end, the length proportioned to the height of the matrass, that it may be put in motion. Expose the matrass in a vessel filled with water, made at first a little warm, and which must afterwards be maintained in a state of ebullition for one or two hours. The matrass may be made fast to a ring of straw.

When the solution is sufficiently extended, add the turpentine, which must be kept separately in a phial, or pot, and which must be melted, by immersing it in a balneum mariæ for a moment; the matrass must be still left in the water for half an hour, when it may be taken off, and the varnish stirred till somewhat cool. Next day draw off and filter through cotton. By these means it will become exceedingly limpid. The addition of glass may appear extraordinary; but it divides the parts of the mixture, which has been made with the dry ingredients, and the same quality is retained when placed over the fire. It obviates with success two inconveniences very troublesome to those who compose varnishes. First, by dividing the matters, it facilitates the action of the alcohol; and in the second, its weight, which surpasses that of resins, prevents these resins from adhering to the bottom of the matrass, and also the coloration acquired by the varnish, where a sand bath is employed, as is commonly the case. The application of this varnish is suited to articles belonging to the *toilette*, such as dressing boxes, cut paper work, &c. The following possesses the same brilliancy and lustre, but have more solidity, and are very drying.

Camphorated Mastic Varnish for Paintings. Twelve ounces mastic, cleaned and washed, one and a half ounces pure turpentine, and a half ounce camphor, five ounces white glass, pounded, and thirty-six ounces ethereous essence of turpentine. Make it according to the method indicated for that of the first genus. The camphor is employed in pieces; the turpentine added, when the solution of resin is completed. If the varnish is to be applied to old paintings, or those which have been already varnished, the turpentine may be suppressed, as it is recommended here, only in cases of a first application to paintings, and just freed from white of egg varnish. The ethereous essence recommended, is that distilled slowly, without any intermediate substance, according to the second process already given for its rectification. The question by able masters has never yet been determined respecting the kind of varnish proper to be employed for paintings. Some artists have paid particular attention to this object, and make a mystery of the means they employ. The real end may be obtained by giving the varnish, destined for painting, pliability and softness, without being too solicitous in regard to what may add to its consistence or durability. The latter quality is particularly requisite in those which are to be applied to articles much exposed to friction, as boxes, furniture, &c.

To make Painter's Cream. Painters who have long intervals between their periods of labour, are accustomed to cover the parts they have painted with a preparation which preserves the freshness of the colours, and which they can remove when they resume their work. The preparation is as follows:

Three ounces very clean nut oil, half an ounce mastic in tears, pulverized, and one-third of an ounce sal saturni, in powder. Dissolve the mastic oil over a gentle fire, and pour the mixture into a marble mortar, over the pounded salt of lead; stir it with a wooden pestle, and add water in small quantities, till the matter assumes the appearance and consistence of cream, and refuses to admit more water.

Sandarac Varnish. Eight ounces gum sandarac, two ounces pounded mastic, four ounces clear turpentine, four ounces pounded glass, and thirty-two ounces alcohol, mix and dissolve as before.

Compound Sandarac Varnish. Three ounces pounded copal, of an amber colour; once liquified, six ounces gum sandarac, three ounces mastic, cleaned, two and a half ounces clear turpentine, four ounces pounded glass, and thirty-two ounces pure alcohol. Mix these ingredients, pursuing the same method as above.

This varnish is destined for articles subject to friction, such as furniture, chairs, fan sticks, mouldings, &c. and even metals, to which it may be applied with success. The sandarac gives it great durability.

Camphorated Sandarac Varnish for Cut Paper Work, Dressing Boxes, &c. 1. Six ounces sandarac, four ounces gum elemi, one ounce gum anima, half an ounce camphor, four ounces pounded glass and thirty-two ounces pure alcohol. Make the varnish according to directions already given. The soft resins must be pounded with the dry bodies; the camphor to be added in small pieces·

2. Six ounces gallipot or white incense, two ounces gum anima, two ounces pounded glass, and thirty-two ounces alcohol. Make the varnish with the precautions indicated for the compound mastic varnish. The two last varnishes are to be used for ceilings and wainscoats, coloured or otherwise: they may be employed as a covering to parts painted with strong colours.

Spirituous Sandarac Varnish for Wainscotting, Small Articles of Furniture, Balustrades, and Inside Railing. Six ounces of gum sandarac, two ounces of shell-lae, four ounces of colophonium or resin, four ounces white pounded glass, four ounces of clear turpentine and thirty-two ounces of pure alcohol. Dissolve the varnish as before directed for compound mastic varnish. This varnish is sufficiently durable to be applied to articles destined to daily and continual use. Those composed with copal, in these cases ought to be preferred.

2. There is another composition, which without forming part of the compound varnishes is employed with success for giving a polish and lustre to furniture made of wood: wax forms the basis of it. Many cabinet makers are contented to wax common furniture. This covering by means of repeated friction, soon acquires a polish and transparency which resembles those of varnish. Waxing seems to possess qualities peculiar to itself: but like varnish is attended with inconveniences as well as advantages. Varnish supplies better the part of glazing; it gives a lustre to the wood which it covers, and heightens the colours of that destined in particular, for delicate articles. These real and valuable advantages are counterbalanced by its want of consistence; it yields too easily on the shrinking or swelling of the wood, and rises in scales or slits, on being exposed to the slightest shock. These accidents can be repaired only by a new strata of varnish. Waxing stands shocks, but has not the property of giving lustre to the bodies on which it is applied, in the same degree as varnish, and of heightening their tints. The lustre it communicates is dull, but the inconvenience is compensated, by the facility which any accident that may have altered its polish can be repaired, by rubbing it with a piece of fine cork. The application of wax under some circumstances, therefore ought to be preferred to that of varnish. This seems to be the case in particular with tables, exposed to daily use, and all articles subject to constant employment. The stratum of wax should be made as thin as possible, that the veins of the wood may be more apparent; therefore the following process may be acceptable to the reader. Melt over a moderate fire, in a very clean vessel, two ounces of white or yellow wax; when liquified, add four ounces good essence of turpentine; stir the whole, until entirely cool, and a kind of pomade is produced, which must be rubbed over furniture according to the usual method. The essence of turpentine is soon dissipated, but the wax by which its mixture is reduced to a state of very great division, may be extended with more ease, and in a more uniform manner. The essence soon penetrates the pores of the wood, calls forth the colour of it, causes the wax to adhere better, and the lustre which then results is equal to that of varnish.

Coloured Varnish for Violin, and other stringed Instruments, also for Plum Tree, Mahogany and Rose Wood. Four ounces of gum sandarac, two ounces of seed-lac, two ounces of mastic, one ounce of Benjamin in tears, four ounces of pounded glass, two ounces of Venice turpentine, and thirty-two ounces of pure alcohol. The gum sandarac and lac render this varnish durable; it may be coloured with a little dragon's blood or saffron.

Fat Varnish of a Gold Colour. Eight ounces of amber, two ounces of gum lac, eight ounces of drying linseed oil, and sixteen ounces essence of turpentine. Dissolve separately the gum lac, and then add the amber, prepared and pulverized with the linseed oil and essence very warm. When the mixture has lost part of its heat, mix in relative proportions, tinctures of arnotto, terra merita, gum guttæ and dragon's blood. This varnish when applied to white metals, gives them a gold colour.

Fat Turpentine, or Gold Varnish, being a mordant to gold and dark colours. Sixteen ounces boiled linseed oil, eight ounces Venice turpentine, and five ounces Naples yellow. Heat the oil with the turpentine, and mix the Naples yellow pulverized. Naples yellow is an oxyde of lead; it is substituted here for resins on account of its drying qualities, and in particular, of its colour, which resembles that of gold; great use is made of the varnish in applying gold leaf. The yellow may be omitted when this species of varnish is to be solid and used on coloured coverings; in this case an ounce of litharge to each pound of composition may be substituted, without this mixture doing an injury to the colour of which it is to constitute the ground.

Turner's Varnish for Boxwood. Five ounces seed-lac, two ounces gum sandarac, one ounce and a half gum elemi, two ounces Venice turpentine, five ounces pounded glass, and twenty-four ounces pure alcohol. The artists of St. Claude do not all employ this formula, which required to be corrected on account of its too great dryness, which is here lessened by the turpentine and elemi. This composition is secured from cracking, which disfigures these boxes after having been used for some months.

2. Other turners use gum lac united to a little elemi and turpentine digested some months in pure alcohol exposed to the sun. In pursuing this method, substitute for the sandarac, the same quantity of gum lac reduced to powder, and not to add the turpentine to the alcohol (which ought to be very pure) till towards the end of the fusion. Solar infusion requires care and attention; vessels of sufficient size to allow the spirituous vapours to circulate freely, ought to be employed, because it is necessary that the vessel should be closely shut. Without this precaution the spirits would become weakened, and abandon the resin which they laid hold of during the first days of exposure. This perfect obituration will not admit of the vessels being too full. In general, the varnishes applied to articles which may be put in the lathe acquire a great deal of brilliancy by polishing; a piece of woollen cloth is sufficient for the operation. If turpentine predominates too much in these compositions, the polish does not retain its lustre, because the heat of the hands is capable of softening the surface of the varnish, and in this state it readily tarnishes.

To varnish Dressing Boxes. The most of spirit of wine varnishes are destined for covering preliminary preparations, which have a certain degree of lustre. They consist of cement coloured or otherwise, charged with landscapes and figures cut out in paper, which produces an effect under the transparent varnish; most of the dressing boxes, and other small articles of the same kind, are covered with this particular composition, which, in general, consists of three or four coatings of Spanish white, poured in water and mixed with parchment glue. The first coating is smoothed with pomice stone, and then polished with a piece of new linen and water. The coating in this state is fit to receive the destined colour, after it has been ground with water. The cut figures with which it is to be embellished, are then applied, and a coating of gum, or fish glue is spread over them, to prevent the varnish from penetrating to the preparation, and from spoiling the figures. The operation is finished by applying three or four coatings of varnish, which, when dry are polished with tripoli and water by means of a piece of cloth. A lustre is then given to the surface, with starch and a bit of doe skin, or very soft cloth.

Gallipot Varnish. Twelve ounces gallipot or white incense, five ounces glass pounded, two ounces Venice turpentine, and thirty-two ounces essence of turpentine. Make the varnish after the white incense has been pounded with glass. Some recommend mastic or sandarac in the room of gallipot; but it is neither more beautiful nor durable; when the colour is ground with the preceding varnish and mixed up with the latter, which, if too thick, is thinned with a little essence, and which if applied immediately, without any sizing to boxes and other articles, the coatings acquire sufficient strength to resist the blows of a mallet. But if the varnish be applied to a sized colour, it must be covered with a varnish of the first or second genus.

Mastic Gallipot Varnish, for Grinding Colours. Four ounces new gallipot or white incense, two ounces mastic, six ounces Venice turpentine, four ounces pounded glass, and thirty-two ounces essence turpentine. With the precautions already indicated, add prepared nut oil, or linseed oil, two ounces. The matters ground with this varnish dry more slowly; they are then mixed up with the following varnish, if it be for common painting, or with particular varnishes destined for colours and for grounds.

Mordant Varnish for Gilding. One ounce mastic, one ounce gum sandarac, half an ounce gum guttæ, quarter of an ounce turpentine, and six ounces essence turpentine. Some artists who make use of mordants, substitute for the turpentine, an ounce of the essence of lavender, which renders this composition less drying. In general the composition of mordants admits of modifications, according to the work for which they are destined. The application of them, however, is chiefly confined to gold. When it is required to fill up a design with gold leaf on any ground whatever, the composition which is to serve as the means of union between the metal and the ground; ought neither to be too thick or fluid; because both these circumstances are equally injurious to delicacy in the strokes; it will be requisite, also, that the composition should not dry till the artist has completed his design.

Other Mordants. 1. Some prepare their mordants with Jew's pitch and drying oil diluted with essence of turpentine. They employ it for gilding pale gold, or for bronzing. Others imitate the Chinese, and mix with their mordants colours proper for assisting the tone

which they are desirous of giving to the gold, such as yellow, red, &c.
Others employ fat varnish, to which they add a little red oxyde of lead.
Others use thick glue, in which they dissolve a little honey. This is
what they call *battuze*. When they wish to heighten the colour of the
gold, this glue is employed, to which the gold leaf adheres extremely
well.

2. The qualities of the following are fit for any kind of application,
and particularly to metals. Expose boiled oil to a strong heat in a
pan; when a black smoke is disengaged from it, set it on fire, and extinguish it in a few minutes after, by putting on the cover of the pan.
Then pour the matter still warm, into a heated bottle, and add to it a
little essence of turpentine. This mordant dries very speedily; it
has body, and adheres to, and strongly retains, gold leaf, when applied
to wood, metal, and other substances.

Varnish for Pails and other coarse Wood work. Take any quantity of tar, and grind it with as much Spanish brown as it will bear,
without rendering it too thick to be used as a paint or varnish, and then
spread it on the pails, or other wood, soon as convenient, for it quickly hardens by keeping. This mixture should be laid on by a large
brush, the work to be kept free from dust and insects as possible, till
the varnish is perfectly dry. On wood it will have a very good gloss,
is an excellent preservative against moisture, on which account, as
well as its being cheaper, it is far preferable to painting, not only for
pails, but for weather-boarding and all other kinds of wood work for
gross purposes. When the glossy brown colour is not liked, the work
may be made of a greyish brown, by mixing a small proportion of
white lead, or whiting and ivory black, with the Spanish brown.

A Black Varnish for old Straw or Chip Hats. Half an ounce of
the best black sealing wax, two ounces of rectified spirits of wine.
Powder the wax, put it with the spirit into a four ounce phial; digest
them in a sand heat, or near the fire till the wax is dissolved; lay it on
warm with a fine soft hair brush, before a fire or in the sun. It produces a stiffness to old straw hats, and gives a beautiful gloss, and resists wet.

To make Varnish for Coloured Drawings. One ounce Canada balsam, two ounces spirits of turpentine: mix them together. Before
this composition is applied, the drawing or print should be sized with
a solution of isinglass in water; and when dry, apply the varnish with
a camel's hair brush.

*To make a Varnish for Wood which resists the action of boiling
water.* One and a half pounds of linseed oil, boil it in a red copper
vessel, not tinned. Suspend over it in a small linen bag, five ounces
litharge, and three ounces pulverized minium, taking care that the bag
does not touch the bottom of the vessel; continue the ebullition till the
oil acquires a dark brown colour, then take away the bag and substitute another in its place, containing a clove or garlic; continue the ebullition, and renew the clove or garlic seven or eight times, or rather
put them all in at once. Then throw into the vessel a pound of yellow amber, when it is melted in the following manner; add to the
pound of amber, well pulverized, two ounces linseed oil; place the
whole on a strong fire. When the fusion is complete, pour it boiling
into the prepared linseed oil, and continue to leave it boiling for two or

three minutes, stirring the whole up well. It is then left to settle; the composition is decanted and preserved, when it becomes cold, in well corked bottles. After polishing the wood on which this varnish is to be applied, give the wood the colour required. When the colour is perfectly dry, apply the varnish with a fine sponge; repeat three or four times, taking care the preceding coat is well dried.

To varnish Drawings and Card Work. Boil some clean parchment cuttings in water, in a glazed pipkin, till they produce a very clear size. Strain it and keep it for use. Give the work two coats of the size, passing the brush quickly over the work, not to disturb the colours.

A Composition for making Coloured Drawings and Prints resemble Paintings in Oil. One ounce Canada balsam, two ounces spirits of turpentine; mix together. Before the composition is applied, the drawing or print should be sized with a solution of isinglass in water. When dry, apply the varnish with a camel's hair brush.

To varnish Harps and Dulcimers. Prepare the work with size and red ochre, then take ochre, burnt umber, and red lead, well ground, and mix up a dark brown colour in turpentine varnish, adding so much oil of turpentine that the brush may just be able to pass over the work fair and even. While yet wet, take a muslin sieve, and sift as much Dutch metal, previously powdered upon it, as is requisite to produce the effect, after which varnish, and polish it.

To varnish Glass. Pulverize a quantity of gum adragant; let it dissolve for twenty-four hours in the white of eggs beat up; then rub it gently on the glass with a brush.

To varnish Balloons. Dissolve elastic gum, cut small, in five times its weight of rectified essential oil of turpentine, by keeping them together; then boil one ounce of this solution in eight ounces drying linseed oil for a few minutes; strain the solution and use it warm. The elastic resin, known by the name of India rubber has been much extolled for a varnish. The foregoing method as practised by M. Blanchard may not prove unacceptable.

To varnish rarified Air Balloons. M. Cavallo, recommends first to soak the cloth in a solution of sal ammonia and common size, using one pound of each to every pound of water: and when quite dry, to paint over the inside with some earthy colour, and strong size or glue, when this paint has dried thoroughly, it will then be proper to cover it with oily varnish, which might dry before it could penetrate quite through the cloth. Simple drying linseed oil will answer the purpose as well as any, provided it be not very fluid.

To paint Sail Cloth, &c. so as to be pliant, durable, and impervious to water. Grind ninety-six pounds English ochre, with boiled oil, add sixteen pounds black paint, which mixture forms an indifferent black. A pound of yellow soap dissolved in six pints of water over the fire, is mixed while hot with the paint. This composition is then laid upon the canvass, (without being wetted, as in the usual way,) as stiff as can be conveniently done with the brush, so as to form a smooth surface; the next day, or still better, on the second day, a second coat of ochre and black, (without any, or but a very small portion of soap,) is laid on and allowing this coat an intermediate day for drying the canvass is then finished with black paint as usual. Three days is allowed for it to dry and harden; it will not stick together when taken down, and folded in cloth, containing sixty or seventy yards each; and canvass finished entirely with the composition, leaving it to dry one day between each coat, will not stick together if laid in quantities. It has been ascertained from actual trials, that the solution of yellow soap is a preservative to red, yellow, and black paints, when ground in oil and put into casks, as they acquire no improper hardness and dry in a remarkable manner when laid on with a brush, without the use of the usual drying articles. It is surprising that the adaption of soap, which is so well known to be miscible with oily substances, or, at least, the alkali of which it is composed, has not been brought into use, in the composition of all colours.

Colouring Compositions for rendering Linen and Cloth impenetrable to water. Begin by washing the stuff with hot water, then dry and rub it between the hands until it becomes perfectly supple; afterwards spread it out, by drawing it into a frame, and give it with the aid of a brush, a first coat, composed of a mixture of eight quarts of boiling linseed oil, calcined amber and acetate of lead seven and a half grammes, to which add ninety grammes of lampblack. Use the same ingredients for the second coat, except the calx of lead. This coat will give a few hours, according to the season, afterwards take a dry plasterer's brush and rub the stuff strongly with it, when the hair, by this operation will become extremely smooth. The third and last coat will give a perfect and durable jet black. Or rather take twelve quarts boiling linseed oil, thirty grammes of amber, fifteen grammes of acetate of lead, seven and a half sulphate of zinc, fifteen Prussian blue, and seven and a half verdigris. Mix them very fine with a little oil, add 120 grammes of lampblack. These coats are used at discretion as is done with painting.

To thicken Linen Cloth for Screens and Bed Testers. Grind whiting with zinc; to prevent cracking, add a little honey; then take a soft brush and lay it upon the cloth; repeat this two or three times, but letting it dry between the layings; and for the last laying smooth it over with Spanish white, ground with linseed oil, the oil being first heated, and mixed with a small quantity of litharge, the better to endure the weather, and to be more lasting.

Common Wax or Varnished Cloth. Common canvass of an open and coarse texture, is stretched on frames, placed under sheds, with the sides open, to afford a free passage to the external air. The cloth is fastened to these frames, by hooks, which catch the edge of the cloth, and by strong packthreads passing through holes at the other extremity of the hooks, which are tied round moveable pegs at the lower edge of the frame. The mechanism by which the strings of a violin are stretched or unstretched will give an idea of the arrangement of the pegs employed for extending the cloth in this apparatus. By this means the cloth can be easily stretched or relaxed, when the oily varnish has exercised an action on its texture in the course of the operation. The whole being thus arranged, a liquid paste made with drying oil, which may be varied at pleasure, is applied to the cloth.

To make Liquid Paste and Drying Oil. Mix Spanish white, or tobacco pipe clay with water, and leave at rest for some hours, to separate the argillaceous parts, and to produce a sediment. Stir the sediment with a broom, to complete the division of earth. After it has rested some seconds, decant the turbid water into an earthen or wooden vessel. By this process the earth will be separated from the sand and other foreign bodies, which are precipitated, and which must be thrown away. If washed by the same process on a large scale, it is divided by kneading it. The supernatant water is thrown aside, and the sediment placed in sieves on pieces of cloth, where it drains; it is then mixed up with oil rendered drying, by a large dose of litharge, about a fourth of the weight of the oil. The consistence of thin paste being given to the mixture, it is spread over the cloth, by means of an iron spatula, the length of which is equal to the breadth of the cloth. The spatula performs the part of a knife, and pushes forward the excess of matter, above the quantity sufficient to cover the cloth. The inequalities of the cloth, produced by its coarseness, are smoothed down by pumice stone The stone is reduced to powder, and rubbed over the cloth with a piece of soft serge or cork dipped in water. The cloth must then be well washed in water to clean it; and after it is dried a varnish of gum lac dissolved in linseed oil boiled with turpentine must be applied to it. This preparation produces yellowish varnished cloth. When wanted black, mix lampblack with the Spanish white, or tobacco pipe clay, which forms the basis of the liquid paste; various shades may be obtained according to the quantity of the lampblack which is added. Umber, Cologne earth, &c. may be used to vary the tints, without causing any addition to the expense.

To prepare fine Printed Varnished Cloth. The process above described may serve to give some idea of that employed for making fine cloths of the same kind, decorated with a coloured impression. The manufactories of Germany have varnished cloths embellished with large and small subjects, figures and landscapes, well executed, and which are destined for covering furniture subject to daily use.

This process, which is only an improvement of the former, requires a finer paste, and cloth of a more delicate texture: the stratum of paste is applied in the same manner, and when dry and polished, the cloth is taken from the frame, and removed to the painter's table, where the art of the colourist and designer is displayed under a thousand forms, and as that in printed cottons, exhibits a richness of tints and a distribution of subjects, which discover taste, and ensure a ready sale for the article manufactured. The processes, however, employed in these two arts, to extract the colouring parts, are not the same. In the art of cotton printing, the colours are extracted by the bath, as in that of dying. In printing varnished cloths, the colouring parts are the result of the union of drying oil, mixed with varnish; and the different colours employed in oil painting and painting in varnish. The varnish applied to common oil cloth is composed of gum lac and drying linseed oil; but that destined for printed varnished cloths requires some choice, both in regard to the oil and the resinous matter which gives it consistence. Prepared oil of pinks and copal form a varnish very little coloured, pliable and solid.

To prepare Varnished Silk. 1. Varnished silk for umbrellas, &c. is prepared in the same manner as the cloths already described; but with some variation in the paste or varnish.

The cloth is placed on a frame as before described; a soft paste

P

composed of linseed oil, boiled with a fourth part litharge; tobacco pipe clay, dried and sifted thro' a silk sieve, sixteen parts, litharge, ground on porphyry with water, dried and sifted in the same manner, three parts, and lampblack, one part.   This paste is then spread in an uniform manner over the surface of the silk by means of a long knife, having a handle at the extremity.   In summer, twenty-four hours are sufficient for its desiccation.   When dry, the knots produced by the inequalities of the silk, are smoothed by a pumice stone.   This operation is performed with water.   When finished, the surface of the silk is washed; when dry, fat copal varnish is applied.

If it is intended to polish the varnish, apply a second stratum; after which polish it with a ball of cloth and very fine Tripoli.   The varnished silk, thus made is very black, exceedingly pliable, and has a fine polish.

2. A kind of varnished silk which has only a yellowish colour, and which suffers the texture of the stuff to appear, is prepared with a mixture of three parts boiled oil of pinks, and one part fat copal varnish, which is extended with a coarse brush or a knife.   Two strata are sufficient when oil has been freed from its greasy particles over a slow fire, or when boiled with a fourth part of its weight of litharge.

The inequalities are removed by pumice stone and water, after which the copal varnish is applied.

To recover Varnish.   Clean off the filth with a lye made of potash, and the ashes of lees of wine; then take forty-eight ounces of potash, and sixteen of the above mentioned ashes, and put them into six quarts of water, and this completes the lye.

To polish Varnish.   This is effected with pumice stone and Tripoli earth.   Reduce the pumice stone to an impalpable powder, and put it upon a piece of serge moistened with water; with this rub lightly and equally the varnished substances.   The Tripoli must also be reduced to a fine powder, and put upon a clean woollen cloth, moistened with olive oil, with which the polishing is to be performed.   The varnish then is to be wiped off with soft linen, and when quite dry, cleansed with starch, or Spanish white, and rubbed with the palm of the hand.

Amber Varnish with Essence Turpentine.   Six or seven ounces of liquefied amber, and separated from the oily portions which alter its consistence.   Reduce the amber to powder, and if the operation of pounding forms it into a paste, break it with your fingers; then mix it with the essence, and heat the whole in a balneum mariæ.   It will speedily dissolve, and the essence will take up, at least, a fourth part of its weight of the prepared amber.   When one coating of it is applied to white smooth wood, but without any preparation, it forms a very pure and durable glazing, which speedily dries, but slower than copal varnish.

Ethereal Copal Varnish.   Half an ounce of ambery copal, and two ounces of ether.   Reduce the copal to a very fine powder, and introduce it by small portions into the flask which contains the ether; close the flask with a glass or cork stopper, and having shaken the mixture for half an hour, let it rest till the next morning.   In shaking the flask, if the sides become covered with small undulations, and if the liquor be not exceedingly clear, the solution is not complete.   In this case, add a little ether, and leave the mixture at rest. The varnish is of a light lemon colour. The largest quantity of copal united to ether, may be a fourth, and at least a fifth. The use of copal varnish made with ether, seems, by the expense attending it, to be confined to repairing those accidents which frequently happen to the enamel of toys, as it will supply the place of glass to the coloured varnishes, employed for mending fractures, or to restoring the smooth surface of paintings which have been cracked and shattered. The great volatility of ether, and in particular its high price, do not allow the application of this varnish to be recommended, but for the purpose here indicated. It has been applied to wood with complete success, and the glazing it produced, united lustre to solidity. In consequence of the too speedy evaporation of the liquid, it often boils under the brush. Its evaporation, however, may be retarded, by spreading over the wood a slight stratum of essential oil of rosemary or lavender, or even of turpentine, which may afterwards be removed by a piece of linen rag; what remains is sufficient to retard the ether.

Turpentine Copal Varnish. One and a half ounces copal, of an amber colour, and in powder, and eight ounces of the best oil of turpentine. Expose the essence to a balneum mariæ, in a wide mouthed matrass, with a short neck; as soon as the water of the bath begins to boil, throw into the essence a large pinch of copal powder, and keep the matrass in a circular motion. When the powder is incorporated with the essence, add new doses of it; and continue in this manner till you observe there is formed an insoluble deposite. Then take the matrass from the bath, and leave it at rest for some days. Draw off the clear varnish, and filter it through cotton. At the moment when the portion of the copal is thrown into the essence, if the powder precipitates itself under the form of lumps, it is needless to proceed any further. This effect arises from two causes; either the essence does not possess the proper degree of concentration, or it has not been sufficiently deprived of water. Exposure to the sun, employing the same matrass to which a cork stopper ought to be added, will give it the qualities requisite for the solution of the copal. This effect will be announced by the disappearance of the portion of copal already put into it.

2. Three ounces of copal liquefied, and twenty ounces essence of turpentine. Place the matrass containing the oil in a balneum mariæ, and when the water boils, add the pulverized copal in small doses. Keep stirring the mixture, and add no more copal till the former is incorporated with the oil. If the oil in consequence of its particular disposition can take up three ounces of it, add a little more; but stop if the liquid becomes nebulous, then leave the varnish at rest. If it be too thick, dilute it with a little warm essence after having heated it in the balneum mariæ. When cold, filter it through cotton, and preserve it in a bottle. This varnish has a good consistence, and is as free from colour as the best alcohol varnish. When extended in one stratum over smooth wood, which has undergone no preparation, it forms a very brilliant glazing, which, in the course of two days, in summer, acquires all the solidity that may be required.

The facility which attends the preparation of this varnish, by the new method here indicated, will admit of its being applied to all coloured grounds which require solidity, pure whites

alone excepted; painted boxes, therefore, and all small articles, coloured or otherwise, whenever it is required to make the veins appear in all the richness of their tones, call for the application of this varnish, which produces a most beautiful effect, and which is more durable
than turpentine varnishes composed with other resinous substances.

Varnish for Watch Cases in imitation of Tortoise Shell.   Six ounces copal, of an amber colour, one and a half ounces Venice turpentine, twenty-four ounces prepared linseed oil, and six ounces essence
of turpentine.   It is customary to place the turpentine over the copal,
reduced to small fragments, in the bottom of an earthen or metal vessel, or in a matrass exposed to such a heat as to liquefy the copal; but
it is more advantageous to liquefy the latter alone, to add the oil in a
state of ebullition, then the turpentine liquefied, and in the last place
the essence.   If the varnish is too thick, some essence may be added.   The latter liquor is a regulator for the consistence in the hands
of an artist.

Resinous Drying Oil.   Ten pounds of drying nut oil, if the paint
is destined for external, or ten pounds drying linseed oil, if for internal articles.   Three pounds of resin, and six ounces of turpentine.
Cause the resin to dissolve in the oil by means of a gentle heat.   When
dissolved and incorporated with the oil, add the turpentine; leave the
varnish at rest, by which means it will often deposit portions of resin
and other impurities; and then preserve it in wide mouthed bottles.   It
must be used fresh; when suffered to grow old, it abandons some of
its resin.   If this resinous oil assumes too much consistence, dilute it
with a little essence, if intended for articles sheltered from the sun or
with oil of poppies.

In Switzerland, where the principal part of the mason's work consists of stones subject to
crumble to pieces, it is often found necessary to give them a coating of oil paint, to stop the
effect of this decomposition.   This painting has a great deal of lustre, and when the last coating is applied with resinous oil, it has the effect of varnish.   To give it more durability, the
first ought to be applied exceeding warm, and with plain oil, or oil very little charged with the
grey colour, which is added to fat copal varnish and the varnish to watch cases, &c.

Fat Copal Varnish.   Sixteen ounces picked copal, eight ounces
prepared linseed oil, or oil of poppies, and sixteen ounces turpentine.
Liquefy the copal in a matrass over a common fire, and then add the
linseed oil, or oil of poppies, in a state of ebullition; when these matters
are incorporated, take the matrass from the fire, stir the matter till the
greatest heat has subsided, and then add the essence of turpentine
when warm.   Strain the whole, while still warm, through a piece of
linen, and put the varnish into a wide mouthed bottle.   Time contributes towards its clarification; and in this manner it acquires a better
quality.

To give a drying quality to Fat Oil.   Eight pounds nut or linseed
oil, one ounce white lead, slightly calcined, one ounce yellow acetate
of lead, (sal saturni) also calcined, one ounce sulphate of zinc, (white
vitriol) twelve ounces vitreous oxyde of lead, (litharge) and a head of
garlic or a small onion   When the dry substances are pulverized,
mix them with the garlic and oil, over a fire capable of maintaining
the oil in a slight state of ebullition; continue it until the oil ceases
to throw up scum, till it assumes a reddish colour, and till the head of
the garlic becomes brown.   A pellicle will then be soon formed on the
oil, which indicates that the operation is completed.   Take the vessel from the fire, and the pellicle, being precipitated by rest, will carry

with it all the unctuous parts which rendered the oil fat. When the oil becomes clear, separate it from the deposite, and put it into wide mouthed bottles, where it will completely clarify itself in time, and improve in quality.

2. One and a half ounces vitreous oxyde of lead, three-eighths of an ounce sulphate of zinc, and sixteen ounces linseed or nut oil. This operation must be conducted as in the preceding case. The choice of the oil is not a matter of indifference. If it be destined for painting articles exposed to the impression of the external air, or for more delicate painting, nut oil or poppy oil will be required. Linseed oil is used for coarse painting, and that sheltered from the effects of the rain and the sun. A little negligence in the management of the fire, has often an influence on the colour of the oil, to which a drying quality is communicated; in this case it is not proper for delicate painting.

This inconvenience may be avoided by tying up the drying matters in a small bag: but the dose of litharge must then be doubled. The bag must then be suspended by a piece of packthread, fastened to a stick, which is made to rest on the edge of the vessel in such a manner as to keep the bag at the distance of an inch from the bottom of the vessel. A pellicle will be formed, as in the first operation, but it will be slower in making its appearance.

3. A drying quality may be communicated to oil by treating, in a heat capable of maintaining a slight ebullition, linseed or nut oil, to each pound of which is added three ounces of vitreous oxyde of lead, reduced to fine powder. The preparation of floor cloth, and all paintings of large figures or ornaments, in which argillaceous colours, such as yellow and red boles, Dutch pink, &c. are employed, require this kind of preparation, that the desiccation may not be too slow; but painting for which metallic oxydes are used, such as preparations of lead, copper, &c. require only the doses before indicated; because these oxydes contain a great deal of oxygen, and the oil by their contact, acquires more of a drying quality.

4. Two pounds of nut oil, three pounds common water, and two ounces sulphate of zinc. Mix these matters and subject them to a slight ebullition, until little water remains. Decant the oil, which will pass over with a small quantity of water, and separate the latter, by a funnel. The oil remains nebulous for some time, after which it becomes clear, and seems to be very little coloured.

5. Six pounds nut or linseed oil, four pounds common water, one ounce sulphate of zinc and one head of garlic or a small onion. Mix these matters in a common iron or copper pan, then place them over the fire, and maintain the mixture in a state of ebullition during the whole day; boiling water must be added from time to time, to make up the loss from that by evaporation. The garlic will assume a brown appearance. Take the pan from the fire, and having suffered a deposite to be formed, decant the oil, which will clarify itself in the vessels; by this process the drying oil is rendered somewhat more coloured; it is reserved for delicate colours.

To give a drying quality to Poppy Oil. Three pounds of pure water, one ounce of sulplate of zinc, two pounds oil of pinks, or poppy oil. Expose this mixture in an earthen vessel, capable of standing the fire, to a degree of heat sufficient to maintain it in a slight state of ebullition. When one half or two-thirds of the water has evaporated, pour the whole into a large glass bottle or jar, and let it rest, till the oil becomes clear. Decant the clearest part by means of a glass funnel, the beak of which is stopped with a piece of cork. When the separation of the oil from the water is completely effected, remove the cork stopper, and supply its place by the fore finger, which must be applied in such a manner as to suffer the water to escape, and to retain only the oil. Poppy oil when prepared in this manner, becomes after some weeks exceedingly limpid and colourless.

To make Varnish for Silk, &c. To one quart of cold drawn linseed oil, poured off from the lees, (produced on the addition of unslacked lime, on which the oil has stood eight or ten days at the least, in order to communicate a drying quality, or brown umber burnt and powdered which will have the like effect,) and half an ounce of litharge; boil them for half an hour, then add half an ounce copal varnish. While the ingredients are on the fire in a copper vessel, put in one ounce Chios turpentine, or common resin, and a few drops neat's foot oil, and stir the whole with a knife; when cool, it is ready for use. The neat's foot oil prevents the varnish from being sticky or adhesive, and may be put into linseed oil at the same time with the lime, or burnt umber. Resin or Chios turpentine may be added, till the varnish has attained the desired thickness.

The longer the raw linseed oil remains on the unslacked lime or umber, the sooner will the oil dry after it is used; if some months so much the better; such varnish will set, that is to say not run, but keep its place on the silk in four hours; the silk may then be turned, and varnished on the other side.

To make pliable Varnish for Umbrellas. Take any quantity of caoutchouc, as ten or twelve ounces, cut into small bits, and put into a ladle, such as plumbers, glaziers, &c. melt their lead in, over a common pit coal or other fire, which must be gentle, glowing, and without smoke. When the ladle is hot, put a single bit into it; if black smoke issues, it will flame and disappear, or it will evaporate without flame; the ladle is then too hot. When the ladle is less hot, put in a second bit, which will produce a white smoke; this white smoke will continue during the operation, and evaporate the caoutchouc; therefore, no time is to be lost, but little bits are to be put in, a few at a time, till the whole are melted; it should be continually and gently stirred with an iron or brass spoon. The instant the smoke changes from white to black, take off the ladle, or the whole will break out into a violent flame, or be spoiled, or lost. Care must be taken that no water is added, a few drops of which, on account of its expansibility, makes it boil over furiously and with a great noise; at this period of the process, one quart of the best drying oil is to be put into the melted caoutchouc, and stirred till hot, and the whole poured into a glazed vessel through a coarse gauze, or wire sieve. When settled and clear, which will be in a few minutes, it is fit for use. The silk should always be stretched horizontally by pins or tenter hooks on frames, and the varnish poured on cold in hot weather, and hot if cold weather. The art of laying it on properly, consists in making no intense motion in the varnish, which would create minute bubbles, therefore, brushes of every kind are improper, as each bubble breaks in drying, and forms a small hole, through which the air will transpire. This varnish is pliant, unadhesive, and unalterable by weather.

Transparent Japan for Tin Ware. Oil of turpentine, eight ounces, oil of lavender, six ounces, copal, two ounces, camphor, one drachm.

Drying Oil. Linseed oil, two pints, litharge or ceruse, one ounce; dissolve with heat; added to paints to make them dry sooner.

Le Blond's Varnish for Prints. Balsam copaiva four pounds, copal in powder, one pound; add by single ounces every day to the balsam, keeping it in a warm place, or in the sun, stirring it frequently; when all is dissolved, add Chios turpentine, q. p.

Sheldrake's Copal Varnish. Oil turpentine, ret. veri. one pint, sal ammoniac two ounces: mix; add copal in small pieces, two ounces; stop the vessel with a cork cut in grooves; bring it quickly to boil, that the bubbles may be counted as they rise; and keep it at that heat; if the least stoppage or overheating takes place, it is in vain to proceed. Then leave the vessel till quite cold, before you open it; otherwise the varnish will be thrown out with violence.

Sheldrake's Oil for Painting. Nut or poppy oil, one pint, boil; add ceruse, two ounces, when dissolved, add a pint of copal varnish, previously warmed, and stir it till the oil of turpentine is evaporated; gives more brightness than common drying oil, but less than varnish only; loses its dry quality in time, therefore, only so much as is sufficient for a month or six weeks' consumption should be prepared at once.

Varnish to be laid on Gilding and Silvering. Grind verdigris, on marble with common water, in which saffron has been infused for eight hours.

A Common Varnish. Sandarac eight ounces, tereb. Venit. six ounces, spirits wine, rectified, two pints.

White Varnish. Gum juniper, one pound, Stratsburg turpentine, six ounces, spirits wine, rectified, two pints, used upon paper, wood, and linen.

White Hard Varnish. Mastic, four ounces, gum juniper, tereb. Venit. of each three ounces (to prevent the gums forming an impenetrable mass,) add four ounces pounded glass, spirits wine rectified, two pints, used upon cards, sheaths, &c.

White Polishing Varnish. Mastic in tears, two ounces, gum juniper, eight ounces, gum elemi, one ounce, tereb. argent. four ounces, spirits wine rectified, two pints; used upon metals, polished with pumice stone.

Transparent Copal Varnish. Spirits wine fully charged with camphor, four ounces, copal in fine powder, one ounce; dissolve, filter; add the filtered liquor to spirits of wine, one part, in which gum elemi one ounce, has been previously dissolved.

2. Spirits wine rectified, one pint, camphor, half an ounce; dissolve; pour it upon copal in small pieces, four ounces; heat it so that the bubbles which rise may be counted; when cold, pour it off and add more spirits to the residuum: used for pictures.

3. Copal, melted and poured into water, three ounces, gum sandarac six ounces, mastic three ounces, terib. argent. two ounces and a half, pounded glass, four ounces, spirits wine rectified, two pints; used for metals, chairs, &c.

Soft Brilliant Varnish.   Gum sandarac, six ounces, gum elemi, four ounces, camphor, four drachms, spirits wine rectified, two pints; used upon wood work and pasteboard.

Reddish Varnish.   Gum sandarac, eight ounces, lava in tabulis, two ounces, resina nigri, four ounces, tereb. Venit. six ounces, spirits wine rectified, two pints; used on wood and metals.

Red Varnish.   Sandarac, four ounces, seed-lac, two ounces, mastic, choice Benjamin, of each one ounce; turpentine two ounces, spirits wine rectified two pints; used for violins and cabinet work.

Nut Oil.   From the kernel of the hazel nut, very fine; substituted for oil of Benjamin, as it will keep better than that of almonds; it has been proposed in the college lists, to be substituted for that oil, being nearly equal to it; is drank with tea in China, probably in lieu of cream; used by painters as a superior article for their colours.

Hemp Oil.   From hemp seed, used by the painters as a drying oil.

Walnut Oil.   Makes good plasters, but will not keep; used by painters; is very drying; they yield about half their weight of oil.

Picture Varnish.   Mastic, twelve ounces, Venit. turpentine, two ounces four drachms, camphor, thirty grains, pounded glass, four ounces, oil turpentine, three pints and a half; pour off the clear; used to oil paintings.

Gold Varnish for Leather.   Tumeric, gamboge, of each one scruple and a half, oil turpentine two pints; add seed-lac, gum sandarac, of each four ounces, dragon's blood four drachms, Venit. turpentine, two ounces, pounded glass, four ounces; pour off the clear.

Copal Varnish.   Oil turpentine, thickened by keeping, eight ounces, copal, two ounces and a half.

2.   Oil turpentine, six ounces, oil lavender, two ounces, copal, one ounce.

Common Turpentine Varnish.   Resin flav. three pounds, eight ounces, oil terebinth. one gallon.

Varnish for Coloured Drawings.   Canada balsam, one ounce, oil turpentine two ounces: size the drawing first with a jelly of isinglass, and when dry, apply the varnish; which will make them resemble oil paintings.

Black Japan Leather.   Boiled linseed oil, one gallon, burnt umber eight ounces, asphaltum, three ounces, boil and add oil terebinth. q. s.

Scouring Drops.   Oil terebinth. scented with essence lemon.

Furniture Oil.   Oil lini, coloured with rad. anchusæ.

Furniture Varnish.   White wax, eight ounces, oil terebinth. one pint.

Bronzing Liquor.   It is blue vitriol, dissolved in water; used to bronze tea urns, &c. the surface being previously well cleaned.

Blue or Green Sympathetic Ink.   Drop a tea spoonful of zaffre into a third of the wine glass of nitro-muriatic acid. After standing awhile, write on paper; the writing will be invisible cold, but on heating the paper the writing will be blue, unless there is a little iron in the zaffre, which will give it a green hue. If a little common salt in solution had been added, the writing would disappear on removing from the fire.

Invisible Ink.   Whittle off a little bismuth into a wine glass. Drop in a little common nitric acid diluted with half as much water. Violent action will commence; when it ceases the nitrate will be formed in the liquid state. Dip a clean pen into it and write as with ink; hold the paper near a fire, but not so near as to heat it, the letters will become invisible; now dip it into water or hold it in a steam over boiling water, and on taking it out, the letters will become visible, and appear as if written with pale ink.

After a short time the writing will disappear, and leave not a vestige to prove a forgotten promise.

Callot's Varnish. Two ounces finest linseed oil, Benjamin in drops, two drachms, white wax the bulk of a filbert, boil all together, till it is reduced to one-third, stirring it constantly. When done, put it into a large mouthed phial. Warm the plate intended to be engraven, and for which this varnish is designed, and with the finger pass it over the place, leaving it slightly coated, and smooth; after which smoke the plate on the varnished side, with a candle, until it is black in every part. Place the plate over a chafing dish, with charcoal fire, and when it has done fuming, the varnish has become sufficiently hardened, when it is prepared to chalk, draw and etch, whatever is desired. This varnish was used by Callot, to engrave his most admired subjects.

CHAPTER XXIII.
COMMERCE AND MANUFACTURES.

Commerce is the interchange of commodities, or the disposal of produce of any kind for other articles, or for some representative of value for which other articles can be procured, with a view of making a profit by the transaction. The term is usually restricted to the mercantile intercourse between different countries. The internal dealings between individuals of the same country, either for the supply of immediate consumption, or for carrying on manufactures, is more commonly denominated trade. Those who engage their capital in commerce or trade, act as agents between the producers and the consumers of the fruits of the earth; they purchase them of the former, and sell them to the latter; and it is by the profits on the sale that capital so employed yields a revenue or income. Commerce or trade increases the wealth of a nation; not by raising produce, like agriculture, nor by working up raw materials, like manufactures; but it gives an additional value to commodities by bringing them from places where they are plentiful, to those where they are scarce; and by providing the means for their more extended distribution, both the agricultural and manufacturing classes are incited to greater industry.

Agriculture never arrives at any considerable, much less at its highest degree of perfection, where it is not connected with trade; that is, where the demand for the produce is not increased by the consumption of trading cities. Though it should be remembered that agriculture is the immediate source of human provision; that trade conduces to the production of provision only as it promotes agriculture; and that the whole system of commerce, vast and various as it is, has no public importance but its subserviency to this end.

The province of a trader is not so contemptible as some would affect to make it. Many prefer to educate their children for what are called the professions, as law, divinity, and physic, rather than merchan-

Q

dise; if such preferment is merely given, as a most likely means of acquiring either honour, preferment, or riches, we will be enabled to convince them in this chapter, their estimation is made by a wrong standard. The celebrated Mr. Locke has observed that trade was a surer and shorter way to riches than any other. And after recommending people to bring up their children to some trade, says, if the mistaken parent, frightened with the name of *trade*, shall have an aversion to any thing of this kind in their children, he recommends teaching them merchants' accounts, as a science well becoming any gentleman. Lord Bacon saith, "that trade enables the subjects to live plentifully and happily; and that the realm is much enriched of late years, by the trade of merchandise." And elsewhere, he stiles the merchants vena porta; and says, 'if they flourish not, a kingdom may have good limbs, but will have empty veins, and flourish little." The learned Bishop of Cambray gives his sentiments on the subject, and says, speaking of the Phœnicians' "trade, which they carry to the farthest quarters of the earth, has so enriched them, that they surpass the most flourishing people in glory."

And again, instructing Telemachus, how to establish a flourishing trade in Ithaca, he says, "do as those people do, receive with kindness and with ease all strangers; and never suffer yourself at any time to be overcome with pride and avarice. Make yourself beloved of all strangers; and even bear with slight inconveniences from them; keep a strict hand over the fraud, negligence, and vain glory of the merchants, which ruins commerce in ruining the traders themselves." The mercantile station affords as large a prospect for opulent acquisitions as any other, and estates got by trade have, perhaps, been far more numerous, than those by any other way whatever. The relation which the merchant stands in to community, is not inferior to any in point of importance. Their zealous attachment to their country, where they have been protected in their commerce, can be fully maintained. History furnishes remarkable instances of this fact. We shall only mention a few, which are sufficient to endear the character of a merchant to every nation.

Charles V. Emperor of Germany, being reduced to great distress, by the unhappy expedition of Tunis, experienced a powerful succour of money from the Fuggers, a single family of merchants only, but at the same time the most opulent and distinguished traders in Augsburg. For security, his majesty gave them written obligations, under his own hand and seal. To give a demonstration of their zeal to the interests of their country, and their inviolable attachment to his majesty, these merchants requested the emperor, one day as he was taking an airing by their house, to do them the honour to regale himself, to which his majesty condescended. When the collation was over, they desired permission of the emperor to burn a faggot of cinnamon in the hall, where the entertainment was made, not only with intent to administer all they could to the emperor's delight, but to give further proof of their affection to his person and government, which they did, by binding up those bonds of security, which they had taken for their money, with the faggot, and set fire to them before his face.

James Cœur, a merchant of Bourges, by the wisdom of his counsel, and the certainty of his cash, humbled the house of Burgundy, secured the crown of France to the lawful heir, Charles VII. and by him to the branches of Valois and Bourbon, who succeeded.

The merchants of St. Malo, being highly exasperated at the demand made at the Congress of Gertruyden burg to Lewis XIV. of employing his troops to compel his grandson Philip V. then King of Spain, to abandon the crown, united all their profits together, which they had made in the Spanish Colonies of America, and produced thirty-two millions of gold at the foot of the throne: and at a time when the finances of France were totally exhausted by a series of unsuccessful events. This succour being timely applied, vigorously renewed the war, and answered the wishes of the nation.

Sir Thomas Gresham, the founder of a college in London, for the promotion of the liberal arts, and of the Royal Exchange, for the convenience of the traders of the metropolis, is another instance of the ability of private merchants to support government under the greatest emergency. This worthy citizen of London lived in the time of Edward VI. who was considerably indebted to the merchants of Antwerp, for the money borrowed to supply the exigencies of the state. Payment of interest, at that time, being a great incumbrance to the nation, many expedients were projected by the king and council, to discharge those debts; which were, either to transport so much treasure out of the country, as would liquidate them, or remit the same by way of exchange. The former was impracticable without being ruinous to trade; and on account of the difference of exchange, the latter appeared equally perplexing. Beside the creditors insisted on their money, or a compliance with such usurious terms, as would have been the highest indignity upon the nation. Under these circumstances, Sir Thomas undertook the affair, and by his great knowledge and skill in the exchanges, exonerated the nation from the incumbrance; and by which negotiations, the king saved not less than an hundred thousand marks, clear. By raising the exchange in favour of England at this critical time, the price of all foreign commodities fell proportionably; and in a very little while between three and four hundred thousand pounds sterling more was saved to the nation. With Queen Elizabeth, he was in so high esteem, that she knighted him, and honoured him in every respect, and came in person to the *Exchange*, which he had erected for the convenience of merchants, and the honour of the city of London, and caused the same to be proclaimed by heralds and a trumpet, the *Royal Exchange*, and Sir Thomas was afterwards honoured by the appellation of *royal merchant*.

Thomas Sutton, Esq. another distinguished English merchant, and founder of the Charter House in London, did an act of benevolence worthy of a great prince, a few years after the death of Sir Thomas Gresham, in being the grand instrument of getting the Spanish bills protested at Genoa, which retarded for a whole year the sailing of the Spanish Armada, designed to invade England; by which means the plan was defeated. Thus we learn the worth of some private merchants; and although great statesmen, admirals, and generals, with the aid of the public purse, and ten thousands to co-operate with them, may perform great achievements, yet we find that one family of merchants has been the support of an emperor in great distress; another single merchant, gave the crown to the house of Bourbon; that one was the principal cause of defeating the Spanish Armada; and another, the restorer of the public credit of England. The merit of persons of distinguished character in trade, cannot, in general, be measured by those who are not well acquainted with trading negotiations; as they pass through life without much noise, the world is little acquainted with their important services and utility to the state.

Whilst the histories of great public capacities are transmitted to posterity with all the pomp and magnificence of representation: yet certainly that is one of the most profitable admonitions, which is drawn from the eminent virtues of men, who move in a sphere nearer levelled to the common reach, than that which is derived from the splendid portrait of the transactions and victories of great statesmen and commanders, which serve but for the imitation of few, and aim rather for the ostentation, than for the true instruction of human life. It is from the practice and examples of private condition, that we are more naturally taught to excel in our private capacities; and, had we the genuine histories of many eminent merchants, giving a lively idea of their rise and progress in business, and of the important service they have been to their respective communities, they would naturally incite the trading class of community to emulate their accomplishments: and this would prove a more effectual means to produce a race of skilful traders, than romantic narratives of a race of heroes. Nor has the security of states and empires been only owing to the occasional zealous exertion of the wisdom and power of the merchants, but they are in a great measure the daily and perpetual support of all trading countries.

For, as nations are at present circumstanced, those which are so situated, subsisting chiefly within themselves, without any intercourse of commerce with others, can never be able to maintain so great a share of power, as those which carry on an extended foreign traffic. Domestic trade, only shifting property from hand to hand, cannot increase the riches and power of a nation; whilst foreign trade under wise laws and regulations, bringing in a constant balance of treasure in favour of a nation, will proportionably augment its weight of interest, and at length give it the balance of power.

The philosopher may arrive to a high pitch of improvement in agriculture, arts and sciences; the husbandman, artisan and manufacturer, may reduce this speculative knowledge to practical uses, with the greatest skill and dexterity on their parts; governments may enact the wisest laws, and give all desirable encouragement to commerce, yet what will these avail without the penetration and sagacity of the merchant, to propagate the produce of our lands, and the labour of our artists and manufacturers into foreign countries, with advantage to the state as well as to himself? "It is foreign trade," says an English lawyer, "that is the main sheet anchor of us islanders; without which, the genius of all our studies, which render men famous and renowned, would make them useless and insignificant to the public. When man has fathomed the bottom of all knowledge, what is it, if not reduced to practice, but an empty notion? If the inhabitants of this island, were learned in all the languages between the rising and setting sun, did know and understand the situation of all places, ports, and countries, and the nature of all merchandise and commodities, were acquainted with the order and motion of all the stars, knew how to take the latitude and longitude, and were perfectly read in the art of navigation, to what purpose would be all, if there were no foreign trade? We should have no ships to navigate to those countries, nor occasion to make use of those languages, nor to make use of those commodities; what would this island be but a place of confinement to the inhabitants, who without it, would be but a kind of hermits, as separated from the the rest of the world; it is foreign trade that renders us rich, honourable and great; that gives us a name and esteem in the world; that makes us masters of the treasures of other nations and countries, and begets and maintains our ships and seamen, the walls and bulwarks of our country; and were it not for foreign trade, what would become of the revenue for customs, and what would the rents of our lands be? the customs would totally fail, and our gentleman's rents of thousands per annum would dwindle into hundreds.'

Since, then, as Lord Chancellor Bacon observes, "*Merchants and Traders are in a state what the blood is to the body*," there naturally arises, the idea of *dignity*, as inseparately annexed to the character of the merchant. Merchants it is true are not exempted from those casualties, to which the whole human species are liable; yet in the way of trade these are often balanced by prosperous contingencies.

When it happens otherwise, the really unfortunate scarce ever want succour in distress. Even when misfortunes have proceeded from unhappy mistakes in point of conduct, yet, where neither integrity nor skill have been wanting, such rarely fail to rise again, in some reputable channel of business or other, dependant on merchants, of which there are numberless instances. No class of citizens are more feeling and energetic in acts of benevolence; of which our own country is fruitful in examples.

That experienced merchant Sir F. Brewster, who lived in the reign of King William III. proposed a way of educating young men of condition and fortune as merchants to practical commerce. "I think it a moral distemper," says Sir Francis, "that we have so few men of university learning conversant in true mercantile employments; if there was as much care to have men of the best heads and education in it, as there is in the law, the nation would fetch more from abroad and spend less in lawsuits at home." He further observes, "that it would be an astonishing observation to any countryman but our own, to see more heads employed in Westminster Hall to divide the gain of the nation, than there are heads on the Exchange to gather it." And further, he says, "we see how the arts and sciences have been improved in this kingdom within the compass of one century, but amongst them all, the merchants part the least; I speak not this to abate the respect due to their profession, and all men in it; but we know it is the vanity of the nation; scarce a tradesman if he has a son, whom a country school master tells him would make a scholar, because he learns his grammar well, whose kindred think it a pity so hopeful a youth should be lost in trade, and that the university is the only soil fit for him to be planted in."

Before we conclude, we request the reader to observe, the above remarks of Sir Francis are not introduced, as applicable to this country generally; for we do rejoice in the belief, the mercantile character of the nation is daily increasing in dignity; that young men of refined taste, requisite qualifications, and most promising talents are engaging in merchandise; and that the public feeling, which hitherto, has been so unnaturally excited against the profession, has nearly subsided. We believe there is a dignity, or as some will have it, *a respectability of character* attached to every profession.   The following article, which we extract from the New-York Courier, headed "*Scale of respectability,*" is expressive of our views in regard to distinction, though rather ludicrous.   "It is a matter of curious investigation, to examine the distinctions which society has made, amongst the different trades and professions, 'a saint in crape is twice a saint in lawn,' says Pope; and yet he tells us, 'that honour and shame from no condition rise;' the latter is true by the laws of nature; the former by the usages of society.   Whether a lawyer is more respectable than a doctor, or a merchant than a farmer, is a question that has not yet been settled by her high mightiness, *Fashion;* but with respect to the different pursuits of trade, she has drawn the distinction, having consulted neither reason or rhyme, and governs solely by her own whims.   A butcher, for instance, is considered as superior to a baker;—and why?   They both cater for the appetite of man; one furnishes the slaughtered calf, and the other the generous grain, which alike support life; one deals in fire, and the other in sword: are they not on a par?   A shoemaker is more respectable than a cobbler;—why? one makes your shoes, and the other mends them—they both use awls and waxed ends; where *is* the difference?

"Is a hatter more exalted than a tailor?   The one covers 'the dome of thought, the palace of the soul!' his vocation is certainly *of the head;* he surmounts the crown; but then the tailor adorns the graceful form and manly chest: the waistcoat that he makes covers the heart, the seat of sensation and the abode of passion.   He makes you either a gentleman or a clown, according to his will.   You are at his mercy with regard to the fit of your habiliments and the effect of your appearance in Broadway.   Thus extensive is his power; and is not power respectability?   A milliner is more respected in society than a mantua-maker; the one makes hats, and the other dresses.   Why is a *female* hatter greater than a *female* tailor?   Why is a grocer considered inferior to a seller of dry goods?   Is not a bottle of mustard as respectable as a yard of tape?   Is not a pound of cheese as honourable as a paper of pins?   A bunch of onions as a skein of thread?   Is not sugar equal to broadcloth, and molasses to ginghams?   Certainly.

"Again, why is a saddler superior to a shoemaker?   He covers the backs of horses, while the latter covers the feet of men.   And is not the foot of lordly man and lovely woman, an object of greater moment than the back of Eclipse himself?   How and why then are these distinctions made?   It is easier to ask than to answer the question; to do the latter, surpasses our wisdom.   But are these distinctions reasonable and natural?   No.   Honest industry is alike respectable in every vocation.   The faithful mason, who piles one brick upon another, is the equal of him who makes the bricks, or him who burns the lime which is used in making the mortar; [and we might add, or him for whose comfort his labour is destined to effect.]   The industrious mechanic is the prop of society, and so long as he labours diligently and honestly in his occupation, he is entitled to respectability, and he will receive it." Nevertheless, it must be acknowledged, and to the de+ gradation of human nature be it said, there are many in all professions, dishonouring them by the flattery of some, and their own unnatural conceit.

Manufactures are the arts by which natural productions are brought into the state or form in which they are consumed or used. They require in general great expenses for their first establishment, costly machines for shortening manual labour, and money and credit for purchasing materials from distant countries. There is not a single manufacture of Great Britain which does not require, in some part of its process, productions from different parts of the globe. It requires, therefore, ships, and a friendly intercourse with foreign nations, to transport commodities and exchange productions. They would not be a manufacturing, unless they were a commercial nation. The two sciences which most assist the manufacturer, are mechanics and chemistry; the one for building mills, working mines, and in general for constructing machines, either to shorten the labour of man by performing it in less time, or to perform what the strength of man alone could not accomplish; the other for fusing and working ores, dying, bleaching, and extracting the virtues of various substances for particular occasions.

It must be observed that though a farmer does not so frequently and rapidly amass wealth as a merchant or manufacturer, yet neither is he so often ruined. The risks a man encounters in trade are much greater than in farming. The manufacturer as well as the merchant is liable to severe losses arising from contingencies in trade; they both must therefore have a chance of making proportionably greater profits. The chances of gain must balance the chances of loss. If he be so skilful or so fortunate as to make more than his average share of gain, he will accumulate wealth with greater rapidity than the farmer; but should either a deficiency of talents or unfortunate circumstances occasion an uncommon share of losses, he may become a bankrupt. The rate of profits, therefore, upon any employment of capital, is proportioned to the risks with which it is attended; but if calculated during a sufficient period of time, and upon a sufficient number of instances to afford an average, these different modes of employing capital, will be found to yield similar profits. It is owing to this that the distribution of capital to the several branches of agriculture, commerce, and manufactures, preserve a due equilibrium, which, though it may be accidentally disturbed, cannot whilst allowed to pursue its natural course, be permanently deranged.

An abundant harvest may occasionally raise the rate of agricultural profits, or a very bad season may reduce them below their level.

The opening a trade with a new country, or the breaking out of a war, which impedes foreign commerce, will affect the profits of the merchant and manufacturer: but these accidents disturb the equal rate of profits, as the wind disturbs the sea; and when they cease, it returns to its natural level.

The division of labour has tended greatly to improve every manufacture. Its utility is exemplified in the manufacture of pins. If a piece of metal were given to a man to make a pin, he could scarcely do it in a day. In pin manufactories, however, each pin passes through twenty-five hands; one draws out the wire, another straightens *it,* another cuts, another points it, three or four prepare the head, two or three put it on, &c.   Twenty-five persons thus make one hundred and twenty-five thousand pins in a day, or five thousand to each person.   Labour likewise divides itself numerously in every branch of the elegant and useful arts, as in building, the arts connected in furnishing a house, in branches connected with the clothing of a man, in the iron and metallic trades, and in connexion with books and literature.

A pack of wool weighing 240 pounds employs 200 persons before it is ready for sale, in the form of stuffs, cloths, &c.   To be made into stockings, it will occupy 184 persons for a week; as ten combers, one hundred spinners, winding, &c. sixty weavers or stocking makers, besides dyers, pressers, &c.   A sword made of steel, the original metal of which was not worth a shilling, is sometimes sold for 300 guineas; and a watch chain has produced fifty guineas, the metal of which before it was wrought, was not worth three pence.   So likewise, a painting, not two yards square, has been valued at 25,000 pounds sterling; and a shawl, which contained but a few ounces of wool, has been said to bring 150 guineas.   As it is with individuals, so it is with nations.   What one possesses in superfluity, it is desirous to exchange for some article it wants, with any other nation which possesses that superfluity.

The Phœnicians, or Philistines were the first people on record, who employed ships to carry the produce and manufactures of one nation to another.   They were followed by the Carthagenians; and these by the Venetians, Genoese and Hanse Towns.   The United States of America, with the advantages of the possession of raw materials of every kind, numerous fine ports, and a free government, are rapidly advancing in the manufacturing system; having numerous ships and a trade extended to all parts of the world.   With this advantage connected with the enterprise, perseverance and industry of our merchants, manufacturers and mechanics, who can doubt the time is not far distant, when this country will rival every other on the whole face of the globe in commerce and manufactures.

CHAPTER XXIV.
THE ART OF DYING.

Dying is a chemical process, and consists in combining a certain colouring matter with fibres of cloth.   The facility with which cloth imbibes a dye, depends upon two circumstances; the union of the cloth and the dyestuff or dying material and the fluid in which it is dissolved.   Wool unites with almost all colouring matters, silk in the next degree, cotton considerably less, and linen the least of all.   To dye cotton or linen, the dyestuff or colouring material, should, in many cases, be dissolved in a substance for which it has a weaker connexion, than with the solvent employed it the dying of wool or silk.   Thus we may use the colour called oxyde of iron, dissolved in sulphuric acid, to die wool; but to die cotton and linen, it is necessary to dissolve it in acetous acid.   Were it possible to procure a sufficient number of colouring substances, having a strong affinity for cloths, to answer all the purpose the art of dying would be extremely simple and easy. But this is by no means the case. This difficulty has, however, been obviated by a very ingenious contrivance. Some other substance is employed which strongly unites with the cloth and the colouring matter. This substance, therefore, is previously combined with the cloth, which is then dipped into a solution containing the colour. The colour then combines with the intermediate substance, which being firmly combined with the cloth, secures the permanence of the die. Substances employed for this purpose are denominated *mordants*.

The method of colouring a scarlet die, was discovered by Cornelius Drebble, a citizen of Alemaar, a man extremely well skilled in chemistry. Among other experiments, he left an account of one, concerning the method of dying wool with a bright flame colour; which his son in law Kufflaar, afterwards put in practice, and by which means he made a fortune. Spirit of nitre has been found to improve the rich colour of cochineal, into the brightness of burning fire; but its acrimony corrodes and damages the wool, which is prevented by dulcifying it with tin, after which, it neither hurts wool or silk. Chemistry is likewise obvious in another point of view. "I once showed," says the learned Boerhaave, "colours which I had prepared from solutions of copper, to some skilful master diers, who were surprised with the beauty of them, and would have given any money to have been able to give colours of such brightness to their stuffs, &c.; and no wonder, since the blue, violet and green of copper, which may be raised and weakened at pleasure, afford such a variety, that a person who can die silk, woollen, cotton or linen cloths therewith will gain an immense estate." It has been said by a Spanish patriot, that "good diers in silk and wool are few every where, and it should be considered," in regard to this art, "we depend upon it as one of the most essential recommendations of our manufactured goods, and what procures them the readiest sale, both at home and abroad; for it will turn to small account that the materials are good, and well wrought up, unless the mixture and colours be answerable and grateful to the eye of the purchaser.

The most important part of dying is the choice and application of *mordants*; as upon them the permanency of almost every die depends. Mordants must be previously dissolved in some liquid, which has a weaker union with the mordant than the cloth has; and the cloth must then be steeped in this solution, so as to saturate itself with the mordant. the most important and most generally used mordant is *alumine*; it is used in the state of common alum, in which it is combined with sulphuric acid, or in that state called acetate of alumine. Alum to make a mordant is dissoved in water, and very frequently, a quantity of tartrite of potash is dissolved with it. Into this solution the woollen cloth is put and kept till it has absorbed as much alumine as necessary. It is then taken out, washed and dried.

Acetate of Alumine, is prepared as a mordant by pouring acetate of lead into a solution of alum, (see page 30, acetate of alumine.) This mordant is employed for *cotton* and *linen*. It answers much better for these than alum; the stuff is more easily saturated with alumine, and takes in consequence, a richer and more permanent colour. The white oxyde of tin has enabled the moderns greatly to surpass many of the

R

ancients, in the fineness of their colours; and even to equal the famous
Tyrian purple; and by means of its scarlet, the brightness of all colours is produced.   It is the white oxyde of tin alone that is the real
mordant.   Tin is used as a mordant in three states: dissolved in nitro-
muriatic acid, in acetous acid, and in a mixture of sulphuric and muriatic acids; but nitro-muriate of tin is the common mordant employed
by diers.   It is prepared by dissolving tin in diluted nitric acid, to which
a certain proportion of common salt, or sal ammoniac is added.   When
the nitro-muriate of tin is to be used as a mordant, it is dissolved in
a large quantity of water, and the cloth is dipped in the solution, and
allowed to remain until sufficiently saturated.   It is then taken out,
washed and dried.   Tartar is usually dissolved in water, along with
the nitro-muriate.

Red Oxyde of Iron, is also used as a mordant in dying; it has a very
strong affinity for all kinds of cloth, of which the permanency of red
iron spots, or iron moulds on linen and cotton is a sufficient proof.
As a mordant it is used in two states; in that of sulphate of iron, or copperas, and that of acetate of iron.   The first, or copperas, is commonly used for *wool*.   The copperas is dissolved in water, and the cloth
dipped into it.   It may be used, also for cotton, but in most cases acetate of iron is preferred, which is prepared by dissolving iron or its
oxyde in vinegar, sour beer, or pyroligneous acid, and the longer it is
kept the better.   *Tan* is very frequently employed as a mordant.   An
infusion of nutgalls, or of sumack, or any other substances containing tan, is made in water; and the cloth is dipped in this infusion, and
allowed to remain till it has absorbed a sufficient quantity.   Tan is
also employed along with other mordants, to produce a compound
mordant.   Oil is also used for the same purpose, in dying cotton and
linen.   The mordants with which it is most frequently combined, are
alumine and oxyde of iron.   Besides these mordants, there are several other substances frequently used as auxiliaries, either to facilitate
the combination of the mordant with the cloth, or to alter the shade of
colour; the chief of these are, tartar, acetate of lead, common salt,
sal ammoniac, sulphur of copper, &c.   Mordants not only render the
die perfect, but also have considerable influence on the colour produced.   The same colouring matter produces very different dies, according as the mordant is changed.   Suppose for instance, that the
colouring matter is cochineal; if we use the aluminous mordant, the
cloth will acquire a crimson colour; but the oxyde of iron produces
with it, a black.   In dying then, it is not only necessary to produce a
mordant, and a colouring matter of such a nature, that when combined together, they shall produce the wished for colour in perfection.
But we must procure a mordant and a colouring matter, of such a nature, that when combined together, they should possess the wished for
colour; even a great variety of colours may be produced with a single
die stuff, provided we change the mordant sufficiently.

To determine the effects of various salts or mordants on colours:
1. *The die of Madder*.   For a madder red on woollens, the best quantity of madder is one half, if the woollens that are to be died; the best
proportion of salts to be used in five parts of alum and one of red tartar, for sixteen parts of the stuff.   A variation in the proportions of the
salts, wholly alters the colour that the madder naturally gives.   If the

alum is lessened, and the tartar increased, the dies prove a *red cinna-mon*. If the alum be entirely omitted, the red wholly disappears, and a durable tawny cinnamon is produced. If woollens are boiled in weak pearlash and water, the greater part of the colour is destroyed. A solution of soap discharges a part of the colour, and leaves the remaining more beautiful. Volatile alkalies heighten the red colour of the madder, but they make the die fugitive.

2. *The Die of Logwood.* Volatile alkaline salts or acids incline this to purple; the vegetable and nitrous acids, render it pale; the vitriolic and marine acids deepen it.

3. *Lime Water.* In dying browns or blacks, especially browns, lime water is found to be a very good corrective, as also, an alternative when the goods are not come to the shades required; but practice alone can shew its utility; it answers well for either woollens, silks, or cottons.

4. *To render colours holding.* Brown or blues, or shades from them, require no preparation to make them receive the die, and hold it fast when they have received it. Alum and tartar, boiled together, when cold, form a mastic, within the pores of the substance, that serves to retain the die, and reflect the colour in a manner transparently. Almost all browns are deemed fast and holding colours, without any preparation, the dying materials containing in themselves a sufficient degree of astringent quality to retain their own colours. Many reds, are also, equally holding, but none more so than those made with madder on woollens prepared with alum and tartar. A very fast red is also made with brazil wood, by boiling the woollen in alum and tartar, and suffering the cloth to remain several days in a bag, kept moist by the preparation liquor. The cause of the solidity of the colour from Brazil wood, died after this method, arises from the alum and tartar masticating itself within the pores of the wool in quite a solid state.

There is not a drug used in the whole art of dying, but may be made a permanent die, by finding out a salt or solution of some metal, that, when once dissolved by acids, or by boiling water, will neither be affected by the air, nor be dissolved by moisture. Such are alum and tartar, the solution of tin, &c. But these salts and solutions do not answer with all ingredients that are used in dying.

To die Wool and Woollen Cloths of a Blue Colour. One part of indigo, in four parts concentrated sulphuric acid, dissolved; then add one part of dry carbonate of potash, and dilute with eight times its weight of water. The cloth must be boiled for an hour in a solution, containing five parts of alum, and three of tartar, for every thirty-two parts of cloth, then throw it into a water bath, previously prepared, containing a greater or smaller proportion of diluted sulphate of indigo, according to the shade which the cloth is intended to receive. Boil it in the bath until the colour desired is obtained. The only colouring matters employed in dying blue are indigo and woad. Indigo has a very strong affinity for wool, silk, cotton and linen. Every cloth, therefore, may be died with it without the assistance of any mordant whatever. The colour thus induced is very permanent. But indigo can only be applied to cloth in a state of solution, and the only solvent known is sulphuric acid. The sulphate of indigo is often used to die wool and silk blue, and is known by the name of Saxon blue. It is not the only solution of that pigment employed in dying. By far the most common method is, to deprive the indigo of its blue colour, and reduce it to green, and then to dissolve it in water by means of alkalies.   Two different methods are employed for this purpose. The first is, to mix the indigo in a solution of green oxyde of iron, and different metallic sulphurets.   If, therefore, indigo lime, and green sulphate of iron, are mixed together in water, the indigo gradually loses its blue colour, becomes green, and is dissolved.   The second method is, to mix the indigo, in water, with certain vegetable substances, which readily undergo fermentation; the indigo is dissolved by means of quicklime or alkali, which is added to the solution.   The first of these methods is usually followed in dying cotton and linen; the second in dying silk and woollen.   In the dying of wool, woad and bran are commonly employed, as vegetable ferments, and lime as the solvent of the green base of the indigo; and by following the common process, indigo may be extracted from it. In the usual state of woad, when purchased by the dier, the indigo which it contains, is probably not far from the state of green pollen.   Its quantity in woad is but small, and it is mixed with a great proportion of other vegetable matter.   When the cloth is first taken out of the vat, it is of a green colour; but it soon becomes blue. · It ought to be carefully washed, to carry off the uncombined particles. This solution of indigo is liable to two inconveniences: 1st. It is apt sometimes, to run too fast, into the putrid fermentation; this may be known by the putrid · vapours, which it exhales, and by the disappearing of the green colour. In this state it would soon destroy the indigo altogether. The inconvenience is remedied by adding more lime, which has the property of moderating the putrescent tendency. 2dly. Sometimes the fermentation goes on too languidly.   This defect is remedied by adding more bran or woad, in order to diminish the proportion of thick lime.

To make Chemic Blue and Green. Chemic, for light blues and greens on silk, cotton, or woollen, and for cleaning and whitening cottons, is made as follows. One pound of the best oil of vitriol, poured on, one ounce of the best indigo, well pounded and sifted; add to this, after it has been well stirred, a small lump of common pearlash, as big as a pea, or from that to double the quantity. When the fermentation which is produced, ceases, put it into a bottle tightly corked, and it may be used the next day. Observe, if more than the quantity prescribed of pearlash should be used, it will deaden and sully the colour. Chemic for green as above for blue, is made by only adding one-fourth more of the oil of vitriol.

To make a solution of Tin in Aqua-Regia. Eight ounces filtered river water, and eight ounces double aqua-fortis; mix; add gradually half an ounce of sal ammoniac, dissolved, piece by piece, and two drachms saltpetre. Then take one ounce of refined block tin; put it into an iron pan, and set it over the fire; when melted, hold it four or five feet over the vessel, and drop it into water, so as to let it fall to pieces. Then put a small piece of this granulated tin into the above aqua-regia, and when the last piece disappears, add more gradually, till the whole is mixed; mind and keep it firmly corked. When finished it will produce a most excellent yellow, though should it fail in that respect, it will not be the worse for use; keep it cool, as heat will injure it, and even spoil it.

To make Muriate of Tin. Take eight ounces muriatic acid, and dissolve in it, by slow degress, half an ounce granulated tin; when this is done, pour off the clear liquid into a bottle, and weaken it if required, with pure river water. [See page 42; *Scarlet Colour.*]

To determine the effect of various Waters on different Colours. Snow water contains a little muriate of lime, and some slight traces of nitrate of lime; rain water has the same salts in a larger quantity, and also carbonic acid; spring water most frequently contains carbonate of lime, muriate of lime, muriate of soda, or carbonate of soda. River water has the same substances, but in less abundance. Well water contains sulphate of lime, or nitrate of potash, besides the above mentioned salts. Should the water contain a salt or a mineral acid, in the first instance no acid will be required to neutralize it; or in the second, an alkali. Thus waters of any quality may be saturated by their opposites, and rendered neutral.

To discharge Colours. The diers generally put all coloured silks which are to be discharged, into a copper, in which half a pound or a pound of white soap is dissolved. They are then boiled off, and when the copper begins to be too full of colour, the silks are taken out and rinsed in warm water. In the interim a fresh solution of soap is to be added to the copper, and then proceed as before till all the colours are discharged. For those colours which are wanted to be effectually discharged, such as greys, cinnamon, &c. when soap does not do, tartar must be used. For slate colours, greenish drabs, olive drab, &c. oil of vitriol, in warm water must be used; if other colours, roche alum must be boiled in the copper, then cooled down, and the silks entered and boiled off, recollecting to rinse them before they are again died. A small quantity of muriatic acid, diluted in warm water, must be used to discharge some fast colours; the goods must be afterwards well rinsed in warm and cold water to prevent any injury to the stalk.

To discharge Cinnamons, Greens, &c. when died too fully, take some tartar pounded in a mortar, sift it into a bucket, then pour over it some boiling water. The silks, &c. may then be run through the clearest of this liquor, which will discharge the colour, but if the die does not take on again evenly, more tartar may be added, and the goods run through as before.

To Re-Die, or change the colour of Garments, &c. depends upon the ingredients by which they have been died. Sometimes when these have been well cleansed, more die stuff must be added, which will afford the colour intended, and sometimes the colour already on the cloth must be discharged and the articles re-died.

Every colour in nature will die black, whether blue, yellow, brown, or red; and black will always die black again. All colours will take the same colour again, which they already possess; and blues can be made green or black; green may be made brown and brown green; and every colour on re-dying will take a darker hue than at first. Yellows, browns, and blues are not easily disengaged; maroons, reds, of some kinds, olives, &c. may be discharged.

Olive Greys, &c. are discharged by putting in two or three table spoonfuls, more or less, of oil of vitriol, then put in the garments, &c. and boil, and it will become white. If chemic green, either alum, pearlash, or soap, will discharge it off to the yellow; this yellow may be mostly boiled off with soap, if it has received a preparation for taking the chemic blue. Muriatic acid used at a hard heat, will dischgare most colours. A black may be died maroon, claret, green, or a dark brown, but green is the principal colour into which black is changed.

To alum Silks. Silks should be alumed when cold, for when they are alumed hot, they are deprived of a great part of their lustre. The alum liquor should always be strong for silks, as they take the die more readily afterwards.

To die Silks Blue. Silk is died light blue, by a ferment of six parts, six of indigo, six of potash, and one of madder. For a dark blue, it must previously receive what is called a *ground colour*; a red die stuff, called archil, is used for this purpose.

To die Cotton and Linen Blue. Take a solution of one part indigo, one part green sulphate of iron, and two parts quicklime.

Yellow Dies. Oxyde of tin is sometimes used when very fine yellows are wanting. Tan is often employed as subsidiary to alumine, and in order to fix it more copiously on cotton and linen. Tartar is also used as an auxiliary, to brighten the colour; and muriate of soda, sulphate of lime and even the sulphate of iron, to render the shade deeper. The yellow die, by means of fustic is more permanent, but not so beautiful as that given by weld or quercitron. As it is permanent, and not much injured by acids, it is often used in dying compound colours, where a yellow is required. The mordant is alumine. When it is oxyde of iron, fustic dies a good permanent drab colour. Weld and quercitron bark yield nearly the same colour; but the bark yields colouring matter in greater abundance, and is cheaper than weld. The method of using each of these die stuffs is nearly the same.

Yellow colouring matters have too weak an affinity for cloth, to produce permanent colours without the use of mordants. Cloth, therefore, before it is died yellow, is always prepared by soaking it in alumine.

To die Woollens Yellow. Let them be boiled for an hour or more, with one-sixth of its weight of alum, dissolved in a sufficient quantity of water as a mordant. Then plunge it without rinsing, into a bath of warm water, containing as much quercitron bark as equals the weight of the alum employed as a mordant. The cloth is to be turned through the boiling liquid, till it has acquired the intended colour. Then a quantity of clean powdered chalk, equal to the hundredth part of the weight of the cloth, is to be stirred in, and the operation of dying continued for eight or ten minutes longer. This method produces a pretty deep and lively yellow. For a very bright orange, or golden yellow, it is necessary to use the oxyde of tin as a mordant. For producing bright golden yellows, some alum must be used along with the tin. To give the yellow a delicate green shade, tartar must be added in different proportions, according to the shade.

To die Silks Yellow. They may be died different shades of yellow, either by weld or quercitron bark, but the last is the cheapest. The proportion is from one to two parts of bark, to twelve parts of silk, according to the shade. Tie the bark up in a bag, and put it into the dying vessel while the water is cold. When it acquires the heat of about 100° the silk having been previously alumed, should be dipped in, and continued, till it assumes the wished for colour. When the shade is required to be deep, a little chalk, or pearlash should be added towards the end of the operation.

To die Linens and Cottons Yellow. The mordant should be acetate of alumine, prepared by dissolving one part of acetate of lead, and three parts of alum, in a sufficient quantity of water. Heat the solution to the temperature of 100°, soak the cloth in it for two hours; then wring out and dry it. This may be again repeated, and if the shade of yellow is required to be very bright and durable, the alternate wetting with limestone and soaking in the mordant may be repeated three or four times.

The dying bath is prepared by putting twelve or eighteen parts of quercitron bark, (according to the depth of the shade required) tied up in a bag, into a sufficient quantity of cold water. Into this bath the cloth is to be put, and turned in it for an hour, while its temperature is gradually raised to about 120°. It is then to be brought to a boiling heat, and the cloth allowed to remain in it for only a few minutes. If kept long at a boiling heat, the yellow acquires a shade of brown.

To fix a fine Mineral Colour on Wool, Silk, Cotton, &c. Mix one lb. sulphur, two lbs. white oxyde of arsenic, and five parts pearlash; and melt in a crucible at a little short of red heat. The result is a yellow mass, to be dissolved in hot water, and the liquor filtrated, to separate from a sediment formed chiefly of metallic arsenic, in shining plates, and in a small part of a chocolate coloured matter, which appears to be a sub-sulphuret of arsenic. Dilute the filtrated liquor, then add weak sulphuric acid, which produces a flacculent precipitate of a most brilliant yellow colour. This precipitate, washed upon a cloth filter, dissolves with the utmost ease in liquid ammonia, giving a yellow solution, which colour is to be removed by an excess of the same alkali.

To prepare the Sulphuret of Arsenic. This produces a very brilliant and permanent yellow. Dip into a solution of this more or less diluted, according to the depth of tint required, wool, silk, cotton or linen. All metallic utensils must be carefully avoided. When the stuffs come out of this bath, they are colourless, but they insensibly take on a yellow hue as the ammonia evaporates. They are to be exposed as equally as possible to a current of open air; and when the colour is well come out, and no longer heightens, they are to be washed and dried. Wool should be fulled in the ammoniacal solution, and should remain in it, until it is thoroughly soaked; then very slightly and uniformly pressed, or else merely set to drain of itself. Silk, cotton, hemp, and flax, are only to be dipped in the dying liquid, which they easily take. They must be then well pressed. The sulphuret arsenic will give every imaginable tint to stuffs, from the deep golden yellow, which has the invariable advantage of never fading, of lasting even longer than the stuffs themselves, and of resisting all re-agents, except alkalies. Hence it is peculiarly fitted for costly tapestry, velvets and other articles of furniture which are not in danger of being washed with alkalies or soap; and to which the durability of colour is a most important object. It may also be used with advantage in paper staining.

To die Woollens Red, Crimson and Scarlet. Coarse woollen stuffs are died red with madder, or archil; but fine cloth is almost exclusively died with cochineal, though the colour it receives from kermes is more durable. Brazil wood is scarcely used, excepting as an auxiliary, because the colour which it imparts to the wool is not permanent. Wool is died crimson, by first impregnating it with alumine, by means of an alum bath, and then boiling in a decoction of cochineal, till it has acquired the wished for colour. The crimson will be finer if the tin mordant is substituted for alum; indeed, it is usual with diers to add a little nitro-muriate of tin, when they want fine crimsons; the addition of archil and potash to the cochineal both render the crimson darker, and gives it the more bloom. But the bloom very soon vanishes. For the paler crimsons, only one half of the cochineal is withdrawn, and madder substituted in its place. Wool may be died scarlet, by first boiling it in a solution of murio-sulphate of tin, then dying it pale yellow with quercitron bark, and afterwards crimson with cochineal, for scarlet is a compound colour, consisting of crimson mixed with a little yellow.

To carry the Colour into the body of the Cloth. Make the moistened cloth pass through between rollers placed within and at the bottom of the die vat, so that the web, passing from one windlass thro' the die vat, and being strongly compressed by the rollers in its passage to another windlass, all the remaining water is driven out, and is replaced by the colouring liquid, so as to receive colour to its very centre. The winding should be continued backwards and forwards from one windlass to the other, and through the rolling press, till the die is of sufficient intensity.

To die Silks Red, Crimson, &c. Silk is usually died red with cochineal, or carthamus, and sometimes with Brazil wood. Kermes does not answer for silk. Madder is scarcely ever used for that purpose, because it does not yield a colour bright enough. Archil is employed to give silk a bloom; but it is scarcely ever used by itself, unless when the colour wanted is lilac. Silk may be died crimson by steeping it in a solution of alum, and then dying it in the usual way, in a cochineal bath. The colours known by the name of poppy, cherry, rose, and flesh colour are given to silks by means of carthamus. The process consists merely in keeping the silk, as long as it extracts any colour in an alkaline solution of carthamus, into which as much lemon juice as gives it a fine cherry red colour, has been poured. Silk cannot be died a full scarlet; but a colour approaching to scarlet may be given to it, by first impregnating the stuff with murio-sulphate of tin, and afterwards dying it in a bath, composed of four parts of cochineal, and four parts of quercitron bark. To give the colour more body, both the mordant and the die may be repeated. A colour approaching scarlet may be given to silk, by first dying it in crimson, then dying it with carthamus; and lastly, yellow without heat.

To die Linens and Cottons Red, &c. Cotton and linen are died red with madder. The process was borrowed from the east; hence the colour is often called Adrianople, or Turkey red. The cloth is first impregnated with oil, then with galls, and lastly with alum. It is then boiled for an hour in a decoction of madder, which is commonly mixed with a quantity of blood. After the cloth is died, it is plunged into a soda lie, in order to heighten the colour. The red given by this process is very permanent, and when properly conducted, it is exceedingly beautiful. The whole difficulty consists in the application of the mordant, which is by far the most complicated in the whole art of dying. Cotton may be died scarlet, by means of murio-sulphate of tin, cochineal, and quercitron bark, used as for silk, but the colour is too fading to be of any value.

Black Die. The substances employed to give a black colour to cloth, are red oxyde of iron, and tan. These two substances have a strong affinity for each other, and when combined, assume a deep black colour, not liable to be destroyed by the action of air or light. Logwood is usually employed as an auxiliary, because it communicates lustre, and adds considerably to the fulness of the black. The decoction is at first a fine red, bordering on violet; but if left to itself, it gradually assumes a black colour. Acids give it a deep red colour, alkalies, a deep violet, inclining to brown; sulphate of iron renders it as black as ink, and occasions a precipitate of the same colour. Cloth before it receives a black colour, is usually died blue; this renders the colour much fuller and finer than it would otherwise be. If the cloth is coarse, the blue die may be too expensive; in that case, a brown colour is given, by means of walnut peels.

To die Woollens Black. Wool is died black by the following process. It is boiled for two hours in a decoction of nutgalls, and afterwards kept, for two hours more, in a bath, composed of logwood and sulphate of iron; kept during the whole time, at a scalding heat, but not boiling. During the operation, it must be frequently exposed to the air; because the green oxyde of iron, of which the sulphate is composed, must be converted into red oxyde, by absorbing oxygen, before the cloth can acquire a proper colour. The common proportions, are five parts galls, five sulphate of iron, and thirty of logwood for every hundred of cloth. A little acetate of copper is commonly added to the sulphate of iron, because it is thought to improve the colour.

To die Silks Black. Silk is died nearly in the same manner. It is capable of combining with a great deal of tan; the quantity is varied at the pleasure of the artist, by allowing the silk to remain a longer or a shorter time in the decoction.

To die Cottons and Linens Black. The cloth previously died blue, is steeped for twenty-four hours in a decoction of nutgalls. A bath is prepared, containing acetate of iron, formed by saturating acetous acid with brown oxyde of iron; into this bath the cloth is put, in small quantities at a time, wrought with the hand for a quarter of an hour; then wrung out and aired again; wrought in a fresh quantity of the bath, and afterwards aired. These alternate processes are repeated till the colour wanted is given; a decoction of alder bark is usually mixed with the liquor containing the nutgalls.

To die Wool, &c. Brown. Brown or fawn colour, though in fact, a compound, is usually ranked among the simple colours, because it is applied to cloth by a single process. Various substances are used for brown dies. Walnut peels, or the green covering of the walnut, when first separated, are white internally, but soon assume a brown, or even a black colour, on exposure to the air. They readily yield their colouring matter to water. They are usually kept in large casks, covered with water, for above a year before they are used. To die wool brown with them, nothing more is necessary, than to steep the cloth in a decoction of them, till it has acquired the wished for colour.

S

The depth of the shade is proportioned to the strength of the decoction. The root of the walnut tree contains the same colouring matter, but in a smaller quantity. The bark of the birch also, and many other trees, may be used for the same purpose.

To die Compound Colours. Compound colours are produced by mixing together two simple ones; or which is the same thing by dying cloth first of the simple colour, and then by another. These colours vary to infinity, according to the proportions of the ingredients employed. From blue, red and yellow, *red olives*, and *greenish greys* are made.

From blue, red and brown, *olives* are made from the lightest to the darkest shades; and by giving a greater shade of red, the *slated* and *lavender greys* are made.

From blue, red and black, *greys* of all shades are made, such as *sage*, *pigeon*, *slate* and *lead greys.*

From yellow, blue and brown, are made *olives* of all kinds.

From brown, blue and black, are produced *brown olives*, and their shades.

From red, yellow and brown, are derived the *orange*, *gold colour, dead carnations, cinnamon, fawn* and *tobacco*, by using two or three of the colours required.

From yellow, red and black, *browns* of every shade are made.

From blue and yellow, *greens* of all shades.

From red and blue, *purples* of all kinds are formed.

To die different shades of Green. Wool, silk and linen are usually died green, by giving them first a blue colour; and afterwards dying them yellow; when the yellow is first given, several inconveniences follow: the yellow partly separates again in the blue vat, and communicates a green colour to it, then rendering it useless for evey other purpose, except dying green. Any of the usual processes for dying blue and yellow may be followed, taking care to proportion the depth of the shades to that of the green required. When sulphate of indigo is employed, it is usual to mix all the ingredients together, and to die the cloth at once; this produces what is known by the name of Saxon, or English green.

To die Violet, Purple, and Lilac. Wool is generally first died blue, and afterwards scarlet, in the usual manner. By means of cochineal mixed with sulphate of indigo, the process may be performed at once.

Silk is first died crimson by means of cochineal, and then dipped into the indigo vat. Cotton and linen are first died blue, and then dipped in a decoction of logwood, but a more permanent colour is given by means of oxyde of iron.

To die Olive, Orange, and Cinnamon. When blue is combined with red and yellow on cloth, the resulting colour is olive. Wool may be died orange, by first dying it scarlet, and then yellow. When it is died first with madder, the result is a cinnamon colour. Silk is died orange by means of carthamus; a cinnamon colour by logwood, Brazil wood, and fustic, mixed together. Cotton and linen receive a cinnamon colour by means of weld and madder; and an olive colour by being passed through a blue, yellow, and then a madder bath.

To die Grey, Drab, and dark Brown. If cloth is previously combined with brown oxyde of iron, and afterwards died yellow with quercitron bark, the result will be a drab of different shades, according to the proportion of mordant employed. When the proportion is small, the colour inclines to olive, or yellow; on the contrary, the drab may be deepened, or *saddened* as the diers term it, by mixing a little sumack with the bark.

To die Olives, Bottle Greens, Purples, Browns, Cinnamons, or Snuffs. Take common iron liquor, or alum dissolved in it, a quantity of each according to the shade wanted, made into a paste or liquid by adding flour, gum, glue, linseed, or one or more of them. Then put the composition into a tub connected with a machine used for such purposes; take them from the machine, and hang them up in a very cool room: where they should remain until dry. Take cow's manure, put it into a large copper of hot water, and mix well together; through which pass the cloth, until thoroughly softened. After this process, cleanse the goods; then take a liquor made of madder, logwood, sumach, fustic, Brazil wood, quercitron bark, peach, or other woods, to produce the colour wanted, or more of them; and if necessary dilute this liquor with water, according to the shade or fulness of the colour wanted to be died. Then work the goods through this liquor; after which pass them through cold or warm water, according to colour, the proper application of which is well known to diers, adding a little alum, copperas, or Roman vitriol, or two or more of them first dissolved in water. Then wash them off in warm water, and dry them. But if the colour is not sufficiently full, repeat the same operation till it is brought to the colour required.

To die a Black upon Cotton, Linen, and mixed Goods, is effected by tar and iron liquor of the best quality, adding to each gallon of the mixture, a pound of fine flour. Some take common iron liquor, and add three quarters of fine flour, and by boiling, bring it to the consistence of a thin paste, or instead of flour, add glue or linseed, or gum, or all of them mixed together, and brought to a proper thickness. The rest of the process is conducted in a similar manner to the last.

To die Crimson, Red, Orange, or Yellow. Take red liquor, such as is generally made from alum, and dilute it with water according to the strength or shade of colour wanted to die, bringing it to the consistency of a paste or liquid, as before described; then pass the cloth through the machine, which, being dried in a cool room, pass it through the operation as described in the article on olives, bottle greens, &c. then take a quantity of liquor made of cochineal, madder, peach wood, Brazil, logwood, woad, fustic, sumach, or any two or more of them, proportioned in strength, to the shade or colour wanted to die, and work the goods through this liquor, till they are brought to the shade of colour required; then wash them in cold or warm water and dry them.

To die Cotton, Wool, and Silk with Prussian blue. Immerse the cotton in a large tub of water slightly acidulated and charged with Prussiate of potash. These sorts of stuffs died in Prussian blue, and then in olive transformed into green, are particularly sought after in trade. By processes analogous to those employed for common stuffs, the inventor has obtained the same shades and colours, on samples of silk; and for many years he has succeeded in fixing Prussian blue on wool; and in producing on cloth the same shades, as on cotton and silk.

To precipitate Acetates of Lead and Copper on Wool, Silk, and Cotton. Soap the stuff to be died, in a solution of acetate, or rather, sub-acetate of lead, wring it when taken out of the bath, dry in the shade; then wash it and immerse it in water charged with sulphuretted hydrogen gas. This process produces in a few minutes, rich and well laid shades, which vary from the clear *vigone* colour, to the deep brown, according to the force of the mordant, and the number of the immersions of the stuffs in the two bathing vessels. From the order of affinities, it is the wool which takes colour the best, afterwards the silk, then the cotton, and lastly the thread which appears little apt to combine with the mordant. The different colours above indicated resist the air well, likewise feeble acids, alkalies, and boiling soap, which modify their shades in an imperceptible manner, and these shades are so striking, that it will appear difficult to obtain them in any other way.

This new kind of die is very economical; the sulphuretted hydrogen gas is obtained from a mixture of two parts of iron filings and one of brimstone, melted in a pot; the brimstone is bruised, introduced into a matrass, and the gas is removed by sulphuric acid, extended in water to a mild heat. The gas absorbs abundantly in cold water.

To die Cotton Cloth Black. Take a quantity of Molacca nuts, and boil them in water, in close earthen vessels, with the leaves of the tree. During the boiling, a whitish substance, formed from the mucilage and oil of the nuts, will rise to the surface; this must be taken off and preserved. The cloth intended to be black must be printed with this scum, and then died, after which, let it be passed through limewater, when the painted figures will be changed to a full and permanent black.

To die Wool a permanent Blue colour. Take four ounces of the best indigo, reduce it to a fine powder and add twelve pounds of wool, in the grease; put the whole into a copper large enough to contain all the wool to be died. As soon as the requisite colour is obtained, let the wool be well washed and dried. The liquor remaining, may be again used, to produce lighter blues. The colour will be very beautiful, and permanent as the finest blue produced by woad; and the wool, by this method will lose less in weight, than if it had been previously scoured.

To produce the Swiss deep and pale red topical Mordants. When the cloth has been freed by steeping and boiling in soap and water, from the paste used by the weaver, and any other impurities it may have acquired, immerse it thoroughly, or as it is called, tramp or pad it in a solution of any alkali, and oil or grease, forming an imperfect soap, or boil in a perfect soap dissolved in water, or in a solution of soda and gallipoli oil, in the proportion of one gallon of oil to twenty gallons of soda lees, at the strength of four degrees and a half; then dry the cloth in the stove, and repeat the process several times, which may be varied at pleasure, according to the lustre and durability of the colour wanted, stove drying the cloth between every immersion. To the above solutions a little sheep's manure for the first three immersions; after the cloth has been immersed in these liquors, steep it in a quantity of water, for twelve hours, at 110°, Fahrenheit; the cloth being again stove dried is immersed in a solution of alkali and oil, or grease, or boiled in perfect soap dissolved; which process must be repeated, according to the brilliancy of the colours wanted; stone drying as before between every immersion; these are called the *white liquors.* Steep the cloth for twelve hours, at 125° Fahrenheit, which forms what is called the white steep. The cloth being now thoroughly washed in cold water, and dried, is ready to receive, first, the pink mordant, composed as follows: equal quantities by measurement of a decoction of galls, at the strength of four to six, and a solution of alum at one half degree, the alum being previously saturated with whitening, or any other alkali, in the proportion of one ounce to the pound weight of alum; mix them together, and raise the temperature to 140°, of Fahrenheit, or as hot as can be handled. By immersion, as formerly mentioned in this mixture, the cloth when died and cleared, exhibits a beautiful pink, equal, if not superior to that produced by cochineal.

To die Silks and Satins Brown, in the small way. Fill the copper with river water; when it gently boils, put in a quarter of a pound of chipped fustic, two ounces of madder, one ounce of sumach, and half an ounce of camwood, but if it is not required to be so red, the camwood may be omitted. These should boil at least, from half an hour to two hours, that the ingredients may be well incorporated. The copper must then be cooled down by pouring in cold water; the goods may then be put in and simmered gently from half to an hour.

If this colour should appear to want darkening, it may be done by taking out the goods; and adding a small quantity of old black liquor; a small piece of green copperas may be used; rinse in two or three waters, and hang up to dry.

To die Silk Fawn Colour Drabs. Boil one ounce fustic, half an ounce of alder bark, and two drachms of archil From one to four drachms of the best madder must be added to a very small quantity of old black liquor, if it be required darker.

To die a Silk Shawl Scarlet. Dissolve two ounces of white soap in boiling water, handle the shawl through the liquor, rubbing such places with the hands as may appear dirty. A second or third liquor may be used, if required; after which rinse out the shawl in warm water. Then take half an ounce of the best Spanish arnotto, dissolve it in hot water; pour the solution into a pan of warm water, handle the shawl in it a quarter of an hour, then rinse it in clean water. In the meanwhile dissolve a piece of alum, of the size of a horse bean in warm water, let the shawl remain in this half an hour, then rinse it in clean water. Now boil a quarter of an ounce of the best cochineal for twenty minutes, dip it out of the copper into a pan, let the shawl remain in this from twenty minutes to half an hour, when it will become a blood red: then take it out and add to the liquor in the pan, a quart more out of the copper, if there is as much remaining, and about half a small wine glass full of the solution of tin; when cold, rinse it out slightly in cold water.

To die a Silk Shawl Crimson. Take about a tablespoonful of cudbear, put it into a small pan, pour boiling water upon it, stir and let it stand a few minutes, then put in the silk, and turn it over a short time, and when the colour is full enough, take it out; but if it should require more violet or crimson, add a spoonful or two of purple archil to some warm water, and dry it within doors. To finish, it must be calendered, and then pressed.

To die thick Silks, Satins, Silk Stockings, &c. Flesh Colour. Wash the stockings clean in soap and water, and rinse in hot water;

if they should not appear perfectly clear, cut half an ounce of white
soap into slices, put it into a sauce pan half full of boiling water; when
it is dissolved, cool the water in the pan, then put in the stockings,
and simmer twenty minutes, when they should be rinsed in hot water;
in the interim pour three table spoonfuls of purple archil into a wash
basin half full of hot water; die the stockings in this liquor, and when
nearly of the shade of half violet or lilac, slightly rinse them in cold
water; when dry, hang them up in a close room, in which sulphur is
burnt; when they are evenly bleached to the shade required, finish by
rubbing the right side with a flannel. Some prefer calendering them
afterwards. Satins and silks are done in the same way.

To die Silk Stockings Black. These are died like other silks, excepting they must be steeped a day or two in black liquor, before
they are put into the black silk die. At first they will look like an
iron grey, but to finish and black them, they must be put on wooden
legs, laid on a table and rubbed with the oily rubber or flannel, upon
which is oil of olives. For each pair it will require half a tablespoon-
full of oil, and half an hour's rubbing, to finish them well.

To die Straw and Chip Bonnets Black. Chip hats are stained black
in various ways.   1st. By being boiled in strong logwood liquor three
or four hours; they must be often taken out to cool in the air, and occasionally a small quantity of copperas must be added. The bonnets may be kept in the vessel containing the liquor one night, and in
the morning dried in the air, and brushed with a soft brush. Lastly, a
sponge is dipped in oil, and squeezed almost to dryness; with this rub
them all over. Some boil them in logwood, and instead of copperas,
use steel filings steeped in vinegar; when they are finished as above.

To die Black Cloth Green. Clean the cloth well with bullock's gall
and water; rinse in warm water; make a copper full of river water boiling hot, and take from one to one pound and a half of fustic; add to the
water, and boil twenty minutes; put in a lump of alum of the size of a
walnut; when dissolved, put in the article to be died, and boil twenty
minutes; then take it out, and add a small wine glass three parts full
of chemic blue, and boil again from half to an hour, when the cloth
will become a beautiful green; then wash out and dry.

CHAPTER XXV.

ARTIST AND MECHANIC.

It is well understood that artificers, or artisans, or mechanics, are
those who carry on any mechanical trade; that they are very numerous in all great trading states and empires; still, perhaps, their importance in society is not generally considered by those, who move (in
what is said to be) a more exalted sphere of life; or more likely, by
those *who flatter themselves* that they have been cast in finer moulds.
It is not expected, that this essay will be very gratifying to the taste
of those *gentlemen*, who measure their consequence either by their
cash or garb; but we hope it will contribute in some measure to produce a better feeling, in regard to those very useful citizens, the
mechanics, and lead all to examine, if they are not alloyed with more
human vanity than ordinarily becomes them. We have not been un-
mindful of the usefulness of the mechanic in former chapters; and we

again repeat, it surpasses our wisdom to answer, why they are not entitled to as much respectability as any class of our citizens? As things are constituted at present among the trading countries of the world, those which subsist upon their natural productions, or merely by bartering or exchanging such commodities, for those of other countries, have never distinguished themselves as a trading people. The Indians in North America, as well as the Negroes in Africa, are plain instances of the fact. If the Chinese were deprived of their useful artificers, (or if you please, manufacturers, for, they may as reasonably be called the one as the other, though custom among us has made a distinction,) they would very probably degenerate into the like savage dispositions with the wildest Africans, or American Indians. And this we presume, also, might be the case with the citizens of the United States. It is the arts which keep the mass of people in useful action, and which keep their minds also on useful invention, beneficial to the whole community; consequently, this is the grand preservative against that barbarism, brutality and a slothfulness in trade, which ever attend an indolent and inactive stupidity. The due cultivation of practical manual arts in a nation, has a greater tendency to polish, and humanize mankind, than mere speculative science, however refined and sublime it may be; and these arts are not only the most naturally adapted to the bulk of the people, but by giving real existence to their ideas, by their practical inventions, improve their minds more sensibly and feelingly, than any ideal contemplation could do, which may have no other being, but in the mind of the speculator. Moreover, it is observable, that those who are fruitful in useful inventions and discoveries, in the practical mechanical arts, are men, not only of the greatest utility, but possess an understanding, which should be most highly estimated. Whether this may be attributed to the constant exercise of their intellectual faculties in those things which they *see* and *feel*, may deserve the consideration of those who contemplate on the most natural way of improving the mind.

The delicate mechanism of a watch, by those great artists, a Graham, or an Ellicot, demonstrate the utility of such artisans to a trading country, as their workmanship is admired amongst all the civilized world. It is the same by other artificers who excel in their peculiar branch. This not only brings credit and honour, but treasures into a nation, in proportion as they are stocked with such celebrated mechanics or artificers. An English writer says, "nothing is more obvious than that the commerce and navigation of the nation, principally depends on the daily improvement made by our artificers, in the infinite and amazing variety in our mechanic and manufactural arts; wherefore, artists, who strike out new inventions, or who improve the old mechanics and manufactures, are deserving of some regard and encouragement, more than they acquire to themselves, by dint of their own peculiar profession only." Experience has manifested the extraordinary effect of those small rewards given in Scotland and Ireland, for the improvement of their manufactures; though it is not always the case, that premiums operate so powerfully, as the motive of emulation; for that credit and reputation, which attends a man's excelling in his employment, has, sometimes, a far greater influence upon the industrious and ingenious mind, than pecuniary rewards only.

Yet these are not to be neglected in trading nations; as it is most commonly the case, that new inventions or improvements, made by one for the benefit of trade, are soon enjoyed equally by all; the inventors very rarely, being able to preserve the benefit to themselves, scarce ever long enough to recompense for the time and expense they have generally been obliged to bestow upon them.

Was it fashionable once for persons of distinctions to devote a proportion of their rural retirements, to practical or experimental philosophy, it might not only prove a salubrious bodily exercise to them, but a great benefit and advantage to our artificers in general, and consequently to the general trade and traffic of the country.

An European author writes, "the mechanic inventions are improved by others, besides the common artificers themselves. This will undeniably appear," says he, " if we will be convinced by instances; for it is evident diverse sorts of manufactures have been given us, by men who were not bred up in trades that resembled those which they discovered. I shall mention three, that of printing, powder and bowdie. The admirable art of composing letters, so far from being started by a man of learning, was the device of a soldier; and powder, to make recompense, was invented by a monk, whose course of life was most averse from handling the materials of war. The ancient Tyrian purple was brought to light by a fisher; and if ever it can be recovered, it is likely to be done by some such accident." The scarlet of the moderns is a very beautiful colour, and it was the production of a chemist and not of a dier. The warmth and vigour which attend new discoveries, is seldom confined to its own sphere; but is generally extended to the ornament of its neighbour. The ordinary method in which this happens, is the introduction of new arts. It is true, indeed, the increase of tradesmen, is an injury to others that are bred up in particular trades, if they are enabled to supply all demands in their various branches; but there can never be too great a surplus of trades. That country is still the richest, and most powerful, which produces and employs the greatest number of artificers and manufacturers.

The hands of men employed, are true riches; the saving of these hands by invention of arts, and applying them to other works, will increase those riches. Where this is done, there will never a sufficient subject for profit be wanting; for, if there be not vent for their productions at home, we shall have it abroad. Thus, in those districts where commerce and manufactures do not flourish to any degree, we find exchange in favour of those places, where they are more extended; hence we learn the balance of trade, particularly in manufactures, is against us, and in favour of Great Britain; but we need not cross the Atlantic to maintain our position, for the argument is applicable to the middle and southern in favour of the New England states; to those who negotiate in bills of exchange, this subject cannot be new, as well as a fact too plain not to have been evident. Where the ways of life are few, the fountains of profit will be possessed by few; whence it is manifest that poverty among a people is caused by a small number, not by having a multitude engaged in a variety of trades. An English writer asserts, that, by the increase of artificers and manufacturers, all things will be dearer, because more must be maintained; for the high rate of things is an argument of the flourishing, and the cheapness, of the scarcity of money, and ill-peopling of all countries. The first is a sign of many inhabitants, which is true greatness, the second is only a fit subject for poets to describe, and to compare to their golden age; for, where all things are without price or value, they will be without arts, or empire, or strength." From the sentiments of this zealous promoter of the useful arts, for the benefit of commerce, it is evident that he makes the prosperity of a trading nation to consist in the multiplying of the number of new trades; that is to say, in multiplying the different species of mechanics, artificers and manufacturers; it is for want of this, that all the old ways of gain become overstocked, and then people complain for want of trade, when the true cause is owing to the want of art, or to the want of the invention of a number of new trades, and new arts, in proportion to the increase of population, and in proportion as other rival states strike into the like trades and arts, with similar advantages. Finally, if our labourers are as diligent as our lawgivers, we shall prove the most laborious, if not the most wealthy nation under heaven. But the true method of increasing industry, and improvement, and wealth, and respectability, is that which was recommended by the Royal Society of London, "by *works and endeavours*, and not be the prescriptions *of words, or paper commands*."

CHAPTER XXV.
THE ART OF CALICO PRINTING.

This art consists in dying cloth with certain colours and figures upon a ground of a different hue: the colours, when they will not take hold of the cloth readily, being fixed to them by means of mordants, as a preparation of alum made by dissolving three pounds alum and one pound of acetate of lead, in eight pounds of warm water. There are added at the same time, two ounces of potash, and two ounces of chalk. Acetate of iron, is also a mordant in frequent use; but the simple mixture of alum and acetate of lead, is found to answer best as a mordant. The mordants are applied to the cloth, either with a pencil, or by means of blocks, on which the pattern, according to which the cotton is to be printed is applied, is cut. As they are applied to only particular parts of the cloth, care must be taken that none of them spread to the part of the cloth which is to be left white, and that they do not interfere with another, when several are applied; it is necessary, therefore, that the mordants should be of such a degree of consistence, that they will not spread beyond those parts of the cloth, on which they are applied. This is done by thickening them with flour or starch, when they are to be applied by the block, and with gum arabic when they are to be put on with the pencil. The thickening should never be greater than is sufficient to prevent the spreading of the mordants; when carried too far, the cotton is apt not to be sufficiently saturated with the mordants, and of course the die takes but imperfectly. In order that the parts of the cloth impregnated with mordants may be distinguished by their colour, it is usual to tinge them with some colouring matter. A decoction of Brazil wood is generally used for this purpose. After the mordants have been ap-

T

plied, the cloth must be completely dried. It is proper for this purpose to employ heat, which will contribute towards the separation of the acetous acid from its base, and towards its evaporation; by which means the mordant will combine in a greater proportion, and more intimately with the cloth. When the cloth is sufficiently dried, it is to be washed with warm water and cowdung, till the flour or gum employed to thicken the mordants which are uncombined with the cloth, are removed. After this the cloth is to be thoroughly rinsed in clear water. Indigo not requiring any mordant is commonly applied at once, either by a block or pencil. It is prepared by boiling it with potash, made caustic by quicklime and orpiment; the solution is afterwards thickened with gum. It must be carefully secluded from the air, otherwise the indigo would soon become regenerated, thus rendering the solution useless. Some have used coarse brown sugar instead of orpiment. It is equally efficacious in decomposing the indigo, and rendering it soluble, while it likewise serves all the purposes of gum.

To paint Yellow. For yellow, the block is besmeared with acetate of alumine. The cloth after receiving this mordant, is died with quercitron bark, and is then bleached.

Nankeen Yellow, is one of the most common colours on prints, is a kind of nankeen yellow, of various shades down to a deep yellowish brown or drab. It is usually in stripes or spots. To produce it, besmear a block, cut out into the figure of a print, with acetate of iron, thickened with gum or flour; and apply it to the cotton, which after being dried and cleansed in the usual manner, is plunged into a potash lye. The quantity of acetate of iron is always proportioned to the depth of the shade.

Red, is communicated by the same process, only madder is substituted for the bark.

Blue. The fine light blues which appear so frequently on printed cottons, are produced by applying to the cloth a block besmeared with a composition, consisting partly of wax, which covers all those parts of the cloth which remain white. The cloth is then died in a cold indigo vat; and after it is dry, the wax composition is removed by hot water.

Lilac and Brown. Lilac, fleece brown, and blackish brown, are given by means of acetate of iron; the quantity of which is always proportioned to the depth of shade. For very deep colours a little sumach is added. The cotton is afterwards died in the usual manner with madder, and then bleached.

Green. To twelve quarts of muriatic acid, add by degrees one quart of nitrous acid; saturate the whole with grain tin, and boil it in a proper vessel, till two thirds are evaporated. To prepare the indigo for mixing with the solution, take nine pounds of indigo, half a pound of orange opiment, and grind it in about four quarts of water; mix it well with the indigo, and grind the whole in the usual way.

To mix the solution of Tin with prepared Indigo. Take two gallons of the indigo prepared as above, then stir into it by degrees, one gallon of the solution of tin, neutralized by as much caustic alkali as can be added without precipitating the tin from the acids. For a lighter shade of green, less indigo will be necessary. The goods are to be dipped in the way of dipping China blues; they must not however be allowed to drain, but moved from one vat to another as quickly as possible. They are to be cleansed in the usual way, in a sour vat of about one hundred and fifty gallons of water to one gallon of sulphuric acid; they are then to be well washed in decoctions of weld, and other yellow colour drugs, then branned or bleached till they become white in those parts which are required colourless.

To print Dove Colour and Drab. Dove colour and drab are given by acetate of iron, and quercitron bark; the cloth is afterwards prepared in the usual manner.

To print different Colours. When different colours are to appear in the same print, a greater number of operations are necessary. Two or more blocks are employed: upon each of which, that part of the print only is cut, which is to be of some particular colour. These are besmeared with different mordants, and applied to the cloth, which is afterwards died as usual. Let us suppose for instance, that those blocks are applied to cotton, one with acetate of alumine, another with acetate of iron, a third with a mixture of those two mordants, and that the cotton is then died with quercitron bark, and bleached. The parts impregnated with the mordants, would have the following colours:

Acetate of alumine,	Yellow.
" iron,	Olive, drab, dove.
The mixture,	-Olive green, olive.

If the part of the yellow is covered over with the indigo liquor, applied with a pencil, it will be converted into green. By the same liquid, blue may be given to such parts of the print as require it. If the cotton is died with madder, instead of quercitron bark; the print will exhibit the following colours:

Acetate of alumine,	Red.
" iron,	Brown, black.
The mixture,	Purple.

When a greater number of colours are to appear; for instance, when those communicated by bark, and those by madder are wanted at the same time, mordants for parts of the pattern are to be applied, the cotton then is to be died in the madder bath, and bleached; then the rest of the mordants, to fill up the patterns, are added, and the cloth is again died with quercitron bark, and bleached.

The second dying does not so much affect the madder colours; because the mordants, which render them permanent, are already saturated. The yellow tinge is already removed, by the subsequent bleaching. Sometimes a new mordant is applied to some of the madder colours, in consequence of which, they receive a new permanent colour from the bark. After the last bleaching, new colours may be added, by means of the indigo liquor. The following table will give an idea of the colours which may be given to cotton by these processes.

I. *Madder Die.*	Acetate of alumine,	Red.
	" iron,	Brown, black.
	" diluted,	Lilac.
	Both mixed,	Purple.
II. *Black Die.*	Acetate of alumine,	Yellow.
	iron,	Dove, drab.

Lilac and acetate of alum.   Olive.
Red and acetate of alum.   Orange.
III. *Indigo Die.*   Indigo,   Blue.
           Indigo and yellow,   Green.

To prepare a Substitute for Gum, used in Calico Printing. Collect half a ton weight of scraps of pelts or skins, or pieces of rabbit or sheep skins, and boil them for seven or eight hours, in 350 gallons of water, or until it becomes a strong size. Then draw it off, and when cold weigh it. Warm it again, and to every hundred weight, add the strongest sweetwort, that can be made from malt, or twenty pounds weight of sugar. When incorporated, take it off, and put it into a cask for use. This substitute for gum may be used by calico printers in mixing up nearly all kinds of colours. By using only a sixth part of gum with it, it will also improve the gum, and be a saving of 200 per cent. and without gum, of 400 per cent. It will also improve and preserve the paste so much used by printers.

To prepare Arnotto for Dying. Arnotto is a colouring fecula of a resinous nature, extracted from the seeds of a tree very common in the West Indies, and which in height never exceeds fifteen feet. The Indians employ two processes to obtain the red fecula of these seeds. They first pound them, and mix them with a certain quantity of water, which in the course of five or six days, favours the progress of fermentation. The liquid then becomes charged with the colouring part, and the superfluous moisture is afterwards separated by slow evaporation over the fire, or by the heat of the sun. The second process consists in rubbing the seeds between the hands in a vessel filled with water. The colouring part is precipitated, and forms itself into a mass like a cake of wax; but if the red fecula, thus detached, is much more beautiful than in the first process, it is less in quantity. Besides as the splendour of it is too bright, the Indians are accustomed to weaken it by a mixture of red sandal wood.

The natives of the East India islands used formerly to employ arnotto for painting their bodies, &c. At present in Europe it is only employed to give the first tints to woollen stuffs, intended to be died red, blue, yellow, green, &c. In the art of the varnisher, it forms part of the composition of changing varnishes, to give a gold colour to the metals on which these varnishes are applied.

To prepare Dying Materials, &c. Arnotto ought to be chosen of a flame colour, brighter in the interior part than on the outside; soft to the touch, and of a good consistence. The paste of arnotto becomes soft in Europe; and it loses some of its odour, which approaches near to that of violets.

Of Litmus. The Cape de Verd islands produce a kind of lichen or moss, which yields a violet colouring part, when exposed to the contact of ammonia disengaged from urine, in a state of putrefaction, by a mixture of lime. When the processes are finished, it is known by the name of litmus. This article is prepared on a large scale at London, Paris, and Lyons. In the latter city, another kind of lichen, which grows on the rocks is prepared.

The ammonia joins the resinous part of the plant, develops its colouring part, and combines with it. In this state the lichen forms a paste of a violet red colour, interspersed with whitish spots, which give it a marbled appearance. Litmus is employed in dying, to communicate a violet colour to silk and woollen.

Of Saffron. The flowers of this plant contain two colouring parts, one soluble in water, which is thrown away; the other soluble in alkaline liquors. The latter colouring part becomes the basis of various beautiful shades of cherry colour, rose colour, &c. It is employed for dying feathers, and constitutes the vegetable red, or Spanish vermilion, employed by ladies to heighten their complexion. Carthamus cannot furnish its resinous colouring part, provided with all its qualities, until it has been deprived of that which is soluble in water. For this purpose, the dried flowers of the carthamus are enclosed in a linen bag, and the bag is placed in a stream of running water. A man with wooden shoes gets upon the bag every eight or ten hours, and treads it on the bank until the water expressed from it is colourless. These moist flowers, after being strongly squeezed in the bag, are spread out on a piece of canvass, extended on a frame, placed over a wooden box, and covered with five or six per cent. of their weight of carbonate of soda. Pure water is then poured over them; and this process is repeated several times, that the alkali may have leisure to become charged with the colouring part, which it dissolves. The liquor when filtered is a dirty red, and almost brown colour. The colouring part thus held in solution, cannot be employed for colouring bodies until it is free; and to set it at liberty, the soda must be brought into contact with a body which has more affinity for it.

It is on this precipitation, by an intermediate substance, that the process for making Spanish vermilion is founded, as well as all the results arising from the direct application of this colouring part in the art of dying.

Of Woad. The preparation for colouring is effected from the leaves of the plant, by grinding them to a paste, of which balls are made, placed in heaps, and occasionally sprinkled with water to promote the fermentation; when this is finished, the woad is allowed to fall into a coarse powder; used as a blue die stuff.

Of Indigo. This die is derived from the leaves of the young shoots of several species of the plant, by soaking them either in cold water, or still better, in water kept warm, and at about 160° Fahrenheit, till the liquor becomes a deep green; it is then drawn off, and the blue sediment dried, and formed into lumps.

Of Potatoe Tops, &c. Cut off the tops when they are in flower, and extract the juice, by bruising and pressing them. Linen or woollen imbibed in this liquor forty-eight hours, will take a brilliant, solid and permanent yellow. If the cloth be afterwards plunged in a blue die, it will acquire a beautiful permanent green colour. As to the mode of execution, it should pass through the hands of a chemist or skilful dier, to derive all the advantages it is capable of furnishing. To prepare cotton and linen to receive certain colours, particularly the red madder, and cross wort, the article of sheep's manure is made use of, as it forms, by impregnating the stuffs with an animal mucilage, of which it contains a large quantity, and thus assimilating them to wool and silk.

To print Carpets. These carpets are made of knitted wool, by means of a machine; they are afterwards pressed and receive all the colours and designs wished for. These designs printed on the tissue, by means of wooden boards, are extremely neat; the colours are very brilliant, and resist rubbing extremely well, provided they traverse the tissue from one part to another.   They are warm, and have the advantage of being cheaper than others.·   They are also as durable, and are not crossed by seams disagreeable to the eye.

CHAPTER XXVII.
FACTORS, AGENTS, &c.

It is generally considered that a factor is a merchant's agent, resident abroad, and constituted by letters of attorney to act for his principal; and one may act for several merchants, who all run a joint risk of his management; factorage is the allowance.   In this country, however, custom ha⸱ distinguished factors as commission merchants, particularly, when they receive goods to dispose of, for and on account, and at the risk of the consignor, or purchase goods to order at a stipulated or customary per centum for sales or services.   Various charges may arise on consignments exclusive of commissions, as a city and state tax, (particularly, in some places, when sales are effected at auction,) guarantee, &c. besides freight or portage, &c.   It is frequent in cases of consignment, to empower the agent to dispose of the goods without limitation in regard to prices, or terms of payment; that is, an agent may act independently, as if the property was his own; but still, it must be remembered, he is subject to a *governing principle*, not to effect a sale at less than a market price, or on an unusually extended term of credit, or for paper, which at the time of sale, would generally be considered, in that market, as doubted: in either case, he would make himself liable for damages to the amount the transaction produced.   In all cases of consignment it is not safe for a commission merchant to effect sales on a credit, without particular orders.

It has been adjudged by chief justice Holt, that every factor of common right shall sell for ready money; but if he be where the usage is to sell on a credit, then, if he sells to a person of undoubted credit, who afterwards becomes insolvent, he is discharged; but otherwise, if the man's credit was bad at the time of sale.   But if there is no such usage, and he on the general authority sells upon trust, he only is chargeable, however able the buyer is;   for having exceeded his authority, there is no contract between the vendee and the factor's principal, and such sale is a conversion in the factor.   *Pasch.* 13,*Will. III.*

If a factor selling goods on credit does, before payment die indebted by specialty more than his effects will pay, this money shall be paid to the principal, and not to the factor's administrator as part of his effects, deducting only the factor's commission.   *Decreed in Equity,* *Hill.* 1708, 2 *Vern.* 638.

If a factor give a man time for payment of money contracted on sale of his principal's goods, and after that time has elapsed, sells him goods of his own for ready money, and he becomes insolvent, the factor in equity and honesty should indemnify his principal, but he is not compelled by the common law.   *Molloy,* 440.

And if any factor sells goods for another, either by themselves, or among other things, not advising his principal, but dealing afterwards with the same man, he becomes insolvent, the factor shall be answerable, because he gave not the owner advice of the sale in due time.

and it is as if he had sold them contrary to commission, for the salary of factorage binds him to it. Also if by a merchant's commission he buys a commodity for his account, with the merchant's money or credit, and he give no advice of it, but sell it again for his own benefit, the merchant shall recover this benefit, and the factor shall likewise be amerced for the fraud.

If a factor by commission buys goods above the price limited to him, or not of the sort and goodness, as by the authority they ought to be, he must take them to his own account, and the merchant may disclaim the buying of them; as he may likewise, if they are shipped for another place than he ordered: but in such case if the price riseth, and the factor thereupon fraudulently ladeth them for some other port, the merchant may recover damages on proof.

A factor selling under the price limited to him, is to make good the difference, unless he gives a good reason for so doing. *Lex Mercat. Malines,* 82.

A factor, and assistant or apprentice differs in this, that the first is made by merchants' letters, to take commission, but the assistant or apprentice is retained with yearly wages, some without: a factor is answerable for loss sustained by misusing his commission, an assistant or apprentice only incurs displeasure; factors must therefore punctually observe their commissions. Factors, most commonly, deal for several; but a servant dealing for others by his master's direction, cannot be a subject for indemnification for losses, for he has only his master's credit; whereupon intimations, citations, attachments, and other lawful causes, are executed against servants and not against factors.

No factor, acting for account of another, can justify receding from his orders, though it might be to advantage, unless commissioned to act for the best. And hence, if four or five merchants remit to one factor four or five distinct parcels of goods, which he disposes jointly to one person, who pays one moiety down, and contracts for the rest at a certain time; before which if he break, the principals shall bear an equal share of loss. *Lex Mercat. Malines,* 81, 82.

If a factor sell at one time to one man, goods belonging to diverse, to be paid for in one or more payments, without distinction made by the buyer for what parcels he pays any sums in part, as shopkeepers do, the factor must make proportionable distribution of the monies received, according to the amount of each parcel, till all be paid; and if loss happen, or all be not paid, it is to be distributed in like manner.

As fidelity, diligence and honesty are expected from the factor, the law requires the like of the principal; if, therefore, a merchant remits counterfeit jewels to his factor, who sells them as if true, if he receives loss or prejudice by imprisonment or other punishment, shall not only make full satisfaction to the factor, but also to the party who bought the jewels: for he shall answer in all cases for his factor, where he is privy to the act or wrong. This was insisted on in the case of Southern vs. How, on a sale made to the king of Barbary; though in that case, after various arguments, given against the plaintiff. *2. Cro.* 468. *Bridgm.* 126, 128.

And so in contracts; if a factor buy goods on account of the principal, especially if used so to do, the contract shall oblige the principal, who is properly to be prosecuted for non-performance. But it has been held, if a factor or servant buy things generally, not declaring on the contract, that it is as a factor only, &c. he is chargeable in his own right. 2. *Keb.* 812.

The actions of factors depend on buying and selling, entering goods, freighting ships, and all other matters of commerce; and their trust being great, they should be provident, for the benefit of their principals. If goods sent to a factor, be through his negligence, false-ly entered, or landed without an officer of the customs, so as they in-cur a seizure, he shall make good the damage: but, if he make his entry according to the invoice, or advice by letter, and there happens a mistake, if any goods are lost, he shall be acquitted. *Lane's Rep.* 65.

If the principal order his factor to insure a ship and goods as soon as laden, having money in hand, and he neglect, if the ship miscarry, by the custom of merchants, he shall answer it; or if he make any composition with the insurers after insurance, without orders so to do, he is answerable for the whole insurance.

A factor entering into charter party of affreightment, with a master of a ship, it obligates him only; unless he lades abroad generally the principal's goods, when both principal and lading are liable and not the factor.

A merchant sends goods to his factor, and about a month after draws a bill on him; which having effects in hand, he accepts, the principal becomes a bankrupt, and the goods in the factor's hands are seized; it has been conceived, that, at law, the factor must answer the bill, and can come in only as a creditor, for what he paid by his ac-ceptance of it. *Molloy,* 442

Goods remitted to a factor must be carefully preserved; yet, if he buys for his principal, and they receive damage afterwards, but not through his negligence, the principal shall bear the loss.

A factor having made considerable profit for his principal, must be careful in the disposal of it. If he sells the principal's goods for coun-terfeit money, the loss is his own; but if he receives money, which is afterwards lessened in value where he resides, the loss is to the mer-chant.

A factor is accountable for all lawful goods coming safe to his hands, and shall suffer for not observing orders: if, having orders not to sell any goods particularly specified, he sells them, he is answerable for the damage that shall be received; goods bought or exchanged without orders the merchant may take or turn them on the factor's hands. And where a factor has bought or sold pursuant to orders, he must immediately give advice of it, lest they should be contradicted, and his reputation suffer: and he is to ship off goods bought, the first opportu-nity, giving the speediest advice, and sending a bill of lading.

Factors should carefully note the contents of their principal's let-ters, and send speedy and particular answers; and should study the nature, value, rise and fall of goods, both at home and abroad, and the want of frequent writing to their principals is often of pernicious con-sequence in diverse respects.

Where a factor deserves money for factorage, it is said he cannot bring an action for it, unless the principal refuse to account; and, if it appears that the factor hath money in his hands, he may detain, and cannot bring any action, but if directed to invest the amount of sales, he may bring an action for factorage, because he cannot detain, and hath no other remedy. *Combert*, 349.

If a factor, by error of account, wrongs a merchant, he is to make good, not only the principal, but interest for the time; and if the error be against himself, the merchant is to answer it in like manner.

CHAPTER XXVIII.
DISCOUNT AND COMMISSION.

Discount is a deduction from a given amount; it is applied in trans-actions between a *factor, commission merchant* or *auctioneer*, &c. and a *merchant* or *manufacturer;* for instance, A consigns B articles amounting to $100, orders sales to be effected at invoice prices, and agrees to discount 25 cents on the dollar for B's services: thus, it will be perceived the factor or agent, clears $33\frac{3}{10}$ per cent.

The principle of *commissions per centum*, in cases of consignment is founded upon the *buying* and *selling* of commodities; and is by some called *factorage*: thus, a merchant buys an article for $1, and sells the same for $1,25, he makes a profit of 25 per cent. if he sells what cost him 75 cents for $1, he clears $33\frac{3}{10}$ per cent. Hence, we learn there is a difference in the term *discount*, and that of commis-sions per cent. and that a commission per cent. is not to be under-stood, as it is generally, a discount on the dollar. It may perhaps be more clearly illustrated as follows: we will suppose A consigns B $1000 worth of goods, at 25 per cent. commission: (not 25 cents dis-count,) now, in order to ascertain the amount of B's commission, we say, as 1,25 is to 1 so is 1250 to 1000, or if $1,25 gives 25 per cent. so does $1000 with the same ratio of advance, produce the same re-sult: or thus, if $1 produces 25 cents, what does $1000? Evidently, $33\frac{3}{10}$ per cent. If $1,25 is only 25 per cent. what is the per cent on $1? As 1,25 is 25 so is 1,00, the answer is 20 per cent; or as 1250 is 25 so is 1000, producing the same answer; which also furnishes us with the fact that 25 per cent. commission, amounts to a discount of 20 cents on the dollar. We are aware that this subject is a matter of frequent disputation among mercantile men, but at the same time our statement is no less correct. We have availed ourselves of the opinion of some of the most eminent practical merchants, and are as-sured that they not only make the distinction, but that the merchants and manufacturers of Europe, govern themselves by the principles which we have laid down, in most instances.

To one who is unacquainted with mercantile transactions and cus-toms, we should suppose it would seem a singular operation to learn, that the merchant with cash furnishing himself with bills of parcels amounting to $1000, in order to make 25 per cent. had to sell them for $1250, while the commission merchant or factor, encountering no risk, either by the depreciation of property, or otherwise, makes the same total as the former in accomplishing a business of 25 per cent. less amount. Notwithstanding, custom may not give her sanction to the correctness of our statement, yet we have no doubt the laws would confirm the fact.

U

CHAPTER XXIX.

BLEACHING.

The mode of bleaching which least injures the texture of the cloth formed of vegetable substances, is that effected by merely exposing it in a moistened state to the atmosphere, having been steeped in a solution of potash or soda, but the length of time and other inconveniences attending this process, led to more active chemical processes. It is by the combination of oxygen with the colouring matter of the cloth, that it is deprived of its hue, and the different processes employed must be adapted to prepare it for this combination, and render it as perfect as as possible, without destroying its texture, an effect which, however, must necessarily ensue in a greater or less degree, from the union of oxygen with all bodies.

To bleach linen, &c. by oxymuriatic acid, it is necessary to ascertain its strength, in which a solution of indigo in the acid is employed. The colour of this is destroyed by the oxygenated muriatic acid; according to the quantity of it that can be discoloured by a given quantity of the liquor its strength is known. In this country, machinery is employed for rinsing and beating; the apparatus must be arranged according to the objects to be bleached; the skeins of thread must be suspended in the tub destined for them, and the cloth must be rolled upon reels in the apparatus. When every thing is thus disposed, the tubs are filled with oxygenated muriatic acid; by introducing a funnel, which descends to the bottom of the tub, in order to prevent the dispersion of gas. The cloth is wound on the frame work, on which the skeins are suspended, is turned several times, until it is judged, by taking out a small quantity of the liquor from time to time, and trying it by the test of the solution of indigo, that it is sufficiently exhausted.

The weakened liquor is then drawn off, and may be again used for a new saturation. In bleaching with the oxymuriate of lime, a large quantity of lime is combined with the oxymuriatic acid gas, to effect which, the lime is mechanically suspended in water, into which the gas is made to pass, and agitated; so as to present fresh matter to the gas. By this means the oxymuriate of lime is formed in a very convenient manner; it is dissolved in water, and used as a bleaching liquor. This liquor is preferable to the oxygenated muriatic acid and potash.

At the great bleach field in Ireland, four lyes of potash are applied alternately, with four weeks exposure on the grass, two immersions in the oxymuriate of lime, a lye of potash between the two, and the exposure of a week on the grass, between each lye and the immersion. During summer two lyes and fifteen days exposure are sufficient to prepare cloth for the oxygenated muriate; the three alternate lyes, with immersions in the liquor, will be sufficient to complete the bleaching; nothing then will be necessary, but to wind the cloth through the sulphuric acid.

The oxygenated muriatic gas may also be combined with lime in a dry state, or the water may be evaporated, when it is employed for the formation of oxymuriates, which may then be very conveniently transported to any distance without injury to its detersive power.

To prepare the sulphate of lime, take sulphur or brimstone in fine powder, four pounds; lime well slacked and sifted, twenty pounds; water sixteen gallons; these are to be well mixed, and boiled for half an hour in an iron vessel, stirring them briskly from time to time. Soon after the agitation of boiling is over, the solution of the sulphuret of lime clears, and may be drawn off free from the insoluble matter, which is considerable, and which rests upon the bottom of the boiler. The liquor in this state, is nearly the colour of small beer, but not so transparent. Sixteen gallons of fresh water are afterwards poured on the insoluble dregs in the boiler, in order to separate the whole of the sulphuret from them. When this clears, being previously agitated, it is drawn off and mixed with the first liquor. Thirty-three gallons more of water may be added to the liquor, thus reducing it to a proper standard for steeping the cloth; and which furnishes sixty gallons of liquor from four pounds of brimstone, making allowance for evaporation. When linen is freed from the weaver's dressing, it is to be steeped in the solution of sulphuret of lime (prepared as above) for about twelve or eighteen hours, then taken out and well washed. When dry, it is to be steeped in the oxymuriate of lime for twelve, or more hours, and then washed and dried. This process is to be repeated six times, that is, by six alternate immersions in each liquor, which has been found to whiten the linen.

Steam has lately been employed with great success. The process was brought from the Levant. Chapel first made it known to the public. The cloth is first immersed in a slight alkaline caustic liquor, and placed in a chamber constructed over a boiler, into which is put the alkaline lye, which is to be raised into steam, after the fire has been lighted, and the cloth has remained exposed to the action of the steam for a sufficient length of time, it is taken out and immersed in the oxygenated muriate of lime, and then exposed for two or three days on the grass. This operation, which is very expeditious, will be sufficient for cotton; but if linen cloth should retain a yellow tint, a second alkaline caustic vapour bath, and two or three days on the grass, will be sufficient to give it the necessary whiteness.

To bleach by alkalized steam, the high temperature swells up the fibres of the cloth; the pure alkali which rises with the elastic fluid, seizes with avidity on the colouring matter; and seldom does the tissue of the flax or hemp resist the penetrating effect of this vapour bath.

The alkali appears to have a much livelier and more caustic action, when it is combined with caloric, than in ordinary lyes, where the temperature never rises above 162° Fahrenheit. By making the cloth pass through the lye of oxygenated muriate of lime, an union is effected between the solution and the carbon, arising from the extracto-mucous matter of the flax; carbonic acid is formed; the water, even, in which this new compound is diluted, concurs to promote the combination; if the cloth is then exposed on the grass, the carbonic acid is dissipated, and the cloth is bleached.

To bleach Cotton. The first operation consists in scouring it in a slight alkaline solution; or what is better, by exposure to steam. It is then put into a basket, and rinsed in running water. The immersion of cotton in an alkaline lye, however it may be rinsed, always leaves with it an earthy deposite. It is well known that cotton bears the action of acids better than hemp or flax; that time is even necessary before the action of them can be prejudicial to it, and by taking advantage of this valuable property in regard to bleaching, means have been found to free it from the earthy deposite, by pressing down the cotton in a very weak solution of sulphuric acid, and afterwards removing the acid by washing, lest too long remaining in it should destroy the cotton.

To bleach Wool.   The first kind of bleaching to which wool is subjected, is to free it from grease. This operation is called scouring. In manufactories it is generally performed by ammoniacal lye, formed of five measures of river water, and one of stale urine; the wool is immersed for about twenty minutes, in a bath of this mixture, heated to fifty-six degrees; it is then taken out, suffered to drain, and then rinsed in running water; this manipulation softens the wool, and gives it the first degree of whiteness; it is then repeated a second, and even a third time, after which the wool is fit to be employed.   In some places scouring is performed with water slightly impregnated with soap; and, indeed, for valuable articles, this process is preferable, but too expensive for articles of less value.   Sulphurous acid gas unites very easily with water, and in this combination it may be employed for bleaching wool or silk.

The most economical way of preparing sulphurous acid, i b y decomposing the acid, by the mixture of any combustible matter, capable of taking from it any part of its oxygen.   When the chemist is desirous to have it in great purity, it is obtained by means of metallic substances, and particularly by mercury, but for the purpose of which we are treating, where great economy is required, we should recommend most common substances.   Take chopped straw, or saw dust, and introduce it into a matrass; pour over it sulphuric acid, applying at the same time heat, and there will be disengaged sulphurous acid gas, which may be combined with water in an apparatus.   The pieces are rolled upon reels, and are drawn through the acid by turning them until sufficiently white.   They are then taken out and left to drain on a bench covered with cloth, lest they should be stained in consequence of the decomposition of the wood by the sulphurous acid; they are then washed in river water, and Spanish white is employed, if it should be judged necessary.   This operation is performed by passing the pieces through a tub of clean water, in which about eight pounds of Spanish white has been dissolved.   To obtain a fine whiteness, the stuffs are generally twice sulphured.   According to this process, one immersion, and reeling two or three hours, are sufficient.   Azuring or bluing is performed by throwing into the Spanish white liquor, a solution of one part Prussian blue to four hundred of water; shaking the cloth in the liquid and reeling rapidly.   The operation is terminated by a slight washing with soap, to give softness and pliability to the stuffs.

A preparation of an improved bleaching liquor; is prepared as follows: by a dissolution in water of the oxygenated muriates of calcareous earths, barytes, strontites, or magnesia.   The earth should be prepared in the dry way, by bringing them in a solid form, in powder, or in paste, in contact with the oxygenated muriatic acid gas.   So prepared, dissolve them in water, and apply them to the substances required to be bleached.   By this mode, colours may be removed from linen, cotton, vegetable and other substances.   (*See also bleaching liquid, page* 45.   *To extinguish colours,* 43.)

To bleach Straw, &c. Cover the bottom of a small plate a quarter of an inch deep with water. Put a small piece of common brimstone upon a sheet iron bench set in the plate, which is sufficiently heated to inflame the brimstone, and shut it over a tubulated bell glass, or a tumbler with a hole in the bottom. This vessel must be of a size just to shut down within the rim of the plate. At first take the stopper out and raise the bell glass a little above the water, to give passage to a current of air. Regulate this by the progress of the burning sulphur. After the bell glass appears well filled with a white vapour, shut it down close and tighten the stopper. The water in the plate will absorb the sulphurous acid gas in about five minutes. Pour part of this water into wine glasses, and you will perceive the nauseous, sulphurous, astringent taste, peculiar to this acid. In the mean time wet several substances, coloured with vegetable colouring matter, and it will extinguish many of them if not all. A yellow straw braid becomes whitened in it; and some colours on calico will be extinguished. The liquid sulphurous acid loses this property by keeping.

It is used by milliners both in the liquid and in the gaseous state for bleaching straw bonnets. If the old straw braid is soaked a while in water and then suspended inside of a hogshead or barrel without a head, and brimstone is inflated at the bottom of a cask, and suffered to commence burning thoroughly, then the top covered over, the straw will soon become whitened by the action of this acid.

To whiten Wax. Melt it in a pipkin without boiling. Then take a wooden pestle, which steep in the wax two inches deep and plunge immediately in cold water, to loosen the wax from it, which will come off like sheets of paper. When you have got all of your wax out of the pipkin, and made into flakes, put it on a clean towel, and expose it in the air, on the grass, till it is white. Then melt it and strain it through a muslin, to take all the dust out of it, if there be any.

Method of purifying Tallow to make Candles. Take five eighths of tallow and three eighths of mutton suet; melt them in a copper cauldron with half a pound of grease; as soon as they are melted, mix eight ounces of brandy, one salts of tartar, one cream of tartar, one sal ammoniac, and two of pure dry potash: throw the mixture into the cauldron and make the ingredients boil a quarter of an hour; then let the whole cool. The next day the tallow will be found upon the surface of the water in a pure cake. Take it out and expose it to the action of the air, on canvass for several days. It will become white, and almost as hard as wax. The dew is very favourable to bleaching; make your wick of fine even cotton, give them a coat of melted wax; then cast your mould candles. They will have much the appearance of wax, and one of six to the pound, will burn fourteen hours and never run.

To make Mutton Suet Candles in imitation of Wax Candles.
1. Throw quicklime in melted mutton suet; the lime will fall to the bottom, and carry with it every impurity, so as to leave it pure and fine as wax itself.
2. Now if with one part of that suet you mix three of real wax, you will be unable to distinguish the mixture; even in the casting and moulding wax figures or ornaments.

CHAPTER XXX.
IMITATION SPIRITS.

We will observe in the article *on rectification*, that the common method of rectifying spirits from alkaline salts, destroys their vinosity, and in its stead introduces a lixivious taste. But as it is absolutely necessary to restore, or at least to substitute in its room, some degree of vinosity, several methods have been proposed, and a multitude of experiments performed, in order to discover this great desideratum: but none have succeeded equal to the spirit of nitre: and accordingly this spirit, either strong or dulcified, has been used by most distillers, to give an agreeable vinosity to their spirits. Several difficulties, however, occur in the method of using it, the principal of which is, its being apt to quit the liquor in a short time, and consequently depriving the liquor of that vinosity it was intended to give. In order to remove this difficulty, and prevent the vinosity from quitting the goods, the dulcified spirit of nitre, which is much better than the strong spirit, should be prepared by a previous digestion, continued some time with alcohol; the longer the digestion is continued, the more intimately will they be blended, and the compound rendered the milder and softer. After a proper digestion, the dulcified spirit should be mixed with the brandy, by which means the vinosity will be intimately blended with the goods, and disposed not to fly off for a very considerable time. No general rule can be given for the quantity of this mineral acid requisite to be employed, because different proportions of it are necessary in different spirits. It should however, be carefully adverted to, that tho' a small quantity of it will undoubtedly give an agreeable vinosity resembling that naturally found in the fine subtile spirits drawn from wines, yet an over large dose of it, will not only cause a disagreeable flavour, but also render the whole design abortive, by discovering the imposition. Those therefore, who endeavour to cover a foul taste in goods by large doses of dulcified spirit of nitre, will find themselves deceived.

But the best, and indeed the only method of imitating French brandies to perfection, is by an essential oil of wine; this being the very thing that gives the French brandies their flavour. It must however, be remembered, that in order to use this ingredient to advantage, a pure tasteless spirit must be first procured; for it is ridiculous to expect that this essential oil should be able to give the agreeable flavour of the French brandies, to our fulsome malt spirit, already loaded with its own nauseous oil, or strongly impregnated with a lixivious taste from the alkaline salts, used in rectification. How a pure insipid spirit may be obtained, will be given in the chapter on distillation. It only therefore remains to show the method of procuring the essential oil of wine, which is this. Take some cakes of dry wine lees, such as are used by hatters, dissolve them in six or eight times their weight of water, distil the liquor with a slow fire, and separate the oil by a separating glass; reserving for the nicest uses, that only which comes over first, the succeeding oil being coarser and more resinous.

Having procured this fine oil of wine, it may be mixed into a quintessence with pure alcohol; by which means it may be preserved a long time fully possessed of all its flavour and virtues; but without such management, it will soon grow resinous and rancid.

When a fine essential oil of wine is thus procured, and also a pure and insipid spirit, French brandies may be imitated to perfection with regard to the flavour. It must, however, be remembered, and carefully adverted to, that the essential oil be drawn from the same sort of lees as the brandy to be imitated was procured from: we mean in order to imitate *cogniac* brandy, it will be necessary to distil the essential oil from cogniac lees; and the same for any other kind of brandy. For as different brandies, have different flavours, and these flavours are owing entirely to the essential oil of the grape, it would be preposterous to endeavour to imitate the flavour of cogniac brandy, with an essential oil procured from the lees of Bordeaux wine. When the flavour of the brandy is well imitated by a proper dose of the essential oil, and the whole reduced into one simple and homogeneous fluid, other difficulties are still behind; the flavour, though the essential part, is not however the only one; the colour, the proof and the softness must be regarded, before a spirit, that perfectly resembles French brandy can be procured. With regard to the proof, it may be easily hit, by using a spirit rectified above proof; which after being intimately mixed with the essential oil of wine, may be let down to a proper standard by fair water. As the softness may in a great measure be obtained by distilling and rectifying the spirit with a gentle fire: and what is wanting of this criterion in the liquor, when first made, will be supplied by time; for it must be remembered, that it is time alone that gives this property to the French brandies; they being at first like our spirits, acrid, foul and fiery. But with regard to the colour, a particular colour is necessary to imitate it to perfection; and how that may be done is considered in the article on colouring spirits.

Our observations respecting the methods of imitating brandies, are not made with a view to favour impositions, by palming them off as real; but we are not sensible of the impropriety of selling them as *imitation spirits.*

We will further suggest to those, who, in order to reduce the price of spirits, mix some of the pure (the spirit which they wish to imitate) with neutral spirit, that quite an improvement can be made in imitating French brandies, by adding a small quantity of rich mountain Malaga wine, commonly called *sweet wine.* The experiment will convince us of the fact, though we still adhere to our first position, that the essential oil obtained from the lees of wine to be the best; but to those who do not deal largely, this last method may be substituted advantageously. The reader is also referred to remarks on apple spirit.

St. Croix Rum. Molasses spirit, commonly called New England rum, rectified, furnishes us undoubtedly with the best body for mixing. We have said, it is quite ridiculous to mix our *malt spirit* with brandies, and it is also true, in regard to the rum of the islands; however, we are sensible a great improvement may be made in neutralizing malt spirits, and that it is not a subject to be esteemed lightly by the distiller. The molasses spirit is manufactured from the same ingredient which the spirit we wish to combine with it, is obtained; the essential oil which gives the flavour to both spirits being the same; the difference then, must be produced by the different processes of manufacturing, and also the quality of the cane must be taken into consideration, even, as we have stated respecting the grape. Enough has already been said, to convince the reader quite a different flavoured spirit must be produced, by mixing malt spirit, with that obtained from cane, than they are intended to represent, when they are blended together. The best neutralized molasses spirit, can be obtained for ten cents per gallon more than that which is usually put up for the trade. It need not be said that the Boston market furnishes the best new rum, and that it produces also the best neutralized, of any which we have ever seen. It can easily be obtained at 60 per cent. above proof; there are considerable quantities manufactured of a very ordinary quality; consequently no article in commerce, requires more care in selecting. The purchaser will do well to observe, that the best is colourless, and free from a burnt or smoky flavour, which in either case, the spirit is unfit to mix.

St. Vincents is next in quality to St. Croix, admits of the same process as described above, in order to reduce the price. However, it must always be considered that much depends on the quality of the goods which you blend with the neutralized spirit; much care and experience is required in selecting that which is high scented and fine flavoured: the difference of cargoes in this respect, is more than we are generally inclined to admit. Hogsheads of rum of prime quality is a very scarce staple, and when found, it should be prized very highly; and indeed it is, by the city dealers, who are generally apprised of its worth; for it will certainly work up a great quantity of neutral rum advantageously.

Grenada Rum, can be imitated very well, with the neutralized molasses spirit, and a small quantity of very high flavoured Jamaica spirits.

Jamaica Spirits, if highly scented, are very much improved by adding the neutralized molasses spirit; the compound would be preferred by most palates, after acquiring a sufficient ripeness.

Neutralized molasses spirit of the first quality will pass for better Windward Island rum, than any rum of the Islands can, with the least addition of malt spirit.

Holland Gin, can be reduced in price, and a very fair flavour retained, by mixing it with that which is manufactured in our own country: some of the American is very nearly as good as imported; and would be quite, if the manufacturers were as careful as the Hollanders in manufacturing it: age, however, is a very necessary qualification to recommend all spirits.

Rectified Whiskey mixes with gin better than any other spirit; and if it must be resorted to, in order to reduce the price of the Holland gin, we would recommend a very small quantity of the oil of juniper, to be added, (first mixed with high wines, and then added to a small quantity of gin, when the whole may be put into the cask,) though we should prefer a few fresh juniper berries, when they can easily be obtained: mash them and digest in alcohol a short while, then pour the tincture into the cask.

CHAPTER XXXI.
CREDITS.

None will deny, that every considerable trader ought to have some stock, or cash capital of his own; the most judicious traders, like bankers, are always careful to keep their dealings within the extent of their capital, that no disappointment may incapacitate them to support their credit. Yet traders of worth, judgment and economy, are sometimes under the necessity of borrowing money, to carry on their business to the best advantage; as when the merchant has commodities on hand, which he wishes to keep for a rising market, or on account of monies accruing to him, which he is disappointed in receiving. On occasions like these, taking up money at interest, is not disreputable, but a great convenience; thus enabling him to carry on his business more successfully; but the borrower ought to be well assured, that he has sufficient effects within his power to liquidate the obligations in due time.

But, if the trader borrows money to the extent of his credit, and launches out into trade, employing it as his own, such management is extremely precarious, and is generally attended with the most preposterous consequences: for trade is subject to losses and disappointments; and when once a trader brings his credit into doubt, it may and will draw all his creditors, at the same time, upon him; consequently rendering him incapable of drawing in so much of his scattered effects as will discharge his debts, and thereby ruin his credit, altho' he might have believed he had more than enough to satisfy the whole world.

As, therefore, a wise man will trade so cautiously, as not to hazard the loss of his own proper estate at once, much more, should an honest man be careful not to involve the estates of others, in his personal trading adventures. But he that knows he has lost his own fortune, and endeavours to recover it by trading with the stock of other men, although he may be actuated by good motives, still cannot have a pretence to the character of being judicious. The dealing for goods on a credit, was, probably, at first introduced, by trusting young men commencing in trade, whose chief, and perhaps only stock, might be the opinion of their capacity, industry, and honesty: and as this is continued to retailers, and those who trade on a small stock, it may be reckoned a commendable, and useful practice; but whether the practice of this liberality should be extended to the wholesale trader, in so unlimited a manner, as is customary in most of our trading cities, is a consideration which admits of great doubt. This maxim may, however be advanced with some confidence, that a merchant should never purchase goods on short credit, with intent to meet the time of payment by remittances from cash sales of the same goods, as consequences might follow, not only ruinous to those who try the experiment, but injurious to trade in several ways. -Under such circumstances, the trader finding his expectances failing, is induced to offer his articles at reduced prices, as a last resource from impending ruin; but ten to one, and a most fortunate occurrence, if he does not find his financial system on the debit side of profit and loss. There may, and certainly are cases when a merchant may be justified in forcing

W

sales, though it has ever been found, as a *general principle,* unwise: it disturbs the whole current of trade, and drives it out of its natural channel; hundreds falling into the stream, in this way, float among breakers, and finally split on rocks, or are cast on quicksands, hardly ever to be recovered.   The forcing of trade produces a general introduction of goods of an ordinary quality.   Is it not a fact, that when one among a number of traders, introduces a financial trade, his neighbours are induced to replenish their stocks with inferior articles (in order to retain their customers,) which will afford them the same profit at less prices, as when accustomed to keep prime articles?   And after obtaining the reputation of selling goods of indifferent quality, is it not the case that other places receive the trade, which otherwise might not have been thus imprudently lost?·

"Cheap Stores" are not always found to have the cheapest goods, if we reckon by *principles of profit* to the purchaser; for the qualities of most goods, correspond with the prices.   It is observable that those merchants generally succeed the best, who have the reputation of keeping prime articles, and are not so very tenacious of acquiring the fame of selling remarkably cheap.

It is no doubt to be considered an established principle among traders, when they have occasion to make use of their credit, it should be for the borrowing of money, but never for the buying of goods; thus enabling them to purchase at the best possible advantage.

There is another evil in trade, which we have seen and which we believe deserves some consideration.   Some traders exhibit a wonderful diffidence or modesty, fearing to offend, in collecting their dues; particularly, when they are against persons of acknowledged responsibility, who certainly ought to be the most prompt, as they are most enabled to make their payments.   It could be said many, and very many merchants have suffered on this account.

But is it often the case, that the debtor under such circumstances is unwilling to avail himself of the advantage thus offered? However such customers may consider the subject, certainly, they are not to be estimated among the number in building up a shopkeeper.   It is an acknowledged fact, that gentlemen of estates generally require those articles which the traders esteem as *cash goods;* and is it not most commonly the case, that those traders who reside at some distance from the city, could have sold all such goods which they dispose of on a credit *for cash,* before they can replenish?   We speak of those who do not keep heavy stocks, though, perhaps, it might be applicable in some cases; but is it not a matter worthy of examination, if an unforced and natural business, effected with cash, or short credit, does not produce, ultimately, more actual gain, than that which is more extended, and on long and unlimited credits?   Those who have been in trade a great number of years, can, perhaps, answer this question satisfactorily.

We shall close this chapter with an extract from Mr. Williams' Almanack, for 1826, published at Utica, which we think is not too old to be forgotten; hoping our readers will not be too unsavoury in their comments on what has been already advanced.

"*Hints to Mechanics.* Avoid giving long credits, even to your·best customers.   A man who can pay easily, will not thank you for the delay; and a *slack, doubtful* paymaster is not too valuable a customer to *dun sharply* and *seasonably*. A fish may as well attempt to live without water, or a man without air, as a mechanic without punctuality and promptness in collecting and paying his debts. It is a mistaken and ruinous policy to attempt to keep on and get business by delaying collections. When you lose a slack paymaster from your books, you only *lose* the chance of *losing* your money—and there is no man who pays more money to lawyers than he who is least prompt in collecting for himself.

"Take care how you agree to pay money for your stock, your provisions, your rent, or your fuel, and take *dog skins* for your work. One hand must wash the other, as poor Richard says, or both will go to jail dirty. Every man's trade ought to bring him money enough to pay all demands against him: and no man can stand it long, who does not get money enough from his business to pay the cash expenses of carrying it on."

CHAPTER XXXII.
COLOURING SPIRITS.

Colouring Brandy. The art of colouring spirits owes its rise to observations on foreign brandies. A piece of French brandy that has acquired by age a great degree of softness and ripeness, is observed at the same time to have acquired a yellowish brown colour; and hence our distillers have endeavoured to imitate this colour in such spirits as are intended to pass for *French brandy*. And in order to this a great variety of experiments have been made on various substances, in order to discover a direct and sure method of imitating this colour to perfection. But in order to do this it is necessary to know from whence the French brandies themselves acquire their colour, for, till we have made this discovery, it will be in vain to attempt an imitation; because, if we should be able to imitate exactly the colour, which is indeed no difficult task, the spirit will not stand the test of different experiments, unless the colour in both be produced from the same ingredient. This being undeniably the case, let us try to discover this mighty secret, the ingredient from whence the French brandy acquires its colour. We have already observed, that this colour is only found in such brandies as have acquired a mellow ripeness by age; it is therefore not given it by the distiller, but has gained it by lying long in the cask; consequently the ingredient from whence this colour is extracted, is no other than the wood of the cask, and the brandy in reality is become a dilute tincture of oak. The common experiment used to prove the genuineness of French brandy proves that this opinion is well founded. The experiment is this: they pour into a glass of brandy a few drops of a solution of calcined vitriol of iron in a diluted spirit of sulphur, or any other mineral acid, and the whole turns of a blue colour, in the same manner as we make ink of a tincture of galls and vitriol. Since, therefore, the colour of French brandies is acquired from the oak of the cask, it is not difficult to imitate it to perfection. A small quantity of the extract of oak, or the shaving of that wood, properly digested, will furnish us with a tincture capable of giving the spirit any degree of colour required; but it must be remembered, that as the tinc-

ture is extracted from the cask by the brandy, that is alcohol and water, it is necessary to use both, in extracting the tincture, for each of
these menstruums dissolve different parts of the wood. Let therefore, a sufficient quantity of oak shavings be digested in strong spirits
wine and also, at the same time, other oak shavings be digested in
water: and when the liquors have acquired a strong tincture from the
oak, let both be poured off from the shavings into different vessels,
and both placed over a gentle fire till reduced to the consistence of
treacle.   In this condition let the two extracts be intimately mixed together; which may be done effectually by adding a small quantity of
loaf sugar, in fine powder, and well rubbing the whole together.   By
this means a liquid essential extract of oak will be procured, and always ready to be used as occasion shall require.

There are other methods in use for colouring brandies; but the best
besides the extract of oak above mentioned, is common treacle and
burnt sugar.   The treacle gives the spirits a fine colour nearly resembling that of French brandies; but as its colour is but dilute, a
large quantity must be used; this is not however attended with any
bad consequences, for notwithstanding the spirit is really weakened
by this addition, yet the bubble proof, the general criterion of spirits,
is greatly mended by the tenacity imparted to them by the treacle.
The spirit also acquires from this mixture, a sweetish or luscious taste,
and a fulness in the mouth, both of which properties render it very
agreeable to the palates of the common people, who are in fact, the
principal consumers of these spirits.   A much smaller quantity of burnt
sugar than of treacle will be sufficient for colouring the same quantity
of spirits: the taste is also very different; for, instead of the sweetness
imparted by the treacle, the spirit acquires from the burnt sugar, an
agreeable bitterness, and by that means recommends itself to nicer
palates, which are offended with a luscious spirit.   The burnt sugar is
prepared by dissolving a proper quantity of sugar in a little water, and
scorching it over the fire till it acquires a black colour.   Either of the
above ingredients, treacle or burnt sugar, will nearly imitate the genuine colour of the French brandies, but neither of them will succeed
when put to the test of the vitriolic solution.

CHAPTER XXXIII.

DISTILLATION, &c.

By the distillation of spirits is to be understood the art by which all
inflammable spirits, brandies, rum, arracs, and the like, are procured
from vegetable substances, by the means of a previous fermentation,
and a subsequent treatment of the fermented liquor by the alembic or
hot still, with its proper worm and refrigeratory.   But as it is impossible to extract vinous spirits from any vegetable subject without fermentation; and previous to this, brewing is often necessary, it will
be requisite to consider these operations.

To extract spirits is to cause such an action by heat, as to cause
them to ascend in vapour from the bodies which detain them.   If this
heat be natural to bodies, so that the operation be made without any
adventitious means, it is called fermentation, which will be hereafter
explained; if it be produced by fire or other heating power in which

the alembic is placed, it is called digestion, or distillation; digestion, if the heat only prepares the materials for distillation of their spirits; and distillation when the action is of sufficient efficacy to cause them to ascend in vapour and distil. This heat is that which puts the insensible parts of a body, whatever it be, into motion, divides them, and causes a passage for the spirits enclosed herein, by disengaging them from the phlegm, and the earthy particles by which they are enclosed. Distillation considered in this point, is not unworthy the attention and countenance of the learned. This art is of infinite extent: whatever the whole earth produces, flowers, fruits, seeds, spices, aromatic and vulnerary plants, odoriferous drugs, &c. are its objects, and come under its cognizance; but it is generally confined to liquids of taste and smell, and to the simple and spirituous waters of aromatic and vulnerary plants: with regard to its utility, we shall omit saying any thing here, as sufficient proofs of it will be given in some of the articles respecting it.

Of Brewing in order to the Production of Inflammable Spirits. By brewing is meant the extracting a tincture from some vegetable substance, or dissolving it in hot water, by which means it becomes proper for a vinous fermentation; a solution, or fermentable tincture of this kind may be procured, with proper management, from any vegetable substance, but the more readily and totally it dissolves in the fluid, the better it is fitted for fermentation, and the larger its produce of spirits. All inspissated vegetable juices therefore, as sugar, honey, treacle, manna, &c. are very proper for this use, as they totally dissolve in water, forming a clear and uniform solution: but malt, from its cheapness, is generally preferred in England; though it but imperfectly dissolves in hot water. The worst sort is commonly chosen for this purpose, and the tincture without the addition of hops, or the trouble of boiling it, is directly cooled and fermented. But in order to brew with malt to the greatest advantage, the three following particulars should be carefully attended to: 1. The subject should be well prepared, that is, it should be justly malted and well ground; for if it be too little malted, it will prove hard and flinty, and consequently, only a small part of it dissolve in the water, and on the other hand, if too much malted, a great part of the finer particles or fermentable matter will be lost in the operation. With regard to grinding, the malt should be reduced to a kind of coarse meal, for experience has shown, that by this means the whole substance of the malt may, through the whole process, continue mixed with the tincture, and be distilled with it; whereby a larger quantity of spirit will be obtained, and also great part of the trouble, time and expense in brewing saved. This secret depends upon thoroughly mixing or briskly agitating the meal, first in cold water, and then in hot, and repeating the agitation after the fermentation is finished, when the thick turbid wash must be immediately committed to the still. And thus the two operations of brewing and fermenting may very commodiously be reduced to one, to the great advantage of the distiller. The second particular to be attended to, is that the water be good, and properly applied. Rain water is the best adapted to brewing, for it not only extracts this tincture of the malt better than any other, but it also abounds in fermentable parts, whereby the operation is quickened, and the yield of the spirit increased. The next to that of rain, is the water of rivers and lakes, particularly such as wash any large tract of a fertile country, or receive the sullage of populous towns. But whatever water is used, it must stand in a hot state upon the prepared malt, especially if judicious distillers always take care to have their wash sufficiently diluted, and constantly find their spirits the purer for it.

With regard to the fire, it may be easily kept regular, by a constant attendance, and observing never to stir it hastily, or throw on fresh fuel; and the stirring the liquor in the still is to be effected by means of a paddle, or bar kept in the liquor, till it just begins to boil, which is the time for luting on the head, and after which there is no great danger, but from the improper management of the fire; this is the common way; but it is no easy matter to hit the exact time; and the doing of it, either too late or to soon, is attended with great inconvenience, so that several have discovered other methods, some put more solid bodies into the still with the wash; others place some proper matter at the bottom and sides of the still, which are the places where the fire acts with the greatest force. The use of the paddle, would however, answer better than either of these methods, could it be continued during the whole time the still is working; and this may be done by the following method; let a short tube of iron or copper be soldered in the centre of the still head, and let a cross bar be placed below in the same head, with a hole in the middle corresponding to that at the top; through both these, let an iron pipe be carried down in the still, and let an iron rod be passed through this, with wooden sweeps at its end; this rod may be continually worked by a wrench at the still head, and the sweeps will continually keep the bottom and sides scraped clean, the interstices of the tube being all the time well crammed with tow, to prevent any evaporation of the spirit. The same effect may in a great measure be produced, by a less laborious method, namely, by placing a parcel of cylindrical sticks lengthwise, so as to cover the whole bottom of the still, or by throwing in a loose parcel of faggot sticks at a venture, for the action of the fire below moving the liquor, at the same time gives motion to the sticks, making them act continually like a parcel of stirrers upon the bottom and sides of the still, which might if necessary be furnished with buttons and loops, to prevent them from starting. Some also use a parcel of fine hay laid upon the loose sticks, and secured down by two cross poles, laid from side to side, and in the same manner fastened down with loops. Care is to be taken in this case not to press the hay against the sides of the still, for that would scratch nearly as soon as the wash itself; but the sticks never will; these are simple, but effectual contrivances, and in point of elegance, they may be improved at leisure.

There is another inconvenience attending the distillation of malt spirit, which is, when all the bottoms or gross mealy feculence is put into the still along with the liquor, the thinner part of the wash going off in the form of spirit, the mealy mass grows by degrees, more and more stiff, so as to scorch towards the latter part of the operation; the best method of remedying this, is to have a pipe, with a stop cock, leading from the upper part of the worm tub into the still, so that upon a half or a quarter turn, it may continually supply little a stream of hot water, in the same proportion as the spirit runs off, by which means the danger of scorching is avoided, and the operation at the same time, not in the least retarded.

In Holland, the malt distillers work all their wash thick, with the whole body of meal among it, yet they are so careful in keeping their stills clean, and so regular and nice in the management of their fires, that though they use no artifice at all on this head, only to charge the still, while it is hot and moist, they very rarely have the misfortune to scorch, except now and then in the depth of winter. When such an accident has once happened in a still, they are very careful to scrape, scrub and scour off the remains of the burnt matter, otherwise they find the same accident liable to happen again in the same place. But beyond all other methods in use on this occasion, would be the working the stills, not by a dry heat, but in a balneum mariæ, which might be possibly contrived by the basin being large and capable of working a great many stills at once, so as to be extremely worth the proprietor's attention in all respects. Another requisite to be observed is, that the water in the worm tub be kept cool; this may be effected by placing in the middle of the tub a wooden pipe or gutter, about three inches square within, reaching from the top nearly to the bottom. By this contrivance cold water may, as often as necessary, be conveyed to the bottom of the warm tub, and the hot water at the top forced either over the sides of the tub, or, what is better, through a leaden pipe of a moderate size, called a waste pipe, soldered into the top of the tub, and extended to the gutter formed to carry away the water.

How to choose good Malt. Malt is chosen by its sweet smell, mellow taste, full flower, round body and thin skin; there are two sorts in general use, the pale and the brown. The former is more generally used in gentlemen's houses and private families, the latter in public brew houses, as seeming to go further, and make the liquor higher coloured. Others again mix one third brown with two thirds pale; but this depends upon the liking of the drinkers. The sweetest malt is that which is dried with coak or cinders. In grinding it, see that the mill be clean from dust, cobwebs, &c. Set it so as to crush every grain, without grinding it to powder; for you had better have some small grains slip through untouched, than to have the whole ground too small, which will cause it to take together, so that you cannot get the goodness out of it.

Hops. Hops are chosen by their bright green colour, sweet smell and clamminess when rubbed between the hands.

Water for Brewing. Water out of rivers or rivulets is best, except polluted by the melting of snow or land water from clay on ploughed lands. Snow water will take near one-fifth part more of malt to make the beer good. If you have no river water, a pond that has a bottom not over muddy, and is fed by a spring, will do; for the sun will soften and rarify it. Very hard water drawn from a deep well into a wide cistern or reservoir, and exposed to the air or sun, in two or three days has been brewed with success, by the addition of malt. Rain water comes next to river for brewing. In short, all water that will raise a lather with soap, is good for brewing.

Brewing Vessels. To a copper that holds thirty-six gallons, the mash tun ought to be at least large enough to contain six bushels of malt, and the copper of liquor, and room for mashing or stirring it. The under back coolers and working tuns, may be rather fitted to the convenience of the room, than to a particular size, for if one vessel be not sufficient to hold your liquor, you may take a second.

Of what is procured by Distillation. By distillation are procured spirits, essence, simple waters, and phlegm. Spirits are very difficult to be defined. We consider them as the most subtile and volatile parts of a body. All bodies, without exception have more or less spirits. These parts are an ignited substance, and consequently by their own nature disposed to violent motion. These volatile particles are more or less disposed to separate themselves as the bodies are more or less porous, or abound with a greater or less quantity of oil. By the term essence, we understand the oleaginous parts of a body. An essential oil is found in all bodies, being one of their constituent principles. We have observed in all distillations, spirits of wine excepted, a soft unctuous substance floating on the phlegm; and this substance is oil, which we call essence, and this is what we endeavour to extract. Simple waters are those distilled from plants, flowers, &c. without the help of water, brandy, or spirit of wine. These waters are commonly odoriferous, containing the odour of the body from whence it is extracted, and even exceeds in smell the body itself. Phlegm is the aqueous particles of bodies, but whether an active or passive principle, we shall leave to the decision of chemists. It is of the last importance to a distiller to be well acquainted with its nature. Many mistaking for phlegm, several white and coloured drops, which first fall into the receiver, when the still begins to work. These however are often the most spirituous particles of the matter in the alembic, and consequently ought to be preserved. What has given occasion to this mistake, is some humidity remaining in the head, &c. of the alembic. And had it been thoroughly wiped, the first drops would have been equally bright with any, during the whole operation.

The following remark deserves attention. In bodies that have been digested, the spirits ascend first. Whereas in charges not digested, the phlegm ascends before the spirits. The reason of this is very plain and natural. In substances previously digested, the action of fire no sooner causes the matter in the alembic to boil, than the spirits, being the most volatile parts, detach themselves, and ascend into the head of the alembic. But when the matter to be distilled has not undergone a proper digestion, the spirits being entangled in the phlegm, are less disposed to ascend till the phlegm itself separates and gives them room to fly upwards. The phlegm being aqueous, rises first— this is more particularly observable in spices. We are, however, inclined to believe, that were the operation performed in an alembic, when the head was at a great distance from the surface of the charge, they would not ascend high enough to come over the helm, but fall back again by their own gravity, and by that means leave the spirits at liberty to ascend. But in the common refrigeratory alembic this always happens. If this observation be not readily admitted, we appeal to experience, which we desire may be the test of every thing we advance. Another observation which has verified the above assertion by innumerable instances is, that in an extraordinary run of business, when we had not time sufficient to digest the substances, we used to bruise them in a mortar; but notwithstanding the trituration, the phlegm first came over and afterwards the spirits. But we desire to be understood, that we speak here only of the volatile parts of the plants, not drawn with vinous spirits, but contained in a simple water.

Another remark we must add, and which we hope will be acceptable to the curious, as it has not yet been made public, though doubtless the observation has often occurred to others; it is this: that in mixed charges, consisting of flowers, fruits, and aromatic plants put into the alembic, without any previous digestion, the spirits of the flowers ascend first; and, notwithstanding the mixture, they contracted nothing of the smell or taste of the fruits and plants. Next after the spirits of the flowers, those of the fruits ascend, not in the least impregnated with the smell or taste of either of the flowers or plants. And in the last place the spirits of the plants distil no less neat than the former. Should this appear strange to any one, experience will convince him of the truth. Another observation we have made on aromatic herbs, is, that whether they are or are not digested, or if the spirits or phlegm ascend first, the spirits contain very little of the taste or smell of the plants from whence they were extracted; and we have always been obliged to put to these spirits a greater or less quantity of the phlegm, in order to give the spirits we had drawn, the taste of an aromatic odour of the plants, the phlegm containing the greatest quantity of both. This observation we insert as of great use to those who practise distillation.

As the term digestion often occurs in this essay, we cannot avoid pointing out its advantages, and even show the necessity of using it in several circumstances. Substances are said to be in digestion when they are infused in a menstruum over a very slow fire. This preparation is often necessary in distillation, for it tends to open the bodies, and thereby free the spirits from their confinements, whereby they are better enabled to ascend. Cold digestions are the best; those made by fire, or in hot materials, diminish the quality of the goods, or some part, as the most volatile will be lost. In order to procure essences, the bodies must be prepared by digestion. It is even of absolute necessity for extracting the spirits and essences of spices.

Bodies proper for Distillation. This article alone might make a volume, were a particular enumeration of all its parts made; but as it has been already observed, we shall confine ourselves to the distillation of simple and compound waters. If we acquit ourselves to the satisfaction of the public, we shall enjoy the pleasure of having treated on one part entirely new: and the only one, indeed, that has been overlooked. The bodies proper for distillation, are flowers, fruits, seeds, spices and aromatic plants. By distillation and digestion, we extract the colour and smell of flowers, in simple waters and essences. We extract from fruits, at least from some, colour, taste, &c. From aromatic plants the distiller draws spirits, essences, simple and compound waters. From spices are procured essences, or in the language of the chemist, oils and perfumes, and also pure spirits. From seeds or berries are drawn simple waters, pure spirits, and from some, as those of anise, fennel and juniper, oil. The colour of flowers is extracted by infusion and likewise by digestion in brandy or spirits of wine; the smell is extracted by distillation; the simple water with

X

brandy or spirits of wine.. What is extracted of the colour of flowers by infusion in water, by a gentle heat or by digestion in brandy or spirits of wine, is called, in the distiller's phrase, tincture of flowers. The colour of fruits is extracted in the same manner, either by infusion or digestion, their taste is also procured by the same processes. But let it be observed that the time of these operations must be limited; for otherwise the fruit, after fermentation, would render it acid. The taste is also extracted by distillation in spirits of wine. From aromatic plants, are extracted by the alembic, pure spirits, odours, simple waters, but these require different methods of distillation. The first by water or brandy only, the second by rectified spirit, which will give them the greatest excellency they are capable of receiving.

The plants themselves with their flowers may also be distilled, which is still better. From spices are drawn spirits and oily or spirituous quintessences. The spirits are drawn by brandy, or spirits of wine, with very little water; the oils are distilled *per descensum;* and the spirituous quintessences by pounding the spices, and after infusing them in spirits of wine, decanting it gently by inclination. From seeds are extracted simple waters, spirits and oils. Very few of the first and last spirits being what is generally extracted from seeds and berries. Some distillers, through a notion of frugality, distil seeds with water, but their liquors are not to be compared with those which are distilled with spirits. When oils are drawn from seed, the operation is performed either by the balneum mariæ, or vapour bath.

Anise Seed Cordial. Take of anise seed bruised two pounds, proof spirit twelve and a half gallons, water one gallon; draw off ten gallons with a moderate heat.

This water should never be reduced below proof, because the large quantity of oil with which it is impregnated, will render the goods milky and foul, when brought down below proof. But if there is a necessity for this, their transparency may be restored by filtration.

Peppermint Cordial. Oil of peppermint seventy-five drops, sugar one ounce, grind together; add spirits of wine rectified one pint; dilute with spirits of wine rectified ten pints, water ten gallons, and fine with alum three drachms. On a similar principle, most cordials can be made, though with a little variation in the formula in some cases. Taste and the habits of the place are to be consulted. In general, it is advisable to filter.

In dulcifying or sweetening spirits, weigh the sugar, and dissolve it in one or more cans of the water, with which the compound is to be made up; bruise the sugar, and stir it well, till all is dissolved; then empty it into the cask containing the spirits; mixing all together, by drawing off several cans by the cock, and emptying them into the casks by the bung holes. Now rummage all well together, till they are perfectly compounded. Spirits or compounds that are strong, require no assistance in settling and becoming clear, but those that are weak, must be refined by the addition of some other substance. To every hogshead of Geneva or other spirituous compound, put six ounces powdered alum, previously dissolved in three or four gallons of the compounds, stir all well together. In the course of twenty-four hours, the whole will be rendered completely clear. It is a good practice to leave the bung holes of the casks (containing spirits or compounds newly made,) open for several days; this improves their flavour, and renders them clear, sooner than they otherwise would be.

Table salt thrown into the still, in the proportion of six ounces to ten gallons of any liquid to be distilled, will greatly improve the flavour, taste and strength of the spirit. The viscid matter will be fixed by the salt, whilst the volatile matter ascends in a state of great purity. The flavour of malt spirits is highly improved by putting three and a half ounces finely powdered charcoal, and four and a half ounces ground rice, into a quart of spirits, and letting it stand fifteen days, frequently stirring it; then let the liquor be strained, and it will be found nearly of the same flavour as brandy.

Raisin Wine. Raisins one hundred weight, water sixteen gallons, soak for a fortnight, stirring every day; press, put the liquor in a cask with the bung loose, till it has done hissing; then add four pounds of brandy and bung up close. Some use little more than half, or two-thirds of this quantity of raisins.

Gooseberry Wine. Ripe berries, bruised, ten gallons, water thirty gallons, soak twenty-four hours, strain: to each gallon add two pounds of sugar and ferment.

2. Bruised berries eighty pounds, water ten gallons, soak for a day, strain; to each gallon add six pounds of loaf sugar, and ferment.

3. Juice ten gallons, water twenty gallons, sugar seventy pounds, ferment.

4. Berries one hundred pounds, brown sugar six pounds, water a sufficient quantity to fill a fifteen gallon cask; yields a good yellowish white, and very transparent wine.

5. Gooseberries forty pounds, water four gallons, bruise together; the next day press out the juice: to every gallon add three pounds of sugar; ferment.

Currant Wine. Red currants seventy pounds, bruised and pressed, brown sugar ten pounds, water a sufficient quantity to fill up a fifteen gallon cask; yields a pleasant red wine, rather tart, but keeping well.

2. White currants one sieve, red currants one gallon; press. To each gallon of juice, add three gallons of water, to ten gallons of liquor add thirty pounds of sugar and ferment; when you bung it up, add two pounds of brandy to each ten gallons of wine.

3. Juice eleven quarts, that is, the produce of one sieve, sugar twenty pounds, water a sufficient quantity to fill up a nine gallon cask, ferment, and when it has done working, add four pounds of brandy; for a half hogshead use three sieves of currants, sugar three-fourths of a hundred weight, brandy one gallon.

Black Currant Wine. Berries twenty pounds, brandy two to four pounds, water twelve to fourteen gallons, yeast two spoonfuls, fermented for eight days, then bottled and well corked; yields a pleasant, rather vinous, cooling liquor of a purple colour; or they may be made into wine like the common currants; by the first process the wine is dark purple, rather thick, but good.

London Porter. For five barrels: malt eight bushels, a sufficient quantity of water, mash at twice; add in the boiling, hops eight to twelve pounds, treacle six pounds, liquorice root eight pounds, moist sugar sixteen pounds, one half of which is usually made into essential bine and the other half into colour, capsicum four drachms, Spanish liquorice two ounces, linseed one ounce, cinnamon two drachms, heading two drachms; cool, add one to two gallons of yeast when it has got a good head, cleanse it with three ounces of ginger; coculus indicus one ounce; then barrel and finish the working; fine with isinglass. The public brewers use a mixture of pale amber, and brown malt, but amber alone is best for private families.

Six pounds of sugar is esteemed equal in strength, and one pound coriander seed in intoxicating power, to a bushel of malt; the sugar employed is burnt to colour the beer instead of brown malt, and it has been proposed to use roasted coffee for the purpose. The other substances are merely to flavour the liquor and may be varied at pleasure.

The desire to evade the duty on malt in England produced the discovery of its being necessary to malt only one-third of the corn, as this proportion will convert the other into its own nature during the process.

Ginger Beer. Three pounds of lump sugar, ten ounces bruised ginger, one ounce cream tartar, lemons number four, pour on them four gallons boiling water, add eight ounces of yeast, work for four days, then bottle in half pints, and tie the corks down.

2. Six pounds of moist sugar, five ounces of ginger, two ounces of cream tartar, lemons number four, eight ounces of yeast, seven gallons of water, work two or three days, strain, add one pound of brandy, bung very close, and in fourteen days bottle it; a cooling effervescent drink in summer.

Orange Wine. Sugar twenty three pounds, water ten gallons, boil, clarify with the white of six eggs, pour the boiling liquor, upon the parings of one hundred oranges; add the strained juice of these oranges, and six ounces of yeast, let it work for three or four days then strain it into a barrel, bung it up loosely; in a month add four pounds of brandy; and in three months it will be fit to drink.

Wines, may also be made of blackberries and other English fruits upon the same principle. Those mentioned are the methods generally employed, but most persons have peculiar ways of proceeding, which may indeed be varied to infinity, and so as to produce at pleasure a sweet or dry wine; the sweet not being so thoroughly fermented as the dry. The addition of brandy destroys the proper flavour of the wine, and it is better to omit it entirely (except for elder and port wine, whose flavour is so strong that it cannot well be injured) and to increase the strength by augmenting the raisins or sugar. In general the must for wines ought to be made of six pounds of raisins, or four pounds of sugar, to the gallon, allowing for that contained in the fruit.

Southampton Port. Cider thirty six gallons, elder wine eleven gallons, brandy five gallons, damson wine eleven gallons, M.

English Madeira. Pale malt ground four bushels, boiling water forty-four gallons, infuse, strain; of this wort, while warm, take twenty-four gallons, sugar candy fourteen pounds; when dissolved, add two pounds of yeast; ferment; keep scimming off the yeast; when the fermentation is nearly finished, add two gallons and a half of raisin wine, brandy, port wine, each two gallons; bung it down for six or nine months. A second infusion of wort may be brewed for beer.

Rectification. The principal business is to separate the spirit from the essential oil the spirit contains. Care should be taken in the first distillation; the spirit, especially malt spirit should be drawn by a gentle fire, which will keep a great part of the essential oil from mixing with the spirit, as it is abundantly proved easier to keep asunder than to separate when mixed, as this is almost impossible. To draw low wines the best method of separating the oil from the spirit is by re-distillation and percolation. To rectify low wines, they should be put into a tall body, or alembic, and gently distilled in balneum mariæ; by this means both the oil and the phlegm will remain in the body, but if the spirit should be found after this operation, to contain some of the essential oil, it must be let down with fair water and re-distilled in the same manner. And thus it may be brought to any degree of purity, especially if in working, the spirit be suffered to fall into a proper quantity of the balneum mariæ. But it must be remembered, that it is much more difficult to cleanse alcohol or proof spirit, than low wines, because the oil is more intimately mixed with the two former than with the latter; this oil may however be separated from proof spirit, &c. by the method already proposed, especially if it be previously filtrated through paper, thick flannel, sand, stone, &c. But this method, though it effectually answers the intention, is generally rejected by distillers, because of the slowness of the operation, and others substituted in its stead; though instead of freeing the spirit from the oil, they only abolish the natural flavour of the spirit, and make a more intimate mixture between the particles of the spirit and those of the essential oil. It is impossible to enumerate all the methods practised by distillers, as almost every one pretends to have a secret nostrum for this purpose. The principal methods in use for rectifying malt spirits are however reducible to three, namely, by fixed alkaline salts, by acid spirits mixed with alkaline salts, and by saline bodies and flavouring additions. The method of rectifying by alkaline salts is thus performed. To every piece of proof spirit add fourteen pounds dry salt of tartar, fixed nitre, or calcined tartar; lute on the head, and distil by a gentle heat, but be careful to leave out the faints. By this method a large proportion of the fetid oil will be left in the still, and what comes over with the spirit will be greatly attenuated. But this operation is generally performed in a very different manner; for instead of distilling the spirit in a gentle and equable manner, the still is worked in its full force; by which means the oil, which should have remained in the still, is driven over and intimately mixed with the spirit, and consequently the whole operation frustrated, and the spirit rendered much harder to cleanse than it was before. But even when the operation is performed according to the rules of art, it is far from being perfect, for it is well known that part of the fixed salts become volatile in the operation, passes over the helm, and intimately mixes with the essential oil still contained in the spirits; by this means the oil becomes more perfectly united with the spirits, and consequently much harder to be separated by repeated distillations: nor is this all, for the still being worked in its full force, the bitter oil of the malt formed into a kind of liquid soap in the still, by means of the alkaline salt, is brought over the helm with the faints and suffered to mix with the spirit, whereby it is rendered almost as nauseous and ill tasted as before the operation. Besides, if this operation were performed in its utmost perfection, it would never answer the intention, for the alkaline salt destroys the vinosity of the spirit, and consequently deprives it of one of its most valuable properties. Our distillers are well acquainted with this defect in the operation, and endeavour to supply it by an addition of acids. This is what we call the second method by alkalies and acids.

The operation of rectifying by the method of fixed alkalies and acids is the same as that above described: the spirit is drawn over from fixed alkalies as before, but in order to mortify the alkali in the spirit, and restore its vinosity, a proper quantity of some acid spirit is added. Various kinds of acids are used on this occasion, but principally those of the mineral kind, because of their cheapness; as the oil of vitriol, spirit of nitre, oil of sulphur,&c. we would however caution young distillers from being too busy with these corrosive acids. The sulphurous spirit of vitriol, dulcified spirit of nitre, or Mr. Boyle's acid spirits of wine well rectified will much better answer their purpose.

The third method of rectification, is that by saline bodies and flavouring ingredients. There is no difference in the operation, between this and the two foregoing methods: fixed alkaline salts, common salt depreciated, or dried calcined vitriol, sandiver, alum, &c. is put into the still with the low wines and the spirit drawn off as before. When the quantity is drawn off, the flavouring ingredients are added to give the spirit the flavour intended. But as the spirit is not by this means rendered sufficiently pure, the disagreeable flavour of the spirit generally overpowers that of the ingredients, whereby the whole intention is either destroyed, or a compound flavour produced, very different from that intended. Some distillers, instead of alkaline salts, use quicklime in rectifying their malt spirit: this ingredient cleanses and dephlegmates the spirit considerably; but like that rectified from all alkaline salts, it requires an alkaline disposition, and also a nidorous flavour. Acids, therefore, are as necessary to be mixed with those spirits rectified with an alkaline salt. If chalk, calcined and well purified bones of animals, &c. were used instead of quicklime, the spirit would have much less alkaline or nidorous flavour; and consequently, the flavouring ingredients might be added to it with more success than can be expected from a spirit rectified from alkaline salts. But perhaps if neutral salts were used instead of the alkaline ones, the spirit might be rendered pure without contracting an alkaline flavour. Soluble tartar might be used for this purpose, though the spirit acquires a little saponaceous flavour.

Dr. Cox has mentioned another method for this purpose, namely, to deprive the volatile salts of their oil, by rendering them neutral with spirit of salt, and afterwards subliming them with salt of tartar. The acid may be varied if the spirit of salt should not be found so well adapted to the purpose as could be wished; but fine dry sugar seems the best adapted to the purpose of rectifying these spirits; as it readily unites with the essential oil, detains and fixes it, without imparting any urinous, alkaline or other nauseous flavour to the spirits rectified upon.

We shall conclude this article with remarking that there is no other method of rectifying to perfection, besides what is first laid down, viz. by gentle distillation: but then it must be remembered, that the whole process must be of a piece, viz. that the first distillation from the wash must be performed in a gentle manner, for otherwise the essential oil will be so intimately blended with the spirit as not to be easily separated by re-distillation. Another good property attending this method is its universality; all kinds of spirits, from whatever ingredients extracted, require rectification; and this is adapted to all kinds.

Fermentation. The tincture, or the wash, as distillers call it, being prepared as you will find described under the head of *Brewing in order to the production of inflammable spirits*, it is next to be fermented; for without this operation no vinous spirit can be produced. By fermentation is meant that intestine motion performed by the instrumental efficacy of water, whereby the salt, oil, and earth of a fermentable subject are separated, attenuated, transposed, and again collected, and recomposed in a particular manner. The doctrine of fermentation is of the greatest use, and should be well understood by every distiller, as it is the very basis of the art, and perhaps, if more attended to, a much purer spirit, as well as a greater quantity of it might be procured, from the same materials than at present. We shall therefore lay down a concise theory of fermentation, before we proceed to deliver the practice.

Every fermentable subject is composd of salt, oil, and a subtile earth; but these particles are so small, that when asunder, they are imperceptible to the senses; and therefore, when mixed with an aqueous fluid, they leave it transparent; neither have fermentable bodies any taste, except that of sweetness. These particles are composed of salt, oil and earth, intimately mixed in an actual cohesion, connexion and union; and therefore, when any one of these principles too much abounds in any subject, so that an intimate union is prevented, the whole efficacy of the fermentation is either stopped or impaired, or at least limited to one certain species. This equal connexion of salt, oil and earth, into a single compound particle, forms a corpuscle soluble in water; or to speak more philosophically, this compound corpuscle is, by means of its saline particles, connected with the aqueous corpuscles, and moved up and down with them. But when these corpuscles are not thus connected with the water, a number of them join together, and form either a gross or a loose chaffy and spungy matter. When these compound particles are diluted with a small quantity of aqueous fluid, they feel slippery, clammy, and unctuous to the touch, and affect the taste with a kind of rosy sweetness; and when a proper quantity of the fluid is added, a commotion is presently excited, and afterwards a subtile separation. This commotion and separation first begins in the whole substance, for before the addition of water, the subject may remain in dry, solid, and large pieces, as in malt, sugar, &c. which being reduced to powder, each grain thereof is an agreement of many compound corpuscles; then being put into water, dissolve and separately float therein, till at length they become so small as to be invisible, and only thicken the consistence of the liquor.

These corpuscles being thus separated from one another, there next ensues a separation of their component particles; that is, the salt, the oil and the earth are divided by the interposition of aqueous particles. The first commotion is no more than a bare solution; for the saline particles being easily dissolvable in water, they are immediately laid hold of by the aqueous particles, and carried about with them. But the suceeeding separation or fermentative motion is a very different thing; for by this, the saline particles are divided from those of oil and earth, partly by the impulse of the others in their motion, and partly by the force of the aqueous particles, which are now continually meeting and dashing against them. This motion is performed by the water, as a fluid or aggregate of an infinite number of particles in actual and perpetual motion, their smallness being proportionable to that of the fermenting corpuscles, and their motion, or constant susceptibility of motion, by the warmth and motion of the air, disposing them to move other subtile moveable corpuscles also. The certain agreement of figure or size, between the aqueous particles, and those of the salt in the fermentable subject, tends greatly to increase this commotion: for by this means they are readily and very closely connected together; and move almost like one and the same compound corpuscle, while the water is not at all disposed to cohere immediately with either the oil or earth; and thus an equal concussion is excited in the compound corpuscles of the fermentable subject which concussion at length strikes out the saline particles, loosens the others, and finally produces a separation of the original connexion of the subject.

An aqueous fluid, therefore, is the true and indeed the only instrument for procuring a fermentable motion in these compound corpuscles of the subject, for were an oily fluid poured upon any fermentable subject, no vinous fermentation would ensue; as the oil could neither give a sufficient impulse on the compound corpuscles which are grosser than its own constituent particles, nor divide the oily or saline particles of the subject, from their connexion with the others, which detain, and as it were, envelop or defend them from its action. The compound corpuscles of the fermentable subject being affected by the perpetual motion of the particles of the aqueous fluid, a proper degree of motion is necessary, or that the particles move with a proper degree of velocity, which depends on external heat. A considerable degree of cold, indeed, will not absolutely prevent fermentation, though it will retard it; and a boiling heat will prevent it still more. A tepid or middle degree of heat, between freezing and boiling is therefore the most proper for promoting and quickening the operation. The admission of air, also, though not of absolute necessity, yet greatly promotes and quickens the action, as being a capital instrument in putting in a proper degree of motion the oily particles of the subject; but whilst the air thus contributes to hasten the effect, it causes at the same time by its activity, some remarkable alterations in the oily particles; for it not only moves but absolutely dissolves and displaces them from their original connexions; and thus carries them off itself from the whole mass. And therefore, though the consideration of the air does not so properly belong to fermentation in the general, yet it does in particular; as having an accidental power to alter every species of this operation, consequently its agency ought to be well understood, either to procure alterations at pleasure, in the fermenting mass, or to prevent or correct impending dangers. The oily particles thus separated and dissolved by the air, are also elastic, though they probably derive that property from their intercourse with the air itself, and these being rendered extremely minute. When, therefore, an aqueous fluid is added to a fermentable subject, exposed to a temperate heat, a fermentative struggle immediately arises, the saline part of the compound particles being dissolved by the continual intestine motion of the water, and carried up and down with it in all directions, amidst an infinite number of other particles, as well fermentable as aqueous ones, whence by this collision and attrition, the saline particles are dissolved and separated from their connexion with the oily and earthy. And as the oily particles are the most subtile and elastic, they would by this means, be thrown up to the surface of the liquor, and carried off by the air, were they not closely connected with the earthy ones, whose gravity prevents their evaporation, and by coming in contact with others of the same kind, form aggregations, and sink down with the oily particles to the bottom.

But before these can form a bulk too large to be supported by the water, many of the oily particles are, by their frequent collisions with the aqueous fluid, separated from the earthy ones, and by degrees more strongly connected again with the saline ones; whilst on the other hand, the same saline particles imbibe some of the earthy ones, which being left single upon their separation from the oily particles, float about separately in the fluid. And hence proceed the several different consequences of fermentation; namely, 1. From the separation of the saline particles of the fermentable subject, proceeds the tart, saline or acid taste of the liquor which is more sensible at first, before the liquor is duly composed and settled, or the due arrangement and connexion of the saline particles with those of the oily and earthy kinds, completed; after which the liquor becomes milder, softer or less pungent. 2. From the oily particles being set at liberty, proceeds the strong smell of the liquor, and the head or shining skin upon the surface. 3. The earthy particles collecting together in clusters, cause the fluid to appear turbid, and afterwards a visible, earthy or clay like matter, to be precipitated; and some of the earthy parts in their motion, arriving at the head or oily skin on the surface cause it to thicken, and afterwards taking it down along with it, thus constitute the lees which abound in oil. 4. From this new struggle or collision, which is productive both of solution and a new connexion in the saline and earthy corpuscles, proceeds the ebullition in fermentation; and lastly, by the same repeated coalition of the oily with the aqueous and saline particles, the inflammable spirit is produced.

Having thus laid down a concise theory of fermentation, we shall now proceed to the practice. The wash being brought to a tepid or luke warm state in the backs, a proper quantity of a good conditioned ferment is added; but if the ferment be soiled, it should be previously broke into small pieces, and gently thinned, either with the hand, wisp, &c. in a little of the tepid liquor. A complete and uniform solution, should not be attempted, because that would greatly weaken the power of the ferment, or destroy its future efficacy. The whole intended quantity being thus loosely mixed with a moderate portion of the liquor, and kept in a tepid state, either by setting it near the fire or otherwise, and free from the too rude commerce of the external air, more of the insensibly warm liquor ought to be added at proper intervals, till at length the whole quantity is properly set to working together, and thus by dividing the business into parts, it may much more speedily and

Y

effectually be performed, than by attempting it all at once. The whole quantity of liquor being thus set at work, secured in a proper degree of warmth, and defended from a too free intercourse of the external air, nature itself, as it were, finishes the process, and renders the liquor fit for the still. By ferments is meant any substance, which being added to any rightly disposed fermentable liquor, will cause it to ferment much sooner and faster, than it would of itself, and consequently render the operation shorter, in contradiction to those abusively called so, which only corrects some fault in the liquor, or gives it some flavour. Hence, we see, that the principal use of ferments is to save time, and make despatch in business, whilst they only occasionally, and as it were by accident, give a flavour, and increase the quantity of spirits. And accordingly, any fermentable liquor, may without the addition of any ferment, by a proper management of heat alone, be brought to ferment, and even more perfectly, though much slower, than with their assistance. These ferments are in general the flowers and fæces of all fermentable liquors, generated and thrown to the surface, or deposited at the bottom, either during the act of fermentation or after the operation is finished. Two of these are procurable in large quantities, and at a small expense: beer yeast and wine lees; a prudent and artificial management, or use of which might render the business of distillation much more certain and advantageous. It has been esteemed very difficult and a great discouragement in the business of distillation, to procure a sufficient stock of these materials, and preserve them at all times ready for use. The whole secret consists in dexterously freeing the matter from its superfluous moisture; because in its fluid state, it is subject to a further fermentation, which is productive of corruption, in which state it becomes intolerably fetid and cadaverous. The method of exposing it to the air till it has acquired a proper consistence, is subject to great inconveniences: and so peculiar and careful management is necessary, that it rarely succeeds. The best way therefore, is to press it very slowly and gradually, in a thick, close and strong canvass bag, after the manner of wine lees, by the toil press, till it becomes a kind of cake, which though soft, will easily snap, or break between the fingers. Being reduced to that consistence, and closely packed up in a tight cask, it will remain a long time uncorrupted, preserve its fragrancy, and consequently fit to be used for fermenting the finest liquor.

The same method is also practicable, and to the same advantage, in the flowers of yeast or wine, which may be thus commodiously imported from abroad; or if these cannot be procured, others of equal efficacy may be procured from fresh wine lees by barely mixing and stirring them into a proper warm liquor, when the lighter and more volatile and active parts of the lees will be thrown to the surface, and may easily be taken off and preserved by the above mentioned method, in any desired quantity. And hence, by a very easy process, an inexhaustible supply of the most useful ferments may be readily and successively procured, so as to prevent for the future, all occasion of complaint for the want of them, in the distiller's business. Experience has demonstrated, that all ferments abound much more in essentials, than the liquor which produced them; and consequently, they retain in a very high degree, the smell and flavour of the subject. It is therefore requisite, before the ferment is applied, to consider what flavour is introduced, or what species of ferment is most proper for the liquor. The alteration thus caused by ferments, is so considerable as to render any neutral fermentable liquor of the same flavour of that which yields the ferment. This observation is of much greater moment than will readily be conceived, for a new scene is hereby opened, both in the business of distillation, and others depending upon fermentation. It must however be observed, that its benefit does not extend to malt treated in the common method; nor to any other subject but what affords a spirit tolerably pure and tasteless. For otherwise, instead of producing a simple, pure, and uniform flavour, it causes a compound, mixed, and unnatural one. How far the fine distiller may profit by it, well deserves his attention, and whether our native cider spirit, crab spirit, &c. which have very little flavour of their own, may not by this artifice, be brought nearly, if not entirely, into the state of some foreign brandies, so highly esteemed, is recommended to experience. It is common with distillers, in order to increase the quantity of spirit, to give it a particular flavour, to improve its vinosity, to add several things to the liquor during the time it is in a state of fermentation, and these additions may properly be reduced to salts, acids, aromatics, and oils.

All rich vegetable juices, as treacle, honey, &c. which either want a natural acid, have been deprived of it, or contain it in too small a quantity, will be greatly improved by adding at the beginning of the operation, a small quantity of the vegetable or fine mineral acids, as oil of sulphur, glaubers, spirit of salt, juice of lemon, or an aqueous solution of tartar. These additions will either give or greatly improve the vinous acidity of the subject, but not increase the quantity of the spirits; that intention being performed by aromatics and oils. All pungent aromatics have a surprising quality of increasing the quantity of the spirits, as well as in altering or improving the flavour; but their use requires that the fermentation should be performed in close vessels, and if a large quantity be intended to be added, care must be taken not to do it all at once, lest the oiliness of the ingredients should check the operation. But if the flavour be the principal intention, they should not be added till the operation is nearly finished. After the same manner a very considerable quantity of any essential vegetable oil may be converted into a surprisingly large quantity of inflammable spirits; but great caution is here also necessary, not to drop it too fast, or add too large a quantity at a time, which would damp the fermentation, it being the surest method of checking, or totally stopping this operation at any point of time required. The best method thererefore, of adding the oil, so as to avoid all inconveniences, is to rub the oil in a mortar with sugar, which the chemists call making an olæsaccharum, by which means the tenacity of the oil will be destroyed, and the whole readily mix with the liquor, and immediately ferment with it. The distiller would do well to consider these observations attentively, as he may thence form an advantageous method of increasing the quantity of spirits, and at the same time greatly improve their quality and flavour. But in order to put these observations in practice, particular regard must be had to the containing vessel in which the fermentation is performed, the exclusion of the air, and the degree of the external heat or cold. With regard to the containing vessel, its purity, and the provision for rendering it occasionally close, are chiefly to be considered. In cleansing it, no soap or other unctuous body should be used, for fear of checking the fermentation; and for the same reason, all strong alkaline lixiviums should be avoided.   Limewater, or a turbid solution of quicklime may be employed for this purpose, without producing any ill effect: it will also be of great service in destroying a prevailing acetous salt, which is apt to generate in the vessels when the warm air has free access to them; and tends to prevent the order of fermentation, and instead of a wine or wash, produce a vinegar.   Special care must also be had that no remains of yeast, or cadaverous remains of former-fermented matters hang about the vessels; which would infect whatever should be afterwards put into them, and cannot, without the utmost difficulty, be perfectly sweetened and cured.   The occasional closeness of the vessels may, in the large way, be provided for by covers properly adapted; and in the small way, by valves placed in light casks.   These valves will occasionally give the necessary vent to preserve the vessel, during the height of the fermentation; the vessel otherwise remaining perfectly close, and impervious to the air.   It is a mistake of a very prejudicial nature in the business of fermentation, to suppose that there is an absolute necessity for a free admission of the external air: the express contrary is the truth, and very great advantages will be found by practising according to this supposition.   A constant influx of the external air, if it does not carry off some part of the spirit already generated, yet certainly catches up and dissipates the fine subtile or oleaginous and saline particles, whereof the spirit is made, and thus considerably lessens the quantity.   By a close fermentation, this inconvenience is avoided; all air except that included in the vessel, being excluded.   The whole secret consists in leaving a moderate space for the air at the top of the vessel unpossessed by the liquor; when the liquor is once fairly at work, to bung it down close, and thus suffered to finish the fermentation without opening or giving it any more vent than that afforded it by a proper valve placed in the cask, which however, is not of absolute necessity, when the empty space, or rather that possessed by the air, is about one tenth of the guage; the artificial air, generated in the operation, being then seldom sufficient to open a strong valve, or at most not to endanger the cask.   This method may be practised to great advantage by those whose business is not very large; but it requires too much time to be used by the large dealers, who are in a manner forced to admit the free air, and thus sustain a considerable loss in their quantity of spirits, that the fermentation may be finished in the small time allowed for that purpose.   It may however be said, that the silent, slow, and almost imperceptible vinous fermentation, is universally the most perfect and advantageous.   During the whole course of this operation, the vessel should be kept from all external cold, or considerable heat, in an equal, uniform, and moderate temperature.   In the winter, stove rooms, such as are common in Germany would be very convenient for this purpose, the vessel being placed at a proper distance from the stove; but at other seasons no particular apparatus is necessary in England, or even in the central part of the United States, if the place allowed for the business be but well defended from the summer's heat and the ill effects of cold, bleak, northern winds.   The operation is known to be perfect when the hissing, or small bubbling noise can be no longer heard upon applying the ear to the vessel; and also, by the liquor itself appearing clear to the eye, and having a pungent sharpness on the tongue. And that it may fully obtain these properties and be well fitted to yield a pure and perfectly vinous spirit by distillation, it should be suffered to stand at rest in a somewhat cooler place, if practicable, than that in which it was fermented, till it has thoroughly deposited, and cleansed itself of the gross lee, and become perfectly transparent, vinous and fragrant, in which state it should be committed to the still; and the spirits obtained will not only exceed that obtained in the common way in quantity, but also in fragrance, pungency and vinosity.

To make Spirits of Wine, Is in England in general obtained from ground meal, either of wheat, rye or barley, with from one-tenth to one-third of the same, or another grain, malted and ground and then called malt spirits; or from treacle, and then called molasses spirits; some is made from apples, or cider wash. The fermentation is carried on quicker and farther, than in brewing, or making cider in order that all the sugar in the wash may be converted into spirits and water. The infusion of the malt and meal is made so strong, that its specific gravity is reduced from 1.083 to 1.14, whereas that for strong ale, is generally 1.06, and for small beer, 1.015 to 1.04, and is mixed with a large quantity of yeast, added by successive portions, until in about ten days, the specific gravity is reduced to 1.002, when it is fit for the still. In general, a third part is drawn off at the first stilling, under the name of low wines, the specific gravity being about 0.975.

On re-distilling the low wines, a fiery spirit, of a milky cast, comes over first, and is returned into the still; then follows the clear spirit; when it begins to grow too watery, the remaining spirit that comes over, as long as it will take fire, is kept apart, under the name of faints, and mixed with the next parcel of low wines. Instead of these trials, the head of the still may have a bulb of a thermometer inserted into it, and by observing the temperature of the steam, an accurate judgment may be formed of the strength of the spirit that distils over.

It is computed that one hundred gallons of malt, or corn wash, will produce about twenty of spirit, containing about half its weight of water; molasses wash twenty-two gallons, cider wash fifteen gallons. The best French wines yield from twenty to twenty-five gallons. The spirit thus obtained is used for pharmaceutical purposes, mixed with water, to separate the oil it contains, and re-distilled several times in tall vessels, with a very gentle heat until its specific gravity is reduced to 0.82; though that usually sold is only 0.837, at 60° Fahrenheit. By distilling spirits of wine with purified pearlashes, salt of tartar, muriate of lime, or common salt, all previously heated to redness, and cooled, its specific gravity may be reduced still lower, even as low as 0,792, at 68° Fah. but there is reason to think that it not only parts with water, but undergoes some change, or acquires some impregnation, by these additions, as its taste is altered. This spirits of wine from which every particle of water is separated, is called by the Arabic name of alcohol.

Of Filtration. Filtration consists in passing liquors through a porous substance in order to free them from those particles which obscure their brightness. Nothing is finer than a liquor newly distilled, but the syrup and colouring particles, render it thick and opaque: in order therefore to restore their brightness they are filtrated, which is done by passing them through sand, paper, cloth, &c. All the attention of the distiller in ordinary operations, cannot always prevent some aqueous particles from rising with the spirits, either in the beginning of the process, in those compositions where they ascend first, or at the conclusion when they rise last; as this is almost unavoidable, so it is sometimes necessary.

In distilling flowers, or aromatic plants, fresh gathered, the phlegm rises first; and this part cannot be taken out of the receiver, without depriving the spirits of a considerable part of their fragrancy.

In distilling spices, their odour being more entangled, will remain in the alembic, till part of the phlegm is drawn off. But when instead of these substances their quintessence is used, the necessity ceases. But the phlegm commonly causing a cloudiness in the liquor, it may be rendered tolerably fine by pouring it gently off by inclination, without the trouble of filtration; the aqueous particles, by their gravity, falling to the bottom; but to render it entirely bright and fine, put some cotton in a funnel, and pour the liquor through it, by which means the aqueous particles will be retained in the cotton. You must however remember to cover the top of the funnel, to prevent the most volatile parts of the spirits from evaporating.

English Sherry. Loaf sugar thirty-two pounds, sugar candy ten pounds, water sixteen gallons, boil; add pale ale wort, (as for English Madeira,) six gallons, yeast one pound; on the third day add ten pounds of stoned raisins, and in another two or three days one gallon of brandy; bung it down for four months; draw it off into another cask, add one gallon of brandy, and in three months bottle it. Imitations for foreign wines, for those who wish to make a show above their circumstances, but far inferior to our own fruit wines.

Elder Wine. Juice of the berries eight gallons, water twelve gallons, brown sugar sixty pounds, dissolve by boiling, add yeast, and ferment; then add four pounds of brandy, and bung it up for three months: disagreeable when cold, but is mulled with allspice and drank warm in winter time as a stimulant.

Ginger Wine. Bruised ginger twelve pounds, water ten gallons; boil for half an hour, add twenty-eight pounds of sugar, boil till dissolved, then cool, and put the liquor along with fourteen lemons sliced, and three pounds of brandy; add a little yeast and ferment.

White Spruce Beer. To ten gallons of water, put six pounds of sugar, four ounces essence of spruce, add yeast, work as in making beer, and bottle immediately in half pints.

Mixed Fruit Wine. White currants three sieves, red gooseberries two sieves: these should yield forty pints of juice; to each gallon add two gallons of water, sugar three pounds and a half; ferment.

2. White, red, and black currants, cherries, especially black heart, raspberries, of each, pounded, equal quantities. To each four pounds of the bruised fruit add one gallon of water, steep for three days, press, and to each gallon of liquor add three pounds of yellow sugar; ferment, and when finished add to each nine gallons two pints of bran-

dy; if it does not fine soon enough, add half an ounce of isinglass, dissolved in a pint of water, to each nine gallons.

Cherry Wine. Cherries thirty pounds, moist sugar five pounds, water a sufficient quantity to fill a seven gallon cask; ferment.

Parsnip Wine, may be made by cutting the roots into small, thin slices, boiling them in water, pressing out the liquor, and fermenting it. This wine, when made strong, is of a rich and excellent quality and flavour.

Metheglin. Honey one hundred pounds, boiling water a sufficient quantity to fill a half hogshead or thirty-two gallon cask, stir it well for a day or two; add yeast, and ferment. Some boil the honey in the water for an hour or two, but this hinders its due fermentation.

Mead, is made from the honey-combs from which honey has been drained out, by boiling in water, and then fermenting, generally confounded with metheglin.

English Champaign. Raw sugar ten pounds, loaf sugar twelve pounds, water nine gallons, concrete acid of lemon, or crystallized acid of tartar six drachms; dissolve by a gentle boil; before it grows cold add about one pound of yeast, and ferment. When the working is nearly over, add perry one gallon, brandy three pounds, and bung it up for three months; then draw out two pounds of the wine, dissolve one ounce of isinglass in it, pour it again into the cask, and in a fortnight bottle it; it may be coloured pink by adding one ounce of cochineal when first bunged up.

English Port. Cider twenty-four gallons, juice of elder berries six gallons, port wine four gallons, brandy one gallon and a half, logwood one pound, isinglass twelve ounces, dissolved in a gallon of the cider: bung it down; in two months it will be fit to bottle, but should not be drank till the next year. If a rough flavour is required, four to six ounces of alum may be added.

To restore Wine fusted or tasting of the cask. Draw that wine entirely out of its own lee and put it in another cask over a good lee. Then through the bung hole, hang up a bag with four ounces of laurel berries in powder and a sufficient quantity of steel filings at the bottom of the bag, to prevent its swimming on the top of the wine: and in proportion as you draw a certain quantity of the liquor, let down the bag.

To prevent Wine from Pricking. Put in the cask half a pound spirits of tartar, or when the wine is new throw in two ounces of common alum for every hogshead.

To clarify Wine easily. Put in the cask two quarts of boiling milk, after having well skimmed it.

To prevent Wine from turning. Put in the cask one pound of fine shot.

To correct a musty taste in Wine. Knead a dough of the best wheat flour, and make it in the form of a rolling pin, or a short thick stick. Half bake it in the oven and stick it all over with cloves; replace it in the oven and bake it quite. Suspend it in the cask over the wine without touching it, and let it remain there, or else plunge it in the wine.

To correct a bitter or sour taste in Wine. Boil a quart of barley in four quarts of water to the reduction of two. Strain what remains through a cloth, and pour it in the cask; stirring all together with a stick without touching the lee.

To restore spoiled Wine. Change the wine from its own lee upon that of good wine. Pulverize three or four nutmegs and as many dry orange peals, and throw them in; stop well the bung, and let it ferment one fortnight. After that term is over you will find it better than ever. This method has gone through many experiments.

To prevent tartness in Wine. Take in the month of March two basins full of river sand, and after having dried it in the sun or in the oven throw it in the cask.

To fine Spirits. Mix a small quantity of wheat flour in water, as if for making paste, and pour the same into the vessel. The whole is then to be well roused, and in a short time the contents will become bright.

Clove Cordial. Cloves, bruised, four pounds, pimento half a pound, proof spirit sixteen gallons.

Digest the mixture twelve hours in a gentle heat, and then draw off fifteen gallons with a pretty brisk fire. The water may be coloured red with tincture of cochineal, or other colouring matter.

To preserve Lemon Juice. Wash the lemons and after expressing the juice, strain; then sift on half a pound pulverized chalk, to the juice obtained from a box of lemons: let it stand twenty-four hours; strain, and bottle tight. This is undoubtedly the best method to preserve lemon juice.

Ratafia des Cerisis. Morello cherries with their kernels bruised, eight pounds, proof spirits eight pints; digest for a month; strain with expression; add sugar one pound eight ounces.

Ratifia de Grenoble. Small wild black cherries with their kernels bruised twelve pounds, proof spirits six gallons; digest for a month; strain; add sugar twelve pounds; a little citron peel may be added at pleasure.

Ratafia de Noyeaux. Peach or apricot kernels, with their shells, bruised in number 120, proof spirits four pints, sugar ten ounces. Some reduce spirits of wine rectified to proof, with the juice of apricots or peaches to make this liquor.

Brandy Shrub. Brandy nine pints, lemon juice, orange juice, of each one pint, orange peels four in number, lemon peels two in number, sugar two pounds, water five pints.

The same formula will answer for making rum shrub, using rum instead of brandy.

Chreme des Barbadoes. Orange peels, lemon peels, of each three in number, cinnamon four ounces, mace two drachms, cloves one drachm, rum eighteen pints; distil in balneum mariæ, and add sugar p. æq.

Chreme des Barbadoes—English. Lemons sliced in number twenty-four, citrons sliced, in number six, spirits wine rectified two gallons four pints, fresh balm leaves eight ounces, water three gallons four pints; digest for a fornight; strain.

Cedrat. Lemon peels in number twelve, spirits wine rectified two gallons; distil in balneum mariæ, and add simple syrup p. æq.

Parfait Amour. The same coloured with a little cochineal.

Rum Shrub. Concrete acid of lemons eight ounces, water five gallons, raisin wine four gallons, rum ten gallons, orange flower water four pints, honey six pounds.

Chreme de Noyaux—English. Bitter almonds blanched four ounces, proof spirits two pints, sugar one pound.

Chreme de Orange—English. Oranges sliced in number thirty-six, spirits wine rectified two gallons, sugar eighteen pounds, water four gallons four pints, tincture of saffron one ounce four drachms, orange flower water four pints; digest for a fortnight; strain.

All the aforementioned liquors are stimulant and taken *ad libitum* for pleasure.

Syrup Lemon Juice. Juice rendered clear by settling and subsequent filtering one pint, white sugar two pounds.

Syrup citri medicæ. Juice rendered clear as before three pounds, sugar five pounds; cooling, expectorant, pleasanter than oxymuriate.

Syrup d' Orgeat—Syrup hordeatus. Amygd. dulc. one pound, Amygd. amar. two drachms, make an emulsion by adding decoct. hord. two pounds; strain; to the strained liquor ten ounces, add sacch. alb. one pound and a half, and when the sugar is dissolved, aq. flor. aurant. one drachm.

2. New almonds eight ounces, bitter almonds four ounces, rub with a little water into an emulsion; strain, rub what is left upon the strainer afresh with the emulsion; to make it as rich as possible add white sugar three pounds, orange flower water two ounces, spirits of lemon peel six drachms, strain through flannel and put up into bottles; cooling, demulcent.

Brown Spruce Beer, as the white, using treacle in lieu of the sugar. In regard to the white and brown spruce and ginger beer and the wines, it is said the purer kinds are mixtures of spirits of wine, water, and extractive matter: the spirits may be separated by careful distillation, or if the extractive matter be first got rid of by the addition of extractum saturni and filtration, the spirits may be separated by adding very pure kali ppm. when it will swim upon the liquor; the spirit constitutes from twelve to twenty-five per cent. of the proper wines, and from two to eight per cent. of the malt liquors.

The fermentation of these liquors is usually hastened by the addition of yeast, crude tartar, or bruised vine leaves, but this is seldom necessary for wines, if the liquor be kept in a proper warmth; but malt liquors are more sluggish.

If the fermentation is in danger of proceeding too far, it may be stopped by drawing off the liquor clear into another vessel in which some brimstone has been newly burned, or in the case of red wine, some nutmeg powder upon a hot shovel, or which has been washed with brandy; the sediment left in the old cask, may be strained through flannel or paper till clear and added to the other; instead of this a part only may be drawn out of the cask and some rags dipped in melted brimstone and lighted, may be held by a pair of tongs in the bung hole slightly covered, so as to impregnate the liquor with the fumes; about one ounce of brimstone to a hogshead, then returning what had been drawn out, and bunging up very close; or a small quantity of oil of vitriol may be poured in: lastly the addition of black manganese has been proposed on theoretical grounds.

If the fermentation has proceeded too far, and the liquor sours, the

Z

fermentation must be stopped as above, and some lumps of chalk, or burned oyster shells added, to saturate the acid already generated.

If the liquors do not become clear soon enough, for each thirty gallons dissolve one ounce of isinglass in two pounds of water. Strain, and mix this with part of the liquor; beat it up to a froth, and pour it into the liquor. Stir the whole well and bung it up: instead of isinglass some use hartshorn shavings in rather larger quantities. Red wines are fined with twelve eggs to the pipe, beaten up to a froth, and well stirred and mixed in with the wine.

If the liquor has acquired a bad flavour, the best way is to let the fermentation go on, and convert it at once into vinegar.

To make Treacle Beer.   Boil two quarts of water, put it into one pound of treacle, stir them together till they are well mixed; then put six or eight quarts of cold water to it, and about a tea cup full of yeast or balm; put it in a clean cask or tub, cover it over with a coarse cloth two or three times double; it will be fit to drink in two or three days. The second or third time of making, the bottom of the first beer will do instead of yeast; if you make a large quantity, or intend it for keeping, you must put in a handful of hops and another of malt for it to feed on, and when done working, stop it up close.

The above is the best and cheapest way of making treacle beer, though some people add raisins, bran, wormwood, spices, such fruit, &c. as are in season; but that is just as you fancy. Indeed, many pleasant, cheap, and wholesome drinks may be made from fruits, &c. if they are bruised and boiled in water before the treacle is added.

Cherry Brandy.   This liquor is greatly called for in the country, and is made in different ways. Some press out the juice of the cherries, and having dulcified it with sugar, add as much spirits to it as the goods will bear, or the price it is intended to be sold for. But the common method is to put the cherries clean picked into a cask, with a proper quantity of proof spirits, and after standing eighteen or twenty days, the goods are drawn off into another cask for sale, and about two-thirds of the first quantity of spirits poured into the cask upon the cherries. This is suffered to stand about a month to extract the whole virtue from the cherries, after which it is drawn off as before; and the cherries pressed to take out the spirits they had absorbed. The proportion of cherries is not very nicely observed: the general rule is to let the cask be about half filled with cherries and then filled up with proof spirits. Some add to every twenty gallons of spirits, half an ounce of cinnamon, an ounce of cloves, and about three pounds of sugar; by which the flavour of the goods is considerably increased. But in order to save expense, not only the spices and the sugar are omitted, but also a great part of the cherries, and the deficiency supplied by the juice of elder berries. Sometimes adding molasses to sweeten instead of sugar, when the elder berries are not made use of.

Raisin and Apple Spirits, &c.   By raisin spirits are to be understood that extracted from raisins after a proper fermentation. In order to extract the spirits, the raisins must be infused in a proper quantity of water and fermented in the manner described in the article on fermentation. When the fermentation is completed, the whole is to be thrown into the still, and the spirits extracted by a strong fire. The reason why a strong fire is directed, is because by that means a greater quantity of the essential oil will come over the helm with the spirits, which will render it much fitter for the distiller's purpose; for these spirits are generally used to mix with common malt goods: and it is surprising how far it will go in this respect; ten gallons of it being sufficient to give a determining flavour and agreeable vinosity to a whole piece of malt spirits. It is therefore well worth the distiller's attention to endeavour at improving the common method of extracting spirits from raisins; and perhaps the following hint merits attention. When the fermentation is completed and the still charged with fermented liquor as before directed, let the whole be drawn off with as brisk a fire as possible; but instead of the cask or can, generally used by our American distillers for a receiver, let a large glass, called by chemists, a separating glass, be placed under the nose of the worm, and a common receiver applied to the spout of the separating glass; by this means the essential oil will swim upon the top of the spirits, or rather low wine, in the separating glass, and may easily be preserved at the end of the operation. The use of this limpid is well known to distillers, who have made their business a scientific study; for in this resides the whole flavour, and consequently may be used to the greatest advantage in giving that distinguishing taste and true vinosity to the common malt spirits. After the oil is separated from the low wine, the liquor may be rectified in balneum mariæ, into pure and almost tasteless spirits, and therefore well adapted to make the finest compound cordials, or to imitate or mix with the finest French brandies, arracks, &c. In the same manner, spirits may be obtained from cider. But as its particular flavour is not so desirable as that obtained from raisins, it should be distilled in a more gentle way, and carefully rectified in the manner shown in the article on rectification, by which means, very pure and almost tasteless and insipid spirits will be obtained which may be used to very great advantage in imitating the best brandies of France, or in making the finest compound waters or cordials.

Sugar Spirits. It is meant by sugar spirits, that extracted from the washings, scummings, dross and waste of a sugar baker's house. These recrementitious or drossy parts of the sugar are to be diluted with water, in the same manner as molasses or wash, and then distilled in the common method; and if the operation be carefully performed, and the spirits well rectified, it may be mixed with foreign brandies, and even arrack in a large proportion, to great advantage; for these spirits will be found superior to that extracted from treacle, and consequently more proper for these uses.

In closing this chapter we will observe, that the wines of commerce undergo very frequently, a great change, either by being mixed, or adulterated after importation. We should be glad to take up several pages on this subject, but it must suffice to state, that if all purchasers were careful in obtaining the certificates of the casks of wine which they buy, the risk would shortly be in some measure diminished in obtaining spurious goods. We are assured an empty rum hogshead, wine or brandy cask, with a certificate corresponding with the brand on the cask, would bring double the price, of the same cask without a certificate; besides, enough more to pay the freight, from any section of our country to the cities. (See laws relative to spirits, wines, and teas.)

We have no particular formula for compounding wines, as it would depend on the quality of the goods to be blended. An equal quantity of the best Sicily, Madeira and Colmenar, is preferable to most kinds found through the country, besides furnishing a very cheap article.

CHAPTER XXXIV.

LAWS RELATIVE TO SPIRITS, WINES, TEAS, &c.

Extracted from Ingersol's Digest.

24. Sec. XLI. The surveyor or chief officer of inspection, shall give the proprietor, importer, or consignee, of any distilled spirits, wines, or teas, or his or her agent, a particular certificate, which shall accompany each cask, chest, vessel, or case, of distilled spirits, wines, or teas, wherever the same may be sent within the limits of the United States, as evidence that the same has been lawfully imported. Form as follows:

No. District of ————, Port of ————.
I certify that there was imported in this district, on the [here insert the date of importation] by [here insert the name of the proprietor, importer, or consignee] in the [here insert the name of the vessel, the surname of the master, and whether a vessel of the United States, or a foreign vessel] from [here insert the place from which imported] one [here insert whether cask, chest, vessel or case, by the proper name] of [here insert whether spirits, wines, or teas and the kinds of each] numbered and marked as per margin; [the marks of the inspector to be inserted in the margin] containing [here insert the number of gallons, and rate of proof, of spirits, or gallons, if wines, or number of pounds weight net, if teas.]

A. B. *Supervisor.*
Countersigned by C. D. *Inspector.*
26. Sec. XLIII. The proprietor, importer, or consignee, or his or her agent, who may receive said certificates, shall, upon the sale and delivery of any of the said spirits, wines, or teas, deliver to the purchaser or purchasers thereof, the certificate or certificates which ought to accompany the same, on pain of forfeiting the sum of fifty dollars for each cask, chest, vessel or case, with which such certificate shall not be delivered: and if any casks, chests, vessels or cases containing distilled spirits, wines, or teas, by the foregoing provisions ought to be marked and accompanied with certificates, shall be found in the possession of any person unaccompanied with such marks and certificates, it shall be presumptive evidence that the same are liable to forfeiture; and it shall be lawful for any officer of the customs or of inspection to seize them as aforesaid; and if upon trial, the consequence of such seizure, the owner or claimant of the spirits, wines, or teas, seized, shall not prove that the same were imported into the United States according to law, and the duties thereupon paid, or secured, they shall be adjudged to be forfeited.
27. Sec. XLIV. On the sale of any cask, chest, vessel or case which has been, or shall be marked pursuant to the provisions afore-

said as containing distilled spirits, wines, or teas, and which has been emptied of its contents, and prior to the delivery thereof to the purchaser, or any removal thereof, the marks and numbers which shall have been set thereon by or under the direction of any officer of inspection, shall be defaced and obliterated in the presence of some officer of inspection or of the customs, who shall, on due notice being given, attend for that purpose, at which time the certificate, which ought to accompany such cask, chest, vessel, or case, shall also be returned and cancelled; and every person who shall obliterate, counterfeit, alter, or deface any mark or number, placed by an officer of inspection upon any cask, vessel, or case, containing distilled spirits, wines, or teas, or any certificate thereof; or who shall sell, or in any way alienate or remove any cask, chest, vessel, or case, which has been emptied of its contents, before the marks and numbers set thereon, pursuant to the provisions aforesaid, shall have been defaced or obliterated, in presence of an officer of inspection as aforesaid; or who shall neglect or refuse to deliver the certificate issued to accompany the cask, chest, vessel, or case, of which the marks and numbers shall have been defaced or obliterated, in the manner aforesaid, on being thereto required by an officer of inspection or of the customs, shall for each and every such offence, forfeit and pay one hundred dollars, with costs of suit.

124. Sec. XIX. When any goods, wares or merchandise, shall be admitted to entry upon invoice, the collector of the port in which the same are entered, shall certify such invoice under his official seal; and no other evidence of the value of such goods, wares, or merchandise, shall be admitted on the part of the owners thereof, in any court of the United States, except in corroboration of such invoice.

125. Sec. XX. Any person or persons, who shall counterfeit any certificate or attestation made in pursuance of this act, or use such certificate or attestation, knowing the same to be counterfeit, shall, upon conviction thereof, before any court of the United States, having cognizance of the same, be adjudged guilty of felony, and be fined in a sum not exceeding ten thousand dollars, and imprisoned for a term not exceeding three years.

127. Sec. XXII. The collector of the customs shall be required to cause one package at least out of every invoice, and one package at least out of every fifty packages, of every invoice of goods, wares, or merchandise, imported into their respective districts, to be opened and examined, and if the same be found not to correspond with the invoice thereof, or to be falsely charged in such invoice, a full inspection of all such goods, wares, or merchandise, as may be included in the same entry, shall be made; and if any package is found to contain any article not described in the invoice, the whole package shall be forfeited; and in case such goods, wares, or merchandize, shall be subject to an ad valorem duty, the same proceedings shall be had, and the same penalties shall be incurred, as in the eleventh section of this act: provided, that nothing herein contained shall save from forfeiture any package, having in it any article not described in the invoice.

CHAPTER XXXV.

TEA, SUGAR, &c.

On the quality of Sugars, with Practical Remarks. Not having authority, except from that founded on our own experience, we enter upon the subject laid out for us with some diffidence, as there are many whom we consider our superiors; however we are willing to abide the test, and rest the subject on close investigation.

There are few staples so variable in quality as sugar. Havannas are undoubtedly preferable to any brought to our market, and are not only as profitable to the retailer, but most profitable to the consumer. Either white or brown is from ten to fifteen per cent. sweeter; besides the flavour approximates nearer to that of the loaf sugar of the shops: they are imported in boxes, weighing from three to four hundred pounds, free from *foot,* and perfectly dry. Generally every pound, throughout the chest, will correspond with the sample. Chests weighing four hundred pounds, have been known to gain forty pounds; usually twenty-five pounds in the tare. There is a difference in the quality of these sugars, of ten per cent. perhaps more. Some of the Brazils are very fair and profitable. Refiners generally give these sugars a preference.

Of the browns, St. Croix lead in price in some of our markets; they certainly are very superior sugars, very clean, richly grained, and of a lively colour, but wanting in that fine flavour which distinguishes the Havannas.

The Calcutta sugars are mixed advantageously with the ordinary sugars of the islands. These mixtures require some care, or the improvement might be called a deception. Some of these sugars have a very bad flavour, and should be avoided by the purchaser: but those of prime quality are very fair and saleable; they are imported in bags weighing from one to two hundred pounds. There are many other kinds we should be glad to notice, if our limits would permit, but we can only indulge ourselves in a few brief remarks.

The islands furnish sugars of various qualities, precisely as they do of spirits. We have the best rum from St. Croix, (unless Jamaica excepted) so it is with respect to sugars; the difference probably arises in a great measure on account of the sweetness of the cane, and the same inference can be drawn in regard to the flavour of sugars, as will be found in the chapter on flavouring spirits; though much undoubtedly may be attributed to the manufacturers. Vast quantities of sugars are sent into commerce, *unmerchantable,* or rather before they have *ripened,* or been properly drained. This is almost universally the case with New Orleans, which on opening appears very bright, but the air soon decomposes it, and if not of sufficient ripeness or age, the retailer of pounds generally finds it a most unprofitable article.

We can draw a very fair conclusion of the ripeness of a piece of goods, particularly when it has lain some time in the warehouse. If we discover molasses issuing from the crevices; between the staves and about the heads, and it is evident much has been deposited on the floor about the cask, then; it is also evident it will fall short of the custom-house weight. In every case the draining head or side, should always be well probed; indeed every part should be carefully examined, or we shall not be certain of its average quality. Much experience and care are required in selecting sugars: perhaps it may not be unprofitable to examine when purchasing, if the casks are not overcharged with hoops or thick staves, heads, &c. Those pieces which contain the largest quantity, usually produce the greatest gain in the tare. The allowances and tares on sugars will be found under their respective heads.

Tea, is distinguished in name, as it differs in colour, flavour and size of its leaf; though its quality is more generally recognized under the title of *chop*: thus, in the same cargo, we have often seen several chops, (qualities) of young hyson tea, frequently varying to 40 per cent.

It is said the Chinese neither drink it in the manner we do, nor so strong, but use it only as their common drink. It is reckoned among them, a singular diluter and purifier of the blood; a great strengthener of the brain and stomach, and promoter of digestion, perspiration, &c. They drink it in great quantities in high fevers, cholics, &c. think it a sure, though slow remedy against chronic diseases.

As it would be endless to enter into a full detail, we would recommend dealers to attend a cargo sale previously furnishing themselves with a catalogue, and examining the sample chests or boxes. The advantages to be derived by attending public sales, are unnecessary to demonstrate, and it must suffice to assure the reader, at these sales, the merchant can become possessed of every desirable information, not only with respect to the qualities, but the standard prices of almost every staple article. Teas should be selected with the greatest care; and here it may not be improper to remind the purchaser of one very material fact, that *re-weighing* chests, as practised by some retailers, is not *correct*, though it may be called *customary*. We believe we are perfectly familiar with the arguments adduced in favour of the practice; and it is our object to attempt to show their futility, and silence for ever a doubt on the subject. And,

1. *Government* regulates commerce; by its *offices*, tares on imported goods are established, and thereby the importer becomes subject to the regulations of the custom-house.

2. If no other reason can be assigned, this alone is sufficient, why they should be correct, and that *they are* rightly estimated, which is, in order to secure the full amount of duties; and, depend upon it, the importer feels as willing to have his teas marked as much as the box or chest contains, as it is for the benefit of the country the duties on every pound should be secured.

3. The difficulties which might arise are innumerable, provided tares be substituted, varying from those established by the custom-house, in every case when sales are effected; and is it not undeniable none are more likely to be correct, unless the goods are emptied from every hogshead, chest, &c. thus preventing a general average, which in regard to teas, is not desirable, if practicable. It cannot be understood by the tariff bill, that a duty of forty cents per pound, (the duty on young hyson tea) shall be secured on the boxes in which it is imported, any more than permitting a single pound of tea to be exempted from duties.

4. Suppose we should re-ship teas to any port within the jurisdiction of the United States, and either on her passage, or at her port of

entry, the vessel's papers are demanded by the revenue officer, (for it must be remembered the law is explicit, requiring the supercargo or master, not only to produce the certificate of his clearance, but a certificate of each chest of tea, which on failure, both the vessel and cargo are liable at least to be detained, if not forfeited;) we are already apprised of the difficulties which might arise, if not the probable result, (provided the certificate of her clearance only can be procured,) if it could not be proved the teas had been regularly entered at a custom-house.   Is it not reasonable then, that every purchaser of a chest of tea, should be entitled to a certificate?

5. Provided our teas are insured, in case of damage how do we prove the quantity shipped?   We answer, if our invoice of shipment is correct, we can prove the quantity by the custom-house books, if in no other way, provided the certificates are lost.   And on the other hand, if our invoice show teas of a number, with a quantity which the custom house books does not recognize, the consequences which follow, might at least give rise to a great deal of litigation.   We have never known an importer to sell tea different from the custom-house mark, though we believe it is quite customary for the retailer to re-weigh and deduct a tare of his own making.   If the custom-house tares are a rough calculation, as some suggest, does it follow that those substituted by some retailers are to be more approved?   It must be understood that boxes and chests, independent of their contents, vary in weight, quarter chests frequently from two to eight pounds; thus, if one chest weighs eighteen, another twenty-two, a third twenty-six, the average weight is twenty-two; and according to the principles of the custom-house, each chest would be marked with the average tare deducted.   The number of pounds the chest contains is put on the chest, with a pencil or brush, (though sometimes we have seen printed figures) opposite the number of the chest: a careful examination will discover to us this mark, called by dealers, the black mark, unless rubbed out, which may sometimes be practised through motives which cannot be commended.

The certificate of each chest is made, signed by the supervisor of the port where it was landed, corresponding with the custom-house brand on the chest, viz. the number of the box or chest, number of pounds of tea, time of entry, name of the ship in which the tea was imported, &c. We have frequently seen chests of tea after having added to them an additional weight in hoops, have gained to the seller in some instances, over the custom-house mark, nine or ten pounds, generally four or five; by carefully reverting to the custom-house tares, and inspecting the boxes or chests, we will readily perceive whether we have our just weight.   We will now ask which of the two is the most equitable tare, or admits of a *more rough calculation*, the one established by the custom-house, or that substituted by the retailer, the one twenty-two pounds on quarter chests of eighty pounds and upwards, down weight, and twenty pounds on quarter chests weighing seventy pounds, &c. (see custom-house tares,) or the *systematic* deduction of the retailer, with his addition of hoops, and close weight, deducting nineteen pounds on quarter chests without distinction?   The laws are plain on the subject, and they are not passed to be trampled upon. (See laws relative to spirits, wines, teas, &c.)

We have good authority in stating, though personally unacquainted with the fact, teas of a rich quality are sometimes emptied and the chests filled with ordinary kinds; and so nicely done that few are able to detect the deception. However, it is not to be believed there are many so destitute of every good principle as to be engaged in the practice. Those who feel no compunction in making "wooden nutmegs and horn flints," perhaps, might not think it amiss to make a little money in this way.

Of Tobacco. We have something to say respecting this great staple article; and to be short, we advise purchasers to *look out.*

Our ever to be respected master used frequently to say, that "goods well bought were half sold," and that "a penny saved was as good as a penny earned." It matters not to our present purpose whether we were, or otherwise, inattentive to his sage advice, though we have no doubt if we had attended to it *strictly* and *systematically*, we should at least have saved so much, as would have kept our teeth free from expense, in regard to this article, all our lives.

The grand question is easily solved; are we compelled by the laws of our country to pay for staves and hoops, when we purchase tobacco? and are such practices to be suffered with impunity? Thus we leave the article for every one to make his own comments.

Of Flour. We will not be too prolix on this article. The old and lawful rule, which we have never heard contradicted, is 196 pounds of flour to the barrel. Has there not been hundreds of barrels, after inspection, sold in the United States, when the barrel and contents would not weigh more than 200 pounds?

Of Cotton. This article is susceptible of being charged with a considerable per centum of moisture, which without close examination is not easily detected. It seems that there should be a general test for detecting impositions of this kind, but we are unable to point it out at the present moment.

We should be glad to extend our remarks to various articles in merchandise, which require much sagacity in purchasing, besides those mentioned above. But we trust enough has already been said to draw the conclusion, that for the sake of money, many overleap the bounds of right, and it should seem, subject themselves to the loss of respect and confidence, notwithstanding they may evade the laws of the country.

CHAPTER XXXVI.

USEFUL RECEIPTS.

Dover's Sudorific Powder. Take of ipecacuanha in powder, opium purified, each one part, sulphate of potash eight parts, triturate them together in a fine powder.

The sulphate of potash from the grittiness of its crystals, is perhaps better fitted for tearing and dividing the tenacious opium than any other salt; this seems to be its only use in the preparation. The operator ought to be careful that the opium and ipecacuanha be equally diffused through the whole mass of powder, otherwise different portions of the powder must differ in degrees of strength.

A A

This powder is one of the most certain sudorifics, and as such, was recommended by Dr. Dover as an effectual remedy in rheumatism. Modern practice confirms its reputation, not only in rheumatism, but also in dropsy, and several other diseases, where it is often difficult by other means, to procure copious perspiration. The dose is from two to five grains, repeated according to the patient's stomach and strength. It is proper to avoid drinking immediately after taking it, otherwise it is very apt to be rejected, before any other effects can be produced. Perspiration should be kept by diluents.

Plummer's Pills. These pills are diaphoretic, alterative, purgative, and beneficial in cutaneous eruptions.

Take of calomel, sulphate of antimony, of each one drachm, gum guaiacum two drachms. Mix them assiduously with mucilage, and divide into sixty pills, two pills forming the dose. To be taken at night.

Earl Warwick's Powder. Scammonii two ounces, antimonii daph. one ounce, crem. tart. half an ounce.

Storey's Worm Cakes. Calomel, jalap, of each one drachm, ginger two scruples, sacch. one ounce, cinnabar anti. a sufficient quantity to colour them: syrup simp. a sufficient quantity to make into cakes.

Worm Cakes. Scamm. Allep. two ounces, calomel ppd. three ounces, res. jalap two ounces. crem. tart. four ounces, white sugar three pounds, mucil. g. trag. a sufficient quantity.

Worm Pills. Calomel one ounce, sugar two ounces, starch one ounce, mucil. gum traga. a sufficient quantity, to make two hundred and forty-eight pills; dose, number one night and morning, for children.

Refined Juice or Liquorice. Spanish liquorice four pounds, gum Ara. two pounds, water a sufficient quantity; dissolve, strain: evaporate gently to a soft extract, roll in cylinders, cut into lengths, and polish, by rubbing them together in a box; expectorant in coughs, &c.

Pate de Reglisse Noire. Refined liquorice eight ounces, gum Arabic two pounds, sugar one pound, water a sufficient quantity; dissolve and evaporate, till it forms a very thick syrup, add rad. enulæ. camp. rad. irid. flor. of each half an ounce, ess. de cedrat a few drops, put into tin moulds, and dry in a stove.

Young's Purging Drink. Crystallized natron two and a half drachms, crystals of tartar three drachms, water eight ounces, corked up immediately in stone bottles and wired: a pleasant cooling laxative in summer.

Ward's White Drops. Quicksilver twelve ounces, spirits nitre two pounds; dissolve; add ammonia. ppa. fourteen ounces, evaporate so as to form a light salt, which drain and dissolve in rose water, three pounds and a half.

Greek Water, is prepared and used in the same manner for turning the *hair black*.

Some perhaps might give a preference to the following preparation. Quicksilver four ounces, spirits of nitre one pound; dissolve; add ammonia ppa. seven ounces: evaporate and crystallize, then dissolve each pound of salt in three pints and a half of rose water.

Godfrey's Cordial. Dissolve half an ounce of opium, one drachm of sassafras in two ounces spirits of wine: now mix four pounds of treacle, with one gallon of boiling water and when cold, mix both solutions. This is generally used to soothe the pains of children, &c.

Lee's Windham Anti-Bilious Pills. Pul. gamb. three pounds, aloes soc. two pounds, sapon. duc. one pound, sal. nitri half a pound, extra. of cow parsnip one pound, beat them into mass with a sufficient quantity of sp. wine rect.

Lee's New London Pills. Pulv. aloes soc. twelve ounces, pulv. scammon. A. six ounces, pulv. gamb. four ounces, pulv. jalap three ounces, calomel pp. five ounces, sapon. cast. one ounce, syrup buckthorn, one ounce, muc. gum. Arab. seven ounces, m. ft. mass s. a. when incorporated, divide two drachms of the mass, into twenty-four pills.

Smith's British Lavender. Ol. lavend. Ang. two ounces, essence ambergr. one ounce, eau de luce one pint, spirits wine rect. two pints.

Essence of Peppermint. Spirits wine rectified one pint, put into it kali pp. one ounce, previously heated, decant, and add ol. minth. pip. half, an ounce, mix.

2. Ol. minth. pip. one pound, sp. wine rect. two gallons, colour with herb minth. pip. sic. eight ounces, mix.

3. Ol. minth. pip. three ounces, sp. wine rect. coloured i th spinage two pints; mix.

Hill's Balsam of Honey. Bals. Tolu one pound, honey one pound, sp. wine rect. one gallon.

2. Balsam Tolu opt. two ounces, gum styrax two drachms opii pur. half a drachm, mell. opt. eight ounces, sp. wine rect. two pints; pectoral used in coughs and colds.

Ford's Balsam of Hoarhound. Hoarhound, liquorice root, of each three pounds eight ounces, water a sufficient quantity to strain six pints, infuse; to the infusion add proof spirits or brandy twelve pints, camphor one ounce and two drachms, opium pur., Benjamin of each one ounce, dried squills two ounces, oil of anise seeds one ounce, honey three pounds and eight ounces.

Stoughton's Elixir. Rad. gentian two pounds four ounces, rad. serp. verg. one pound, cort. aurant. sicc. one pound and eight ounces, cal. aromat. four ounces, spirits of wine rectified, water, of each six gallons.

2. Rad. gentian four pounds, cort. aurant. two pounds, pis. aurant. one pound, cocin. two drachms, sem. cardam. min. one ounce, spr. of wine rectified eight gallons.

Hooper's Pills. Vitriol. virid. aquæ of each eight ounces; dissolve; add aloes Barb. two pounds eight ounces, canellæ alb. six ounces, gum. myrrhæ two ounces, oponacis four drachms.

2. Sal. martis two ounces pulv. aloes c. canellæ one pound, mucilage gum tragacanthæ, tinct. aloes, of each a sufficient quantity; cut each drachm into eighteen pills, put forty in a box.

Matthew's Pills—Starkey's Pills. Rad. helleb. nigri rad. helleb. albi rad. glycyrrh. opii of each two ounces, sapon. Starkeii six ounces, ol. terebinth. a sufficient quantity.

2. Rad. helleb. nigri rad. glycyrrh. sapon. castill. rad. circumæ, opii puriff. syr. croci. of each four ounces, ol. terebinth. a sufficient quantity.

Barclay's Anti-Bilious Pills. . Extract colocynth. two drachms, resin. jalap one drachm, sapon. amygdal. one drachm and a half, guaiaci three drachms, tart. emet. eight grains, ol. junip. ol. carui, ol. rorismar. of each four gtt. syr. spin. cerv. a sufficient quantity; make into sixty-four pills.

Worm Pills. Calomel one ounce, sugar two ounces, starch one ounce, mucil. gum traga. a sufficient quantity, to make two hundred and forty-eight pills; dose, number one, night and morning for children.

Keyser's Pills. Hydrag. acetat. four ounces, manna thirty ounces, starch two ounces, mucil. gum traga. a sufficient quantity, make into pills of six grains each; dose, number two, nocte maneque, increasing the dose to number twenty-five, or more; a box of 1000 or 1200 is usually sufficient.

Escubæ Usquebaugh. Saffron one ounce, juniper berries four drachms, dates without their kernels, raisins, of each three ounces, jujebs six ounces, anise seed, mace, cloves, coriander seed, of each one drachm, cinnamon two drachms, proof spirits twelve pints, simple syrup six pounds; pectoral, emmenagogue.

Dalby's Carminative. Tinct. opii four and a half drachms, tinct. assa. two and a half drachms, ol. carui three scruples, ol. minth. pip. six scruples, tinct. castor. six and a half drachms, sp. of wine rect. six drachms, put two drachms into each bottle with magnesia one drachm, and fill up with simple syrup and a little sp. of wine. rect.

Scotch Malmelade. Juice of Seville oranges two pints, yellow honey two pounds, boil to a proper consistence.

Botany Bay Cement. Yellow gum and brick dust of each p. aeq. used to cement china ware.

Admirable wash for the Hair to thicken its growth. Take two ounces each of rosemary, maiden hair, southernwood, myrtle berries and hazle bark, and burn them to ashes on a clean hearth, or in an oven; with these ashes make a strong lye, with which wash the hair at the roots every day, and keep it cut short. This lixivium, it is said will destroy that unsuspected enemy to the hair, the worm at the root.

Easy and effectual method of rendering all kinds of Paper fire proof. This surprising effect is produced by a simple cause. It is only necessary that the paper, whether plain, coloured, written, printed or stained, should be immersed in a strong solution of alum water, and afterwards thoroughly dried, when it will immediately become fire proof. The experiment may easily be made, by holding a piece of paper thus prepared over the flame of a candle. Some paper, however, will require to imbibe more of the solution than it can do by a single immersion, in which case the dipping and drying must be repeated till the paper becomes fully saturated. It is asserted that neither the colour nor quality of the paper will receive the least injury from this operation, but that on the contrary they will be improved.

An excellent Paste for stopping Holes or Cracks in Iron Culinary Utensils, so as to render them perfectly tight. To six quarts of potter's clay, add one part steel filings, and of linseed oil a sufficient quantity to render the mixture of the consistence of glazier's putty and fill the holes with it. This will soon become hard, and resist the action both of water and fire.

Eau de Husson. Is probably a mixed tincture or wine of henbane and colchicum. A tincture of colchicum has been proposed for it by Want; a tincture of hedge hyssop is said to be sold for it by Reece; and a wine of white helleb. proposed by Moore, but neither of them is possessed of the same characteristics as the Parisian medicine.

Bateman's Pectoral Drops. Sem. fœnic. dulc. two pounds and eight ounces, sem. anise one pound, proof spirits four gallons, water a sufficient quantity, distil ten gallons, to which add opium seven ounces and four drachms, camphor six ounces, kali pp. one ounce, coral rubr. four ounces.

2. Castor N. A. two ounces, opium, ol. anisi, of each one ounce and four drachms, camph. eight ounces, sem. fœn. dulc. two ounces. tinct. antim. four ounces, proof spirits ten pints, add rad. valerian and cochineal in powder.

3. Castor, camphor, of each four ounces, coccin. one ounce, spirits of wine rectified, two gallons, water one gallon.

4. Opii camph. of each one pound, castor, ol. anisi, santal. rubr. of each four ounces, treacle ten pounds, spirits of wine rectified five gallons, water four gallons.

5. Opii camph. of each ten drachms, coccin. one drachm, kali ppt. four scruples, ol. fœnic. dulc. one drachm, (or seeds three ounces,) proof spirits fourteen pints, water two pints: produce fifteen pints.

6. Castor one ounce, ol. anisi one drachm, camph. five drachms, coccin. one drachm and a half, opii six drachms, proof spirits one gallon.

Daffy's Elixir. Elixir Salutis. Fol. sennæ four ounces, ras. lign. sant. rad. enulæ sicc. sem. anisi, sem. carui, sem. coriand. rad. glycyrrh. of each two ounces, raisins stoned eight ounces, proof spirits six pounds. This is now sold by the name of Dicey's Daffy.

2. *Tincture Sennæ. Tinct. Sennæ, P. L.* Fol. sennæ one pound, sem. carui one ounce and a half, sem. card. min. half an ounce, raisins sixteen ounces, proof spirits one gallon.

3. *T. Sennæ, P. D.* The same but omitting the raisins.

4. *Sennæ Composita.* Fol. sennæ two ounces, rad. jalap one ounce, sem. coriand. half an ounce, proof spirits three pounds and a half by weight, when made, add white sugar four ounces.

5. Fol. sennæ, rad. rhei, sem. anisi, of each two pounds, rad. jalap, sem. carui, of each one pound, sant. rub. eight ounces, proof spirits ten gallons, brown sugar four pounds.

6. Rhubarb, East India, forty pounds, sennæ fifteen pounds, sant. subr. five pounds, sem. carui, sem. anisi, sem. coriand. of each five pounds, cineres Russici eight ounces, spirits of wine rectified ten gallons; digest three days, then add proof spirits eighty gallons, treacle forty-six pounds.

7. Rad. rhei fourteen pounds, sem. anisi ten pounds, sennæ parvæ eight pounds, rad. jalap four pounds, sant. rubr. three pounds eight ounces, ciner. Russ. two pounds, spirits of wine rectified thirty-eight gallons, water eighteen gallons.

8. *Swinton's Daffy.* Rad. jalap three pounds, fol. sennæ twelve ounces, sem. coriand. sem. anisi, rad. glycyrrh. rad. enulæ, of each four ounces, spirits of wine rectified, water, of each one gallon.

9. Rad. enulæ, ras. guaiaci, sem. coriand. rad. rhei, rad. glycyrrh,

sem. anisi, of each three ounces, raisins one pound eight ounces, proof spirits ten pints.

10. Rad. jalap three pounds, fol. sennæ one pound, sem. anisi six ounces, sem. coriand. four ounces, cort. aurant. sicc. two ounces, proof spirits two gallons.

11. Fol. sennæ seven pounds, rad. jalap five pounds, sem. anisi fourteen pounds, sem. carui four pounds, sem. fœnic. dulc. four pounds, brandy coloured two gallons, spirits of wine rectified twenty-six gallons, water twenty-four gallons; let it stand three weeks, strain washing out the last portions with water two gallons, then add treacle twenty-eight pounds. A common remedy in flatulent cholic, and used as a purge by those accustomed to spirit drinking; dose one, two or three table spoonfuls.

Anti-Attrition. Hog's lard ten pounds, camph. four ounces, black lead a sufficient quantity to colour it; used to rub on iron to prevent rust, and diminish friction.

Issue Peas. Ceræ fl. one pound, rad. circum. eight ounces, rad. irid. flor. four ounces, tereb. Venit. a sufficient quantity, make into peas.

2. Ceræ flav. six ounces, rad. irid. flor. two ounces, vermilion four ounces, tereb. Ven. a sufficient quantity, form into peas.

3. Ceræ fl. six ounces, ærug. æris. rad. helleb. albi, of each two ounces, cantharidum one ounce, rad. irid. flor. one ounce and a half, tereb. Ven. a sufficient quantity; this last is caustic and will open issues of itself, the others are used to put into issues that begin to close up to keep them open longer.

Issue Plasters. Ceræ fl. half a pound, minii, tereb. Chiæ, of each four ounces, cinnab., rad. irid. flor. of each one ounce, mosch. four grains; melted, spread upon linen, polished with a moistened calendering glass rubber, and lastly cut into small squares.

2. Diachyl. simpl. one pound, rad. irid. flor. one ounce, spread and polished.

3. Diachyl. simpl. two pounds, pic. Burg. sarcocollæ of each four ounces, tereb. com. one ounce, spread and polished.

Corn Plaster. Ceræ fl. two pounds, pic. Burg. twelve ounces, tereb. comm. six ounces, ærug. ppæ. three ounces, spread on cloth, cut and polished.

Almond Paste. Almonds blanched four ounces, lemon juice two ounces, oil of almonds three ounces, water one ounce, proof spirits six ounces.

2. Bitter almonds blanched, one pound, white of four eggs, rose water, spirits of wine rectified, of each a sufficient quantity.

Brown Almond Paste. Bitter almonds blanched, pulp of raisins, of each one pound, proof spirits a sufficient quantity; cosmetic, softens the skin and prevents chaps.

Almond Paste. Amygd. dulc. decoct. one pound, amygd. amar. decoct. half an ounce, sugar one pound, aq. flor. aurant. a sufficient quantity; beat to a paste sufficiently thick not to stick to the fingers.

Ready made Mustard. Flour of black mustard seed well sifted from the bran three pounds, salt one pound, make it up with currant wine and add three or four spoonfuls of sugar to each pint.

Blacking Paste. Rape oil three ounces, oil vitriol three ounces, mix, the next day add treacle, ivory black, of each three pounds, stone blue six ounces, vinegar a sufficient quantity to form a stiff paste; this will fill one dozen tin boxes.

2. Rape oil three ounces, treacle, brown sugar, each nine ounces; mix, adding ivory black three pounds, flour paste two pounds; when the paste is quite smooth thin it to the consistence of honey with a sufficient quantity of vinegar: used for making blacking for leather.

James' Analeptic Pills. Pil. Rufi. one pound calc. antimonii lotæ eight ounces, gum guaiaci eight ounces, m. and make thirty-two pills from each drachm.

2. Pill. Rufi. pulv. antimonialis, gum guaiaci, of each one scruple; make into twenty pills.

Anderson's Scotch Pills. Aloes Bbds. one pound, rad. helleb. nigr. rad. jalapi kali ppi. of each one ounce, oil anise four drachms, syr. simp. a sufficient quantity.

2. Aloes Bbds. two pounds eight ounces, water eight ounces; soften, add jalap sem. anisi pulv. ebor. ustri, of each eight ounces, ol. anisi one ounce.

3. Aloes (Bermudas) one pound, rad. jalap, flour sulphur ebor. ustri, glycyrrh. of each two ounces, oil anise one drachm, gamboge two drachms, sap. castil. four ounces, syr. sp. cervin. a sufficient quantity.

Ward's Antimonial Pills. Glass of antimony finely levigated, four ounces, dragon's blood one ounce, mountain wine a sufficient quantity, make into pills of one and a half grains each.

Steer's Opodeldoc. Sapo cast. three pounds, spirits wine rectified three gallons, camph. fourteen ounces, oil rorism. three ounces, ol. origani six ounces, aquæ ammon. pur. two pounds.

2. Sap. alb. one pound, camphor two ounces, oil rorism. four drachms, spirits wine rectified two pints.

3. Sap. alb. one pound, camphor four ounces, ol. origan. ol. rorism. of each four drachms, spirits wine rectified q. v. it will bear near six pints.

4. Sap. alb. three pounds, camph. oil rorism. of each six ounces, spir. am. ccmp. fourteen ounces, spirits wine rectified four gallons and a half.

5. Sap. alb. four ounces, camph. one ounce, ol. rorism. two drachms, oil origani thirty drops, spirits wine rectified one pint, water half a pint.

Squire's Elixir. Opium four ounces, camphor one ounce, cocind. one ounce, ol. foeniculi dulc. two drachms, tinct. serpt. one pint, spirits anisi two gallons, water two pints, and add aur. musiv. six ounces.

2. Ra d. glycy. one pound, kali pp. four ounces, cochineal one ounce, water twelve pints; boil till reduced to one gallon, then add tinct. opii twelve ounces, camphor one ounce, spirits wine rectified four pints, aur. musiv. twelve ounces.

3. Opii one ounce and four drachms, camph. one ounce, coccin. kali pp. of each one drachm, burnt sugar two ounces, tinct. serpent. one pint, sp. anisi two gallons, aur. musiv. eight ounces.

Essence of Spruce is prepared by boiling the twigs of Scotch fir in water, and evaporating the decoction till it grows thick; used to flavour treacle beer instead of hops.

Essence of Malt is prepared by infusing malt in water, first boiled, and then cooled till it reflect the image of a person's face in it, pouring off the infusion, and evaporating it to the consistence of new honey; used in sea voyages and places where malt cannot be procured to make beer.

Ink Powder. Green vitriol one pound; galls two pounds, gum Arab. eight ounces: two ounces make a pint of ink.

Marking Ink. Lunar caustic two drachms, distilled water six ounces, dissolve and add gum water two drachms, dissolve also natron ppm. half an ounce in water four ounces, and add gum water half an ounce; wet the linen on which you intend to write with this last solution, dry it, and then write upon it with the first liquor, using a clean pen.

Red Sealing Wax. Gum lac two pounds, vermilion four ounces, ol. tereb. ol. olive, of each eight ounces, roll in cakes and polish with a rag till quite cold.

2. Shell-lac five pounds, resinæ fl. three pounds, ol. tereb. one pound, vermilion twelve ounces, chalk ppd. four ounces.

3. Resinæ fl. six pounds, shell-lac two pounds, tereb. Venit. two pounds, vermilion eight ounces.

4. Shell-lac, resinæ fl. of each four pounds, tereb. Ven. one pound; add vermilion or bole Armen. ppd. q. p.

Black Ball. Beeswax eight ounces, tallow one ounce, gum Arab. one ounce, lampblack a sufficient quantity.

Court Plaster, or Sticking Plaster. Black silk is stained and brushed over with a solution of one ounce of isinglass in twelve ounces of proof spirits, to which two ounces of tinc. Benzoini is added, when dry this is repeated five times more, after which two coats are given it of a solution of four ounces of tereb. Chiæ, in six ounces of tinc. Benzoini, which renders it less liable to crack; but some finish it with a simple tincture of black balsam of Peru.

Lip Salve. Cera alb. four ounces; ol. olive five ounces; spermaceti four drachms; ol. lavend. twenty drops, rad. anchusæ two ounces.

2. Ol. olive opt. two ounces, cera alb. spermaceti. each three oz. rad. anchusæ six drachms; melt, strain; add ol. lign. rhod. three drops.

3. Ol. amygd. six ounces, spermaceti three ounces, cera alb. two ounces; rad. anchusæ one ounce; balsam Peruv. two drachms.

4. Ol. amygd. spermaceti, cera alb. sacch. candi albi, of each p. æq. this is white—the others are red.

Ol. Succini Reductum. Ol. succin. one pound, petrol. bbd. two pounds.

British Oil. Ol. tereb. eight ounces, petrol. bbd. four ounces, ol. rorism. four drachms.

Ol. tereb. five pounds, asphalt. twelve ounces, ol. lateritii eight ounces.

Ol. tereb. five pounds, ol. laterit. ver. eight ounces.

Huile Antique a la Violette. Oil of Ben. olives, or almonds, scented with ovia, in the same manner as in making essence de jasamin, and then pressed out of the wool or cotton.

Huile Antique au melle fleurs. Oil of Ben. or almonds mixed with different essences to the fancy of the perfumer.

Artificial Spa Water. Prepared natron seven grains, magnesia alb. one scruple, iron filings three grains, common salt one grain, water three pounds, and impregnate it with gas from marble powder and oil of vitriol, of each ten scruples, sufficiently diluted with water.

Artificial Pyrmont Water. Epsom salts fifteen grains, common salt five grains, magnesia alb. ten grains, iron filings five grains, water three pounds, and impregnate it with the gas from marble powder and oil of vitriol, of each seven drachms.

Artificial Sheltz Water. Common salt one drachm, magnesia alb. one scruple, natron ppm. fifteen grains, chalk seven grains, water three pounds, and impregnate with the gas from marble powder and oil of vitriol of each six drachms.

A method of making a Superior Black Writing Ink. Take four ounces of the best galls, copperas calcined to whiteness two ounces and a half, and a quart of rain water or stale beer; let them infuse in it cold for twenty-four hours, after which add an ounce and a quarter of gum Arabic, and preserve it in a stone jar covered with paper.

Permanent Red Ink for marking Linen. Take half an ounce of vermilion and a drachm of salt of steel, or copperas, let them be finely levigated with linseed oil to the degree of limpidity required for the occasion. This ink it is said, will perfectly resist the effect of acids, as well as of all alkaline lyes. It may be made of other colours by substituting the proper articles instead of vermilion: used with either types, a hair pencil, or even a pen, but in the latter case it will be necessary to thin it still more than it can be done by oil, by the addition of spirits of turpentine, so as to enable it to flow.

Wine Test. When wine becomes partly acetous, called pricked wine, the disagreeable taste is often corrected by sugar of lead; it is then poisonous, and the fraud ought to be detected. This may be done by dropping it into a little water, charged with sulphuretted hydrogen gas; it will immediately become a dark brown.

To turn Wine into Vinegar in less than three hours. Put in the wine a red beet, and it will be quite sour and true vinegar in less than three hours.

To restore such Wine to its first taste. Take off the red beet, and in its stead put a cabbage root into that wine, and it will return to its primary taste in the same space of time.

Easy method of securing Furs and Woollens from moths. Sprinkle the furs or woollen stuffs, as well as the drawers or boxes in which they are kept, with spirits turpentine, the unpleasant scent of which will speedily evaporate on exposure of the stuffs to the air: some persons place sheets of paper moistened with spirits turpentine, over, under, or between pieces of cloth, &c. and find it a very effectual method.

Easy and effectual method of preserving Eggs perfectly fresh for twelve months. Having provided small casks like oyster barrels, fill them with fresh laid eggs, then pour into each cask, the head being first taken out, as much cold thick lime water as will fill up all the void spaces between the eggs, and likewise completely cover them. The thicker the lime water is made, the better, provided it will fill up all the interstices and be liquid at the top of the cask. This done, lay on the head of the cask lightly. No further care is necessary, than merely to prevent the lime from growing too hard, by adding occasionally a little common water on the surface, should it seem so disposed, and keeping the cask from heat and frost. The eggs when ta-

B B

ken out for use, are to be washed from the adhering lime, with a little cold water, when they will have every appearance of fresh eggs.

To prevent the Oil of a Lamp from smoking.   Distil some onions, and put of the distilled liquor at the bottom of the lamp, and the oil over it, then you will see the oil give no offensive smoke.

To make an incombustible Wick.   Take a long piece of feathered alum, which cut of what size you like, and bore in its length several holes with a large needle; then put this wick in the lamp, the oil will ascend through these holes, and if you light it you will see the effect of it.

Curious and simple manner of keeping Apricots, Peaches, Plums, &c. fresh all the year,—By M. Lemery.   Beat well up together equal quantities of honey and spring water, pour it into an earthen vessel, put in the fruits all freshly gathered, and cover them up quite close. When any of the fruit is taken out, wash it in cold water and it is fit for immediate use.

Blacking.   Ivory black, treacle of each two pounds, neat's foot oil eight ounces, oil of vitriol one ounce, gum traga. two ounces, vinegar six pints; mix.

2. Ivory black six pounds, vinegar, water of each two gallons, treacle eight pounds, oil of vitriol one pound.

3. Ivory black, one ounce, small beer or water one pound, brown sugar, gum Arabic of each half an ounce, or if required to be made shining, the white of an egg.

4. Ivory black four ounces, treacle eight ounces, vinegar one pound, used to black leather.

Ready mode of mending Cracks in Stores, Pipes, and Iron Ovens, as practised in Germany.   When a crack is discovered in a stove, through which the fire or smoke penetrates, the aperture may be completely closed in a moment, with a composition consisting of wood ashes and common salt, made up into a paste, with a little water, and plastered over the crack.   The good effect is equally certain, whether the sto e, &c. be hot or cold.

Liquid to take out Spots or Stains of ink, red wine, iron mould, mildew, &c.   Mix an ounce each of sal ammoniac and salt of tartar, in a quart bottle of water, and keep it for use.   Soak and wash out in this liquid the table linen, &c. thus spotted or stained, and after the colour is discharged, get them up in the usual manner, and there will remain no visible effect of the injury.

Composition for preserving Wood against injury from Fire Works. Put into a pot equal quantities of finely pulverized iron filings, brick dust and ashes, pour over them size or glue water, set the whole near the fire, and when warm, stir them well together; with this liquid composition or size, wash over all the wood work which might be in danger, and on its getting dry, give it a second coat, when it will be sufficient proof against damage by fire.

Cement Water Proof.   Take two parts plaster of Paris to one of good lime, made fine then with oil to a thin paste.   If to stop cracks round chimniés, &c. make it harder; and when dry, another coat that is thinner   To mend broken marble or earthen, make it quite thin and give it time to dry.   No water can penetrate it.

CHAPTER XXXVII.

MENSURATION.—LOG TABLE.

Diameter in inches.	10 ft. in length.	11 ft. in length.	12 ft. in length.	13 ft. in length.	14 ft. in length.	15 ft. in length.
15	90	99	108	117	126	135
16	100	110	120	130	140	150
17	125	137	150	162	175	187
18	155	170	186	202	216	232
19	165	179	197	214	230	247
20	172	189	206	224	246	258
21	184	202	220	238	256	276
22	194	212	232	263	294	291
23	219	240	278	315	332	353
24	250	276	300	325	350	375
25	280	308	336	364	392	420
26	299	323	346	375	404	448
27	327	367	392	425	457	490
28	360	396	432	462	504	540
29	376	414	451	488	526	564
30	412	452	504	535	576	618
31	428	471	513	558	602	642
32	451	496	541	587	631	676
33	490	539	588	637	686	735
34	532	585	638	691	744	798
35	582	640	698	752	805	863
36	593	657	717	821	836	889

This Table shows the number of feet of boards, any log will make when the diameter is from 15 to 36 inches at the smallest end, and from 10 to 15 feet in length.

OF STEAM.

Woolf's table, of the relative pressure per square inch, the temperature and expansibility of steam at different degrees of heat above the boiling point of water, beginning with the temperature of steam of an elastic force equal to five pounds per square inch, and extending to steam able to sustain forty pounds on the square inch.

	pounds per square inch.		Degrees of heat.			
Steam of an elastic force predominating over the pressure of the atmosphere upon a safety valve,	5	requires to be maintained by a temperature equal to about	$227\frac{1}{2}$	and at these respective degrees of heat steam can expand itself to about	5	times its volume & continue equal in its elasticity to the pressure of the atmosphere.
	6		$230\frac{1}{4}$		6	
	7		$232\frac{3}{4}$		7	
	8		$235\frac{1}{4}$		8	
	9		$237\frac{1}{2}$		9	
	10		$239\frac{1}{2}$		10	
	15		$250\frac{1}{2}$		15	
	20		$259\frac{1}{2}$		20	
	25		267		25	
	30		273		30	
	35		278		35	
	40		282		40	

SOLID MEASURE OF ROUND TIMBER.

diam. in inch.	8 ft. long Contents.	9 ft. long Contents.	10 ft. long Contents.	11 ft. long Contents.	12 ft. long Contents.	13 ft. long Contents.	14 ft. long Contents.	15 ft. long Contents.	16 ft. long Contents.
6	1 6	1 8	2 0	2 1	2 3	2 5	2 7	2 9	3 1
7	2 1	2 4	2 7	2 9	3 2	3 5	3 7	4 0	4 2
8	2 8	3 1	3 5	3 8	4 2	4 5	4 8	5 2	5 5
9	3 5	3 9	4 4	4 8	5 3	5 7	6 1	6 6	7 0
10	4 3	4 9	5 4	6 0	6 5	7 1	7 6	8 1	8 7
11	5 3	5 9	6 6	7 4	7 9	8 5	9 3	9 8	10 5
12	6 3	7 1	7 8	8 6	9 4	10 2	11 0	11 8	12 5
13	7 3	8 5	9 4	10 0	11 1	11 9	12 8	13 8	14 6
14	8 5	9 6	10 6	11 7	12 8	13 9	14 9	16 0	17 0
15	9 8	11 1	12 4	13 6	14 9	16 1	17 2	18 5	19 7
16	11 2	12 6	14 0	15 3	16 8	18 2	19 5	20 8	22 3
17	12 6	14 1	15 7	17 3	18 9	20 4	21 8	23 5	25 0
18	14 1	15 9	17 7	19 4	21 3	22 8	24 5	26 4	28 2
19	15 7	17 7	19 7	21 6	23 5	25 5	27 3	29 3	31 3
20	17 5	19 6	21 6	23 9	26 2	28 2	30 3	32 5	34 6
21	19 2	21 5	23 8	26 3	28 7	31 0	33 3	35 8	38 1
22	21 0	23 6	26 3	28 8	31 5	34 0	36 6	39 2	41 8
23	22 9	25 9	28 8	31 5	34 5	37 3	40 2	42 8	45 7
24	25 0	28 4	31 3	35 3	37 6	40 6	43 6	46 7	49 6
25	27 2	30 7	34 0	37 3	40 7	44 0	47 4	50 7	53 9
26	29 4	32 1	36 8	40 4	44 0	47 7	51 3	54 8	58 3
27	31 6	35 6	39 7	43 2	47 4	51 3	55 0	58 9	63 0
28	33 9	38 4	42 5	46 6	51 0	55 2	59 2	63 5	67 6
29	36 3	41 0	45 5	50 0	54 5	58 9	63 4	68 0	72 4
30	39 0	43 9	49 0	53 5	58 4	63 4	68 0	73 3	77 7
31	41 8	47 0	52 2	57 2	62 5	67 7	72 7	78 2	83 3
32	44 5	52 2	55 6	61 2	66 7	72 4	77 5	83 5	88 7
33	47 2	53 3	59 1	65 0	71 0	76 8	82 5	88 6	94 5
34	50 3	56 3	62 9	69 0	75 3	81 4	87 5	94 3	99 6
35	53 0	59 8	66 5	73 0	79 8	86 4	92 8	99 5	106 8
36	56 0	63 2	70 5	79 0	84 4	91 3	98 0	105 5	112 9
37	59 4	67 0	74 5	81 8	89 5	96 8	104 7	112 0	119 5
38	62 8	70 6	78 8	86 3	94 4	102 5	110 0	117 7	126 0
39	66 3	74 4	83 3	91 0	99 3	108 3	115 9	124 7	132 6
40	69 6	78 3	87 3	95 7	104 4	113 4	124 0	130 8	139 5

By the above Table the solid measure of any stick of round timber, can be found at sight from 6 to 40 inches in diameter, and from 8 to 46 feet in length. It rises one inch in diameter and one foot in length at a time. The left hand column on the first page gives the inches in diameter, and the other columns the contents, which are given in cubic feet and tenths of a foot. Over the top of the columns is placed the length of the stick, and to find the contents of any stick, first find the length at the top, then the inches in diameter at the left hand column, and against it under the length, to the right will be found the contents.

MEASURE OF ROUND TIMBER—Continued.

17 ft. long		18 ft. long		19 ft. long		20 ft. long		21 ft. long		22 ft. long		23 ft. long		24 ft. long		25 ft. long		26 ft. long	
Contents.		Contents.		Contents.		Contents.		Contents.		Contents.		Contents.		Contents.		Contents.		Contents.	
3	3	3	5	3	7	3	9	4	1	4	3	4	5	4	7	4	9	5	1
4	5	4	8	5	1	5	3	5	7	5	9	6	1	6	4	6	7	6	9
5	9	6	3	6	6	7	0	7	3	7	7	8	0	8	4	8	8	9	1
7	5	8	0	8	4	9	0	9	4	9	7	10	2	10	3	11	1	11	5
9	3	9	8	10	4	11	0	11	5	12	1	12	6	13	2	13	7	14	2
11	2	11	9	12	6	13	3	13	9	14	6	15	3	15	9	16	6	17	3
13	4	14	2	15	0	15	8	16	6	17	4	18	2	19	1	19	8	20	5
16	7	17	1	17	6	18	5	19	5	20	4	21	3	22	2	23	0	23	9
18	3	19	3	20	7	21	4	22	5	23	6	24	5	25	7	26	7	27	8
21	1	22	3	23	6	24	7	26	2	27	4	28	6	29	7	31	0	32	3
23	8	25	2	26	7	28	2	29	5	31	0	32	3	33	7	35	0	36	5
26	8	28	3	30	0	31	6	33	3	34	9	36	3	38	0	39	6	41	0
30	1	31	9	33	6	35	4	37	2	39	0	40	7	42	5	44	3	46	0
33	5	35	4	37	5	39	4	41	5	43	3	45	2	47	3	49	4	51	2
37	2	39	2	41	5	43	7	46	0	48	3	50	3	52	5	54	7	56	7
40	9	43	1	45	6	48	4	50	4	53	0	55	2	57	7	60	0	62	5
44	7	47	4	50	2	52	7	55	2	58	1	60	7	63	5	66	0	68	7
49	1	51	8	54	8	57	7	60	8	63	7	66	2	69	5	72	3	75	2
53	3	56	1	59	5	62	9	66	2	69	4	72	3	76	4	78	6	81	9
57	7	61	4	64	8	68	3	71	8	75	3	78	5	82	3	85	7	88	5
62	6	66	4	70	2	74	0	77	6	81	5	85	3	88	7	93	5	96	0
67	5	71	5	75	4	79	5	83	5	87	7	91	5	96	0	99	8	103	4
72	6	77	2	81	3	85	6	90	0	94	5	98	5	103	2	107	3	111	3
77	7	82	4	87	2	91	5	96	3	101	0	105	6	110	7	114	8	119	5
83	5	88	4	93	5	98	5	103	4	108	8	113	5	118	6	123	3	128	0
89	4	94	5	99	5	105	3	111	0	116	0	121	4	126	8	131	5	137	0
95	5	101	0	106	8	112	4	118	0	124	0	129	5	135	5	140	6	145	5
101	5	107	3	113	4	119	5	125	4	131	5	138	0	144	0	149	0	155	0
107	5	113	8	120	0	126	7	133	0	139	4	145	7	152	5	158	6	164	0
114	0	120	5	127	2	135	0	141	0	147	7	154	7	161	5	167	5	174	0
120	6	127	5	135	1	142	2	149	0	156	5	163	5	171	0	178	0	186	0
127	6	135	3	143	0	150	9	157	6	164	5	173	5	181	5	188	0	195	5
134	8	142	6	150	8	159	0	166	5	174	5	183	0	191	0	198	0	206	0
142	0	150	5	159	0	167	9	170	0	184	4	192	5	202	0	208	6	217	0
149	5	158	0	167	0	176	0	185	0	193	5	204	0	213	2	218	5	228	0

MEASURE OF ROUND TIMBER—Continued.

27 ft. long	28 ft. long	29 ft. long	30 ft. long	31 ft. long	32 ft. long	33 ft. long	34 ft. long	35 ft. long	36 ft. long
Contents.	Contents.	Contents.	Contents.	Contents.	Contents.	Contents.	Contents.	Contents.	Contents.
5 3	5 5	5 7	5 9	6 1	6 3	6 5	6 7	6 9	7 1
7 2	7 5	7 8	8 0	8 3	8 6	8 8	9 1	9 4	9 6
9 4	9 7	10 1	10 3	10 8	11 1	11 5	11 9	12 3	12 6
11 9	12 4	12 8	13 1	13 7	14 2	14 6	15 1	15 5	15 9
14 8	15 4	15 9	16 4	17 1	17 6	18 2	18 7	19 3	19 7
17 9	18 6	19 2	19 8	20 6	21 2	21 7	22 5	23 2	23 7
21 3	22 1	23 0	23 6	24 4	25 4	26 1	26 7	27 7	28 4
24 9	25 8	26 7	27 7	28 6	29 5	30 6	31 4	32 3	33 3
28 9	30 1	31 2	32 1	33 3	34 3	35 4	36 5	37 6	38 7
33 5	34 7	36 1	37 3	38 5	39 7	41 1	42 2	43 3	44 5
37 9	39 3	40 7	42 0	43 4	45 0	46 3	47 7	49 2	50 4
42 6	44 2	45 6	47 2	48 6	50 5	52 0	53 4	55 2	56 5
47 8	49 7	51 3	52 7	54 6	56 5	58 3	60 1	62 0	63 6
53 3	55 1	57 0	58 8	61 1	63 0	65 0	67 0	69 0	70 9
59 2	61 3	63 5	65 5	67 2	70 2	72 2	74 4	76 7	79 0
65 0	67 2	69 7	72 0	75 5	76 7	79 5	81 7	84 4	86 5
71 5	74 0	76 5	79 0	82 0	84 5	87 2	89 5	92 5	95 4
78 5	81 0	83 7	86 5	89 5	92 4	95 5	98 3	101 2	104 5
85 3	88 0	91 2	94 2	97 5	100 8	104 0	107 0	110 5	113 5
92 5	95 6	99 0	102 7	106 0	109 5	113 0	117 5	119 5	123 0
99 7	103 5	107 5	111 2	114 7	118 5	122 0	125 8	129 5	133 0
107 7	111 7	115 5	119 4	123 3	127 5	131 5	135 2	139 5	142 5
116 0	120 0	124 7	128 8	132 7	137 5	141 5	145 5	150 3	154 4
124 2	128 7	133 0	138 0	142 0	146 4	150 6	155 5	161 0	165 0
133 2	136 0	143 1	148 0	152 4	157 0	162 6	167 0	172 5	177 5
142 3	147 5	152 7	158 3	163 0	169 0	174 0	179 0	182 4	190 0
152 1	157 3	163 0	169 0	174 0	180 0	185 5	191 0	197 0	202 0
161 8	167 0	173 0	179 7	185 4	191 2	197 0	202 5	208 0	214 0
171 5	178 0	184 0	190 5	196 0	202 5	208 2	214 3	220 0	227 0
182 0	188 7	194 7	202 5	208 0	214 0	220 5	227 0	234 0	240 0
192 5	199 0	206 0	213 0	218 5	226 5	233 5	240 0	247 0	255 0
206 0	211 0	217 5	225 0	232 5	240 0	247 5	254 3	262 5	269 5
214 1	222 1	228 5	236 1	244 0	253 5	261 5	268 0	276 4	284 0
226 3	234 0	242 0	251 0	258 0	267 0	275 0	283 2	292 5	300 0
237 5	245 3	254 5	263 7	272 0	280 0	288 5	297 3	206 4	316 2

MEASURE OF ROUND TIMBER—Continued.

37 ft. long Contents.	38 ft. long Contents.	39 ft. long Contents.	40 ft. long Contents.	41 ft. long Contents.	42 ft. long Contents.	43 ft. long Contents.	44 ft. long Contents.	45 ft. long Contents.	46 ft. long Contents.
7 3	7 4	7 7	7 8	8 0	8 2	8 4	8 7	8 8	9 0
9 9	10 2	10 4	10 3	10 5	11 3	11 5	11 7	12 0	12 3
12 9	13 3	13 7	14 0	14 3	14 7	15 1	15 4	15 7	16 1
16 3	16 8	17 3	17 7	18 1	19 0	19 1	19 4	19 8	20 4
20 3	20 7	21 6	21 7	22 3	22 9	23 5	24 0	24 5	25 3
24 4	25 2	25 7	26 4	27 7	28 7	28 4	29 2	29 6	30 5
29 2	29 9	30 8	31 5	32 2	33 0	33 9	34 7	35 4	36 4
34 0	35 0	36 1	36 8	37 7	38 7	39 7	40 5	41 4	42 5
39 6	40 7	41 7	42 7	43 5	44 7	45 9	46 9	48 0	49 4
45 8	47 0	48 4	49 5	50 6	51 7	52 3	53 2	55 5	57 0
51 7	53 3	54 5	55 7	57 0	58 5	60 4	61 5	62 8	64 6
58 2	59 7	62 5	62 9	64 2	66 0	67 7	69 4	70 7	72 7
65 4	67 0	69 0	70 5	72 3	74 2	76 0	77 6	79 5	81 5
72 8	74 7	76 7	78 7	80 4	82 5	84 6	86 5	88 4	90 8
81 0	83 3	85 5	87 5	89 0	91 5	94 5	96 3	98 5	100 5
88 8	91 3	93 7	96 0	98 4	100 8	103 4	105 5	108 3	110 5
97 7	100 5	103 2	106 0	108 6	111 0	113 5	116 0	118 4	121 5
107 3	110 0	113 0	115 5	119 5	121 3	124 5	127 3	129 5	133 0
116 6	119 5	123 0	126 0	129 0	132 0	135 0	138 7	141 5	144 5
127 0	130 0	133 3	137 3	140 4	143 5	147 3	150 5	153 7	157 0
137 5	141 5	144 4	148 0	151 5	155 0	159 0	162 7	166 5	170 5
147 5	151 0	155 5	159 5	163 0	167 0	171 0	175 0	179 0	183 0
159 0	163 0	167 0	172 0	175 2	180 2	184 7	188 5	193 0	197 0
170 7	174 5	178 0	182 0	188 0	192 8	197 0	201 5	213 0	211 0
183 0	187 5	192 5	197 0	202 0	206 5	211 5	215 0	221 0	225 0
195 1	200 5	205 0	211 0	214 5	220 0	225 2	221 0	23 0	242 0
207 2	212 4	218 0	224 0	228 0	334 5	241 0	245 4	252 5	257 5
221 0	226 5	232 5	238 2	243 5	249 0	256 1	262 0	267 5	273 0
234 0	239 0	246 0	253 0	258 0	264 0	271 5	276 5	283 5	289 0
247 0	254 0	262 0	268 0	274 0	282 1	287 0	294 0	301 5	307 5
262 5	267 5	276 0	283 0	289 0	296 0	304 0	310 3	317 5	325 0
276 5	285 0	293 5	300 0	307 0	314 5	322 7	328 0	336 5	344 0
292 5	300 0	309 0	316 5	324 0	332 1	337 5	345 0	355 0	363 2
309 0	316 5	326 2	334 0	341 2	349 0	357 1	366 4	375 0	384 0
325 0	333 0	341 4	349 5	359 0	367 3	377 0	385 2	394 0	403 1

A Table, showing the rates a boat weighing with its load fifteen tons, and a wagon of the same weight, is impelled the one on a canal and the other on a railway, which is stated in pounds and in horse power—reckoning one horse power equal to 180 pounds.

	Boat on a Canal.		*Wagon on Railroad.*	
Miles per hour.	Power in lbs.	Horse power.	Power in pounds.	Horse power.
2	33	$\frac{1}{5}$	100	$\frac{1}{2}$
4	133	$\frac{3}{4}$	102	$\frac{1}{2}$
6	300	$1\frac{3}{4}$	105	$\frac{1}{2}$
8	533	3	109	$\frac{1}{2}$
12	1200	7	120	$\frac{2}{3}$
16	2133	12	137	$\frac{3}{4}$
20	3325	18	156	1

Dr. Armstrong observes, that a horse travelling at the usual rate that wagons move, would with ease, under favourable circumstances, draw twenty tons; but Mr. Fulton says, that five tons to a horse is the average work on railways, descending at the rate of three miles per hour, and one ton upwards with the same speed.

Mr. Telford, an experienced engineer, observes, that on a railway well constructed and laid, with a declivity of fifty feet in a mile, one horse will readily take down wagons containing twelve or fifteen tons, and bring back the same with four tons in them.

The following is a list of the average weight of pipes of different diameters in the clear, with the thickness required to bear a pressure of 300 feet head of water.

Diameter in inches.	Thickness of pipe in inches.	Weight per running yd: cwt.	qrs.	lbs.
2	$\frac{4}{16}$	0	1	2
3	$\frac{4}{16}$	0	1	16
4	$\frac{5}{16}$	0	2	4
6	$\frac{6}{16}$	1	0	0
8	$\frac{8}{16}$	1	1	21
10	$\frac{9}{16}$	2	0	S
12	$\frac{9}{16}$	2	2	18
16	$\frac{10}{16}$	3	2	0
20	$\frac{10}{16}$	5	0	0

SOLID MEASURE OF SQUARE TIMBER.

By the following table the solid contents, and the value of any piece or quantity of timber, stone, &c. may be found at sight, from six to nineteen and a half inches, the side of the square, or one fourth of the girth, from fourteen to sixty feet in length.

It rises from six, half an inch at a time, to nineteen and a half inches, and from fourteen, one foot at a time, till it rises to sixty.

The number of inches which the side of each stick measures, are placed at the top commencing next to the left hand column on the first page. These columns give the contents of each stick, and the first column which runs from the top to the bottom, the length. Half feet are not reckoned; that is, when a stick measures thirty cubic feet and five inches, it is called only thirty feet; if thirty feet and seven inches, it is reckoned thirty-one feet. We believe this method is practised in all the cities in the United States and Canada.

Feet in length.	Side 6 in.	Side 6 1-2 inch.	Side 7 inch.	Side 7 1-2 inch.	Side 8 inch.	Side 8 1-2 inch.	Side 9 inch.	Side 9 1-2 inch.	Side 10 inch.	Side 10 1-2 inch.	Side 11 inch.	Side 11 1-2 inch.	Side 12 inch.	Side 12 1-2 inch.
14	3	4	5	5	6	7	8	9	9	10	12	13	14	15
15	4	4	5	6	6	7	8	9	10	11	12	14	15	16
16	4	5	5	6	7	8	9	10	11	12	13	14	16	17
17	4	5	6	6	7	8	9	10	11	13	14	15	17	18
18	4	5	6	7	8	9	10	11	13	14	15	16	18	19
19	5	6	6	7	8	9	10	12	14	14	16	17	19	21
20	5	6	7	8	9	10	11	12	15	15	17	18	20	22
21	5	6	7	8	9	10	12	13	15	16	17	19	21	23
22	5	6	7	8	10	11	12	14	16	17	18	20	22	24
23	6	7	8	9	10	11	13	14	16	17	19	21	23	25
24	6	7	8	9	10	12	13	15	17	18	20	22	24	26
25	6	7	8	10	11	12	14	15	17	19	21	23	25	27
26	6	8	9	10	11	13	14	16	18	20	22	24	26	28
27	7	8	9	10	12	13	15	17	19	20	22	25	27	29
28	7	8	9	11	12	14	16	18	20	21	23	25	28	30
29	7	9	10	11	13	14	16	18	20	22	24	26	29	31
30	7	9	10	11	13	15	17	19	21	23	25	27	30	33
31	8	9	10	12	14	15	17	19	21	23	26	28	31	34
32	8	9	11	12	14	16	18	20	22	24	27	29	32	35
33	8	10	11	13	14	16	18	20	23	25	27	30	33	36
34	8	10	11	13	15	17	19	21	24	26	28	31	34	37
35	9	10	12	13	15	17	19	22	24	27	29	32	35	38
36	9	11	12	14	16	18	20	23	25	27	30	33	36	39
37	9	11	12	14	16	18	21	23	26	28	31	34	37	40
38	9	11	13	15	17	19	21	24	27	29	32	35	38	41
39	10	11	13	15	17	19	22	24	27	30	33	36	39	42
40	10	12	13	15	18	20	22	25	28	30	33	36	40	43
41	10	12	14	16	18	21	23	25	29	31	34	37	41	44
42	10	12	14	16	18	21	23	26	29	32	35	38	42	45
43	11	13	14	17	19	21	24	27	30	33	36	39	43	46
44	11	13	15	17	19	22	25	27	30	34	37	40	44	48
45	11	13	15	17	20	22	25	28	31	35	38	41	45	49
46	11	13	15	18	20	23	26	29	32	35	38	42	46	50
47	12	14	16	18	21	23	26	29	33	36	39	43	47	51
48	12	14	16	19	21	24	27	30	33	37	40	44	48	52
49	12	14	16	19	22	24	27	30	34	38	41	45	49	53
50	12	15	17	19	22	25	28	31	34	38	42	46	50	54
51	13	15	17	20	22	25	28	32	35	39	43	47	51	55
52	13	15	17	20	23	26	29	33	36	40	43	48	52	56
53	13	16	18	20	23	26	30	33	37	41	44	49	53	57
54	13	16	18	21	24	27	31	34	37	42	45	50	54	58
55	14	16	18	21	24	27	31	34	38	42	46	51	55	59
56	14	16	19	22	25	28	32	35	39	43	47	52	56	60
57	14	17	19	22	25	28	32	36	39	44	48	53	57	62
58	14	17	19	22	26	29	33	36	40	44	49	54	58	63
59	15	17	20	23	26	29	33	37	41	45	49	55	59	64
60	15	18	20	23	26	30	34	37	41	46	50	56	60	65

Cc

Side 13 inch.	Side 13 1-2 inch.	Side 14 inch.	Side 14 1-2 inch.	Side 15 inch.	Side 15 1-5 inch.	Side 16 inch.	Side 16 1-2 inch.	Side 17 inch.	Side 17 1-2 inch.	Side 18 inch.	Side 18 1-2 inch.	Side 19 inch.	Side 19 1-2 inch.
16	17	19	20	22	23	25	26	28	30	31	33	35	37
17	19	20	22	23	25	26	28	30	32	34	35	37	39
19	20	22	23	25	26	28	30	32	34	36	38	40	42
20	21	23	25	26	28	30	32	34	36	38	40	42	45
21	23	24	26	28	30	32	34	36	38	40	43	45	47
22	24	26	27	29	31	34	36	38	40	43	45	47	50
23	25	27	29	31	33	35	38	40	42	45	47	50	53
25	26	28	30	33	35	37	39	42	44	47	50	52	55
26	28	30	32	34	36	39	41	44	47	49	52	55	58
27	29	31	33	36	38	41	43	46	49	52	54	57	60
28	30	32	35	37	40	42	45	48	51	54	57	60	63
29	31	34	36	39	41	44	47	50	53	56	59	62	66
30	33	35	38	40	43	46	49	52	55	58	62	65	68
32	34	37	39	42	45	48	51	54	57	61	64	67	70
33	35	38	41	44	46	50	53	56	60	63	66	70	74
34	36	39	42	45	48	51	55	58	62	65	69	72	76
35	38	41	44	47	50	53	56	60	64	67	71	75	79
36	39	42	45	48	51	55	58	62	66	70	73	77	82
38	40	43	46	50	53	57	60	64	68	72	76	80	84
39	42	45	48	51	55	58	62	66	70	74	78	82	87
40	43	46	49	53	56	60	64	68	72	76	81	85	90
41	44	47	51	54	58	62	66	70	74	79	83	87	92
42	45	49	52	56	60	64	68	72	77	81	85	90	95
43	47	50	54	58	61	66	70	74	78	83	88	93	97
44	48	51	55	59	63	67	72	76	81	85	90	95	100
46	49	53	57	61	65	69	73	78	83	88	92	98	103
47	50	54	58	62	66	71	75	80	85	90	95	100	105
48	52	55	60	64	68	73	77	82	87	92	97	103	108
49	53	57	61	65	70	74	79	84	89	94	100	105	111
50	54	58	63	67	71	76	81	86	91	97	102	108	113
51	55	60	64	69	73	78	83	88	93	99	104	110	116
53	57	61	65	70	75	80	85	90	95	101	107	113	119
54	58	62	67	72	76	82	87	92	98	103	109	115	121
55	59	64	68	73	78	83	89	94	100	106	111	118	124
56	60	65	70	75	80	85	91	96	102	108	114	120	127
57	62	66	71	76	82	87	92	98	104	110	116	123	129
58	63	68	73	78	83	89	94	100	106	112	119	125	132
60	64	69	74	79	85	90	96	102	108	115	121	128	134
61	66	71	76	81	87	92	98	104	110	117	123	130	137
62	67	72	77	82	88	94	100	106	112	119	126	133	140
63	68	73	79	84	90	96	102	108	115	121	128	135	142
64	69	75	80	86	92	98	104	110	117	124	130	138	145
66	71	76	82	87	93	99	106	112	119	126	133	140	148
67	72	77	83	89	95	101	108	114	121	128	136	143	150
68	73	79	84	90	97	103	109	116	123	130	138	145	153
69	74	80	86	92	98	105	111	118	125	133	140	148	156
70	76	81	87	94	100	106	113	120	127	135	142	150	158

CHAPTER XXXVIII.

ABSTRACT OF TONNAGE, DUTIES, &c.

On American vessels six cents per ton; on French vessels one dollar per ton; and on British vessels from other places, and all other foreign vessels, two dollars per ton; fifty cents per ton, light money, if from ports to which vessels of the United States are not permitted to go and trade; but from all other ports fifty cents tonnage and fifty cents light money.

All vessels of the United States arriving from foreign ports, are subject to fifty cents per ton, unless all the officers and two-thirds of the crew are citizens of the United States.

TARIFF OF ARTICLES.

To be Weighed and Gauged.

☞ All articles that are subject to an ad valorem duty, are not specified in this Tariff.

Ale, beer, and porter, in bottles	20 c per gallon.
do do do in casks	15 c do
Alum,	$2,50 per 112 lbs.
Almonds,	3 c per lb.
Anchors, iron and parts of,	2 c do
Anvils,	2 c do
Brandy, see spirits.	
Bacon,	3 c per pound.
Beef	2 c do
Bristles,	3 c do
Butter,	5 c do
Books printed in Latin or Greek, since the year 1775, when bound,	15 c do
" when unbound,	13 c do
" printed in English since 1775, when bound,	30 c do
" when in sheets or boards,	26 c do
Brads, sixteen ounces to the thousand,	5 c per M.
" exceeding sixteen ounces per M.	5 per pound.
Cables, tarred,	4 c per pound
Cordage, do	4 c do
do untarred,	5 c do
Cables or chains of iron or parts, (no drawback)	3 c do
Castings of iron, not specified,	1 c do
Camphor, crude,	8 c do
do refined,	12 c do
Candles, tallow,	5 c do
do wax,	6 c do
do spermaceti,	8 c do
Cassia, Chinese,	6 c do
Cinnamon,	25 c do
Cloves,	25 c do
Cocoa,	2 c do
Chocolate,	4 c do

Coffee,	5 c	per pound.
Cotton,	3 c	do
Currants,	3 c	do
Cheese,	9 c	do
Copper, rods, bolts, spikes, nails, and composition rods, bolts, and spikes,	4 c	do
Copperas,	$2,00	per 112 lbs.
Candy, Sugar,	12 c	per pound
Corks,	12 c	do
Coals,	6 c	per bush.
Figs,	3 c	per pound.
Fish, dried, foreign caught,	$1,00	per 112 lbs.
Flour, wheat,	50	per do
Gin, see spirits.		
Ginger,	2 c	per pound.
Glass, wares of cut, not specified,	3 c	do
All other articles of glass,	2 c	do
Glue,	5 c	do
Gunpowder,	8 c	do
Hammers, blacksmith's,	2 1-2 c	per lb.
Hoops, iron,	3 c	do
Hemp,	$35,00	per ton.
Hams and other bacon,	3 c	per pound.
Herrings, smoked,	1,00	per 112 lbs.
Indigo,	15 c	per pound.
Iron, pig,	50 c	per 112 lbs.
" bars or bolts, not manufactured in whole or in part, by rolling.	90 c	do
" in bars or bolts, manufactured by rolling,	$1,50	do
" round or braziers' rods, of 3 to 7/16 of an inch diameter, inclusive,	3 c	per pound.
" nails or spike rods, slit,	3 c	do
" in sheets,	3 c	do
" for hoops,	3 c	do
" slit or rolled, for band iron, scroll iron, or casement rods, viz. one inch by 1/4, 1 1/2 by 1/8, 1 1/8 by 1/8,	3 c	do
" cast vessels, if not otherwise specified,	1 1/2 c	do
All other castings,	1 c	do
Lard,	3 c	do
Lead, in pigs, bars, or sheets,	2 c	do
" red or white, dry or ground in oil,	4 c	do
Looking-Glasses,	2 c	do
Lines,	5 c	do
Molasses,	5 c	per gallon.
Mace,	100 c	per pound.
Mill cranks, wrought iron,	4 c	do
Mill irons,	4 c	do
Oil, castor,	40 c	per gallon.
" linseed, hemp, and rapeseed,	25 c	do

Oil, olive, in casks,	25 c	per gallon.
" spermaceti, foreign,	25 c	do
" whale and other,	15 c	do
" of vitriol,	3 c	per pound.
Ochre, yellow, dry,	1 c	do
" in oil,	1½ c	do
Oats,	10 c	per bushel.
Potatoes,	10 c	do
Paper, folio and quarto post, all kinds,	20 c	per pound.
" foolscap, and all drawing and writing,	17 c	do
" printing, copperplate, and stainer's,	10 c	do
Sheathing, binder's, boxboards and wrapping paper,	3 c	do
All other kinds,	15 c	do
Packthread, untarred,	5 c	do
Pepper,	8 c	do
" Cayenne,	15 c	do
Pimento,	6 c	do
Plums,	4 c	do
Prunes,	4 c	do
Pork,	2 c	do
Rum, see spirits.		
Raisins, Mus.	4 c	do
" in jars and boxes,	4 c	do
All others,	3 c	do
Rope, ciar or coiar, grass,	5 c	do
Spirits, from grain, 1st proof,	42 c	per gallon.
2d do	45 c	do
3d do	48 c	do
4th do	52 c	do
5th do	60 c	do
Above 5th proof,	75 c	do
Spirits, from other materials than grain,		
1st and 2d proof	38 c	do
3d do	42 c	do
4th do	48 c	do
5th do	57 c	do
Above 5th proof,	70 c	do
Sugars, brown,	3 c	per pound.
" white, clayed,	4 c	do
" do powdered,	4 c	do
" lump,	10 c	do
" loaf,	12 c	do
" candy,	12 c	do
Soap,	4 c	do
Snuff,	12 c	do
Salt Petre, refined,	13 c	do
Salts, Glauber,	2 c	do
" Epsom,	4 c	do
Seines,	5 c	do
Shot,	3½ c	do

Cinnamon, chests,   actual.
  do   mats,   do
Cloves,   do
Cocoa, bags,   1 per cent.
  do   casks,   10   do
  do   ceroons,   10   do do
Chocolate, boxes,   10   do
Coffee, bags,   2   do
  do   do double, 4 lb.   do
  do   bales,   3 per ct. do
  do   casks,   12   do do
Cotton, bales,   2   do
  do   ceroons,   6   do
Currants, casks,   12   do do
Cheese, hampers or
          baskets,   10   do
  do   boxes,   20   do
Copper, casks,   12   do do
Candy Sugar, in bask'ts   5   do do
  do Sugar in boxes,   10   do do
Corks, sacks,   12 and 15 lbs. do
Figs, boxes,   60 lbs. 9 lbs. actual
  do half do   36   5½   do
  do qr. do   15   3¼   do
  do drums,   10 per cent. do
  do frails,   5   do   do
Flour, Wheat,   do
Glue,   actual.
Ginger,   do
Gunpowder,   do
Indigo, bags or mats, 3 per ct. act'l.
  do ceroons,   10   do   do
  do barrels,   12   do   do
  do other casks,   15   do   do
  do cases,   20   do   do
Looking-Glasses,
     French,   30 per ct. actual.
Lines,   do
Lard,   do
Mace, casks or kegs, 33 per ct. act'l.
Nutmegs, liggers,   21 per ct. act'l.
Nails, casks,   8   do
Ochre, French,   12 per ct. act'l.
Pepper, bags,   2 per cent.
  do bales,   5   do
  do casks,   12   do
Pimento, bags,   3   do
  do bales,   5 do actual.
  do casks,   16   do

Prunes,   actual.
Pork,   do
Raisins, Malaga,
          boxes, 6 lbs. 7 lbs. act'l.
  do   do   jars,   5   do
  do   do   casks 12   do
  do   Smyrna, do 12 per cent. do
Sugar, bags or mats, 5 per cent.
  do   casks,   12   do
  do   boxes,   15   do
  do   cannisters,   35   do act'l.
Soap, boxes,   10   do
Salts, Glauber,
       in casks,   8   do
Shot, in casks,   3   do
Steel,   do
Tea, Bohea, chests,   70 lbs.
  do   ½ do   36 "
  do   ¼ do   20 "
  do Hyson, or other Green, chests
     70 or upwards, gross, 20 lbs.
  do Souchong, chests 80 lbs. 20 "
  do Souchong, chests 80 lbs. and
upwards, gross 22 lbs.
  Every box of other tea, not less
than 50 lbs. nor more than 70 lbs.
gross, 18 lbs.
  On all other boxes, according to
invoice, or actual weight.
Twine casks, 12 per cent.
  do bales,   3   do
Tallow, ceroons, 10 per ct. actual.
  do   casks,   12 do   do
Vitriol, blue or Roman,   do
Venitian Red,   do
White, Paris,   do
Whiting,   do
Wheat of all kinds,   do

In some instances as stated in the foregoing, the actual tares have been determined; but the packages may vary as to their make and size; in that case they must be weighed again, provided always, that when the original invoices of any of the said articles are produced at the time of making entry of such articles, and the tare or tares appear therein, it shall be lawful for the collector and naval officer, where there is one, if they see fit, with the consent of the importer, consignee, or consignees, to estimate the said tare or tares according to such invoice; but if not determined at the time of entry, the tare or tares as above shall be granted or allowed.

Check Out More Titles From HardPress Classics Series In this collection we are offering thousands of classic and hard to find books. This series spans a vast array of subjects – so you are bound to find something of interest to enjoy reading and learning about.

Subjects:
Architecture
Art
Biography & Autobiography
Body, Mind &Spirit
Children & Young Adult
Dramas
Education
Fiction
History
Language Arts & Disciplines
Law
Literary Collections
Music
Poetry
Psychology
Science
…and many more.

Visit us at www.hardpress.net

CPSIA information can be obtained
at www.ICGtesting.com
Printed in the USA
BVHW040944270819
556819BV00015B/3718/P